SOVIET STRATEGY

Soviet Strategy

EDITED BY JOHN BAYLIS AND GERALD SEGAL

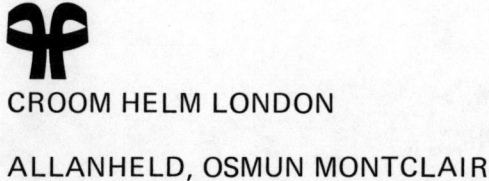

CROOM HELM LONDON

ALLANHELD, OSMUN MONTCLAIR

© 1981 Introduction and selection by John Baylis and Gerald Segal
Croom Helm Ltd, 2-10 St John's Road, London SW11

British Library Cataloguing in Publication Data
Soviet strategy
   1. Russia - Military policy
   I. Baylis, John
   II. Segal, Gerald
   355'.0335'47   UA770
   ISBN 0-7099-0609-9
        0-7099-0629-3 (pbk)

Published in the United States of America in 1981
by Allanheld, Osmun & Co Publishers, Inc
6 South Fullerton Avenue, Montclair, NJ 07042

Library of Congress Cataloging in Publication Data

Soviet strategy.
   1. Russia–Military policy. 2. Russia–Defenses.
I. Baylis, John. II. Segal, Gerald.
UA770.S668   1981   355'.033047   80-28515
ISBN 0-86598-050-0

Printed and bound in Great Britain
by Billing and Sons Limited
Guildford, London, Oxford, Worcester

CONTENTS

Acknowledgements

1. Soviet Strategy: An Introduction *Gerald Segal and John Baylis*   9

Part One: The Evolution of Soviet Strategy

2. Soviet Attitudes Towards Nuclear War: Do They Really Think They Can Win? *Robert L. Arnett*   55

3. The Military Instrument in Soviet Foreign Policy *Ken Booth*   75

Part Two: Contemporary Issues

4. How to Think about Soviet Military Doctrine *Benjamin S. Lambeth*   105

5. Rethinking Soviet Strategic Policy: Inputs and Implications *Dennis Ross*   124

6. The Soviet Military and SALT *Raymond L. Garthoff*   154

Part Three: The Use of the Military Instrument

7. Soviet Risk Taking and Crisis Behaviour *Hannes Adomeit*   185

8. The Rationale for the Development of Soviet Seapower *Michael MccGwire*   210

Notes on Contributors   255

Index   257

ACKNOWLEDGEMENTS

The editors would like to thank Ms Jane Davis of the Department of International Politics, University of Wales, Aberystwyth, for her superb and swift assistance in producing the index for this book.

In fulfilment of their obligations to the holders of copyright for the articles used in this text, the editors would like to acknowledge the kind permission of the following: Frank Cass for Robert L. Arnett, 'Soviet Attitudes Towards Nuclear War: Do They Really Think They Can Win?', *The Journal of Strategic Studies,* vol. 2, no. 2 (Sept. 1979) and Dennis Ross, 'Rethinking Soviet Strategic Policy: Inputs and Implications', *The Journal of Strategic Studies,* vol. 1, no. 1 (May 1978); The Royal United Services Institute for Ken Booth, *The Military Instrument in Soviet Foreign Policy* (London, 1973), pp. 9-25; The International Institute for Strategic Studies for Hannes Adomeit, 'Soviet Risk-Taking and Crisis Behaviour; From Confrontation to Coexistence', *Adelphi Papers,* no. 101 (Autumn 1973), pp. 20-33; The Rand Corporation for Benjamin S. Lambeth, *How to Think About Soviet Military Doctrine,* P-5939 (February 1978); The editors of *Problems of Communism* for Raymond Garthoff, 'The Soviet Military and SALT', vol. 14, no. 1 (Jan.–Feb. 1975) and Raymond Garthoff especially for his revisions to the original text; The United States Naval Institute for Michael MccGwire, 'The Rationale for the Development of Soviet Seapower', in *Proceedings of the USNI, Military Review Issue* (May 1980).

1 SOVIET STRATEGY: AN INTRODUCTION
Gerald Segal and John Baylis

The analysis of the Soviet Union's military strategy has resulted in a wide expression of opinion on the crucial question: what are the intentions of the USSR? The spectrum stretches from those 'hawks' who see expansionism as the motive force behind Soviet actions, to 'doves' who see defensiveness as the key element. If the readers hope to divine in the first paragraph where the editors of this volume fit into these categories, they will be disappointed. It is our intention to compile a series of analyses of Soviet strategy that lie somewhere in the middle of the spectrum, combining the most important arguments of both sides. In recent years, amid the mass of literature from both hawks and doves,[1] there has emerged a balanced and careful analysis by several scattered scholars and we feel that it will be useful, especially in the present climate, to make them readily available in a single book. Their arguments are not as simple as those of their colleagues on the two extremes, and therefore tend to require more careful study. In order to clarify the main issues and opinions, this lengthy introduction will place these moderate analysts' work in the context of the debate on Soviet strategy and extensive references are provided as a guide to the available literature on the subject.[2]

The difficulties in analysing Soviet strategy are manifold and afflict the international relations field as a whole. For example, problems in estimating and imputing intentions are complicated by the difficulties with such basic concepts as the 'image' of the adversary, 'perception and misperception' in interstate politics and ethnocentrism.[3] Another major problem in producing a sophisticated analysis of Soviet foreign policy is the fact that there is no monolithic decision-making process in the Kremlin. A major difficulty has been that Western hawks cite statements of Soviet hawks to support their views of Soviet strategy and likewise Western doves cite statements of moderate Soviet officials. Thus the mere citation of Soviet statements cannot be seen as sufficient 'proof' of a position, and a far more complex discussion of the political context is required.[4] In recent years there has been some selective criticism from scholars of these problems in the Soviet strategic studies field, and if we break down the issues into specific aspects we find that some progress has been made. In this introduction we will begin with a survey of the overarching problem in the debate on Soviet strategy:

i.e. what is Moscow's basic attitude towards nuclear war and its utility as a tool of policy? Continuing in this general vein we will review the historical development of Soviet strategic thought. The following section will deal with more specific contemporary issues in Soviet strategy. We will begin by raising some of the general issues in arms control negotiations and then outline the discussion on deterrence and defence in greater detail. The role of the Soviet military in arms control discussions will also be dealt with in this section. The final cluster of topics will be a more in depth analysis of the use of force in Soviet foreign policy in general and in crisis diplomacy in particular. The sensitive area of naval policy provides a useful case study of these problems.

1. Nuclear War and Victory

We can divide the subject of Soviet military strategy into several clusters of issues, all of which containing differences of opinion regarding the nature of the Soviet view. We can begin with the broadest topic: what is Moscow's view of nuclear war and can such a conflict serve as a useful tool of policy? There are those who argue that the USSR adopts a classic Clausewitzian attitude to all types of war, including nuclear, seeing it merely as a continuation of politics. For example, Richard Pipes argues that Moscow perceives nuclear war as being a practical instrument of policy.[5] On the other hand there are those in the West who see the Soviets as sharing an abhorrence of nuclear war and realising that it would wreak such devastating destruction as to render it useless as a tool of policy.[6]

In many respects this dispute regarding Soviet attitudes towards nuclear war revolves around basic issues of Soviet ideology. There is a vast literature in the West debating whether ideological motives continue to guide Soviet policy, and if so, what kind of ideology with which fundamental principles.[7] In part the disagreement results from the lack of unity in the USSR on these matters and thus Western commentators have a mass of material to draw on in order to support their particular points of view. For example, there are some Soviet voices sounding a more shrill ideological note when discussing the US, and there are those who stress pragmatic aspects when discussing relations with Washington. Some issues create cleavages that cut across those on other ideological problems such that any analysis of uniform opinion in the USSR is difficult to substantiate. Although these

Soviet Strategy: An Introduction

disparate voices have not always been divided up in the same way, there can be little doubt that the Soviet view is not uniform.[8]

The complex debate can in part be resolved by studying the ideological issues in greater detail. Given that one does not dismiss the ideological component to Soviet policy entirely, there is a way to begin to resolve the debate on Soviet attitudes. Soviet ideology does indeed have at its roots the notion that politics is fundamental to the theory of war, indeed politics is fundamental to almost all spheres. Every war is a continuation of politics and can be understood by studying the nature of the struggle between classes and political forces.[9]

However, there is a large leap into the second major statement by those such as Pipes who argue that nuclear war is seen as serving as a useful instrument of politics. Most people would accept that war and politics are connected, but it is a much more dubious argument that such wars can serve as *useful instruments* of policy. Robert Arnett (our Chapter 2) makes this distinction very clear. He argues most persuasively that even though Richard Pipes may not make the distinction between the explanation of the theory of war and the tools of policy, the Soviets, including the military, do make such a differentiation. Nuclear weapons have altered the historical practice and rendered the nuclear variant of war useless for practical policy. This change that Arnett has pointed out in a crucial aspect of Soviet ideology related to strategic issues is not in any way out of keeping with developments in the ideological component of general Soviet foreign policy. It has long been noted by students of USSR policy that the role of ideology is not static.[10] A further variation on that theme is that even if the doctrine is not changing, it is at least flexible enough to encompass various different opinions, some of which are more dominant depending on the historical conditions.

A related debate in the literature is whether the USSR feels it could win a nuclear war. As opposed to the view of Pipes, Arnett argues that once again a differentiation must be made in Soviet statements and that ideological issues lie at the root of the question. It is undoubtedly true that Soviet statements proclaim that their system will inevitably triumph in any conflict, including nuclear war, but this is required by a basic ideological tenet, i.e. that the fate of capitalism is predetermined. However, this view has undergone important changes, especially in the 1950s Soviet strategic debate on the question of the potential decisiveness of surprise in war.[11] Following the death of Stalin the notion of permanently operating factors, which had previously ruled out the discussion of surprise, was cast aside. Thus the military was liberated to seek 'real-world' solutions to the problem while officially maintaining the ideological line on the inevitability of victory.

This pragmatic concern with reality also raises a second problem with this alleged Soviet view of the desirability of war. The hawkish argument ignores the fundamental distinction between types of victory. Those taking a pessimistic view of the USSR would argue that the Soviets foresee the type of victory wherein they suffer minimal damage. However, as Arnett argues, this does not appear to be an accurate description of Moscow's policy. The Soviet view, while accepting that victory is inevitable, also argues that it will be a pyrrhic victory due to the awesome destruction of nuclear war. Thus ideological principles are upheld, as well as another basic ideological motif, recognition of the realities of the world's forces. The USSR, then, prefers to obtain its objectives through peaceful means and so long as it views war as an unproductive path to these goals it will continue to pursue non-military means.[12] The USSR attempts to minimise the total destruction of nuclear war, for example by providing for civil defence, but so far it has been unable to significantly reduce the likelihood of a holocaust.

What emerges in Arnett's discussion is that simplistic explanations do not do justice to the complexity of the Soviet position. While the hawkish view of the USSR contains basic elements of sound analysis, it tends to take an additional leap that distorts the implications of the originally judicious view. As Arnett shows, what is needed is a far more careful and qualified view of the Soviet attitude towards nuclear war.

2. Development of Strategic Thought

While the question of Soviet attitudes towards nuclear war is largely concerned with ideological issues, the purpose of our Chapter 3 is to highlight the historical perspective on Soviet strategy. Clearly it is important to grasp what has gone before in order to understand the present, and this has motivated a great deal of analysis of the development of strategic thought. In large measure, the debates over present Soviet strategy are not carried very far back into the past. The argument has been confined overwhelmingly to the period from the late 1960s when the USSR began to obtain strategic parity. Thus it has been easier to choose a non-contentious account to set the historical framework for this book. Where the element of debate does persist is in the selection of crucial dates and why these turning points occurred. As could have been expected, the latter is far more controversial than the former.

Soviet Strategy: An Introduction

Most analyses begin in the aftermath of World War II when the USSR found itself with dominating conventional power in Europe.[13] To a certain extent the basic security of the Soviet Union was ensured with Germany defeated and the US withdrawing troops from Europe. However, the US had emerged as the major adversary and it was developing several alliance structures surrounding the USSR in co-ordination with its monopoly of nuclear weapons. Atomic forces meant, *inter alia,* that Soviet conventional forces could no longer guarantee the security of the heartland and that the USSR would be required to invest in its own atomic weapons. What is more, the European balance was not all that secure as West Germany was rearmed and NATO developed. The USSR chose an extended type of security encompassing East Europe that held both positive and negative elements for Moscow; positive in the sense of a security line farther from the Soviet heartland, but negative in the sense of potential instability and dependence on the USSR.

This uncertain state of Soviet strategy was most prominent during the Cold War. Although this period is one of fierce debate in the Western literature,[14] it seems clear, that contrary to the belief at the time, there was no Soviet master-plan for expansion. The mutual misperceptions between East and West, and the spiral escalation process that developed when a hostile action reinforced an already paranoid image of the adversary, meant that both the USSR and the US muddled through from one crisis to another. Not until the explosion of the Soviet's first atomic device could they begin to feel less insecure.[15] The sense of inferiority and vulnerability no doubt dominant in Stalin's personality at the time could not be easily overcome.

Soviet strategic thought in the nuclear age was very much frozen during Stalin's lifetime, but his death brought forth a flood of debate.[16] One of the key arguments was whether the Stalinist view that 'permanently operating factors' ensured Soviet success in a nuclear clash was still valid. The question of whether surprise attack could invalidate these factors was vigorously debated and it was soon agreed in Soviet military and civilian circles that surprise could indeed be decisive. The result was not a coherent strategy but at least it was more relevant to modern realities. Even those in the West who reject the notion of the changing nature of Soviet ideology acknowledge the existence of the Soviet strategic debate and the evolution of military thought at this time.

The resolution of this debate was not the same in the US. Washington was essentially to accept that the threat of Mutual Assured

Destruction (MAD) would deter the enemy from believing that surprise could be effective. In the USSR the groundwork was laid for a far less passive deterrence and defence policy stressing an active role for various levels of military force. What emerged was the beginning of a multi-layered Soviet strategy. At its most basic, the forces in Europe were maintained and trained for an 'offensive' in the belief that attack is the best defence. In this respect, Western Europe was seen as a hostage to guarantee Soviet security. More directly, Soviet security was reinforced with air defence systems and naval protection. Simultaneously, a deterrence force was developed based on bombers and basic ICBM forces, thereby for the first time threatening the US heartland directly. These military aspects were reinforced by a political campaign to reduce tension with the main threat in Washington by pursuing a line of peaceful coexistence. The horrors of nuclear war were clearly understood in the Kremlin and the Leninist notion of the inevitability of war was unambiguously amended by Khrushchev when he said 'war is not fatalistically inevitable'. Serious negotiations for arms control were begun by the late 1950s and the fruits of the modernising of Soviet strategic thought began to emerge. The fears of nuclear proliferation, especially to China and West Germany, also helped drive the USSR towards genuine interest in arms control negotiations.

Although there was a brief period of unilateral Soviet reduction in conventional forces and an emphasis on strategic deterrence (late 1959 – mid-1961), by 1961 the Soviet defence posture began to evolve in the form that has basically been retained to date.[17] In part in reaction to President Kennedy's expansion of American strategic forces,[18] as well as the later evidence that the missile gap favoured the US, the USSR embarked on a campaign to establish a deterrence strategy based on war fighting. Essential steps were taken to produce an ICBM counter-force capability coupled with civil and air defence and a blue-water role for the navy. The Cuban missile crisis reinforced this trend and also added impetus to the complementary drive for arms control. The partial test-ban treaty of 1963 and work on a non-proliferation agreement were cases in point. 1963 also marked the open Sino-Soviet rift and the USSR adopted concrete strategic responses in an attempt to deter two powers rather than merely one in the nascent great power triangle. Conventional forces facing China were increased eventually to a point where there were more Soviet troops on the PRC border than were in East Europe. In addition, a significant portion of Soviet strategic forces were also targeted on China and the new ballistic missile defence probably served at least in part an anti-China purpose.[19]

Soviet Strategy: An Introduction

Despite the change in Soviet and American leadership in the last twenty years, little has changed in Soviet strategy. Along with growing concern with China, the Soviet drive for nuclear parity with the US was pursued during the 1960s. The SALT I agreement began the process of ratifying strategic parity and SALT II went further down that road. While the SALT process continues to leave vast gaps for further arms expansion and provides roomy walls and ceilings for arms spending,[20] it is clear that the USSR has engaged in serious and significant arms control talks while at the same time doing its best to secure its definition of Soviet security needs. The significance of SALT for the Soviet Union, as well as the process by which Moscow reached this stage, is well illustrated in our Chapter (see also our discussion of Soviet Strategic policy below) from Ken Booth's longer study on the role of military power in Soviet foreign policy.

3. Some General Aspects of USSR Strategic Thought

Having set the general background to Soviet strategy, it will now be useful to turn to more contemporary issues. One of the better ways to organise this diverse subject is to begin with a broad analysis of contemporary aspects of USSR strategy, comparing it with that of the US. Although we will deal in detail with only some of the issues presented by Benjamin Lambeth (in Chapter 4), this analysis provides an excellent overview of important strategic issues.

To a certain extent it is misleading to attempt a discussion of strategic doctrine, for as we have already begun to make clear, Soviet thinking on these matters is by no means uniform at any one time, nor does it always remain the same. Even in the US these issues are subject to much debate and change, and most recently the US has apparently begun to adopt many aspects of Soviet doctrine.[21] In the USSR as in the US there are competing voices and interest groups constantly affecting policy and we will discuss some of these aspects at greater length below. There are numerous other problems in analysing contemporary doctrine, not the least of which is the disparity in type and quality of evidence. For example, most Soviet comment on military issues is made by the military but that does not necessarily mean that the views are identical with policy. In the US the discussion of strategic issues is more dominated by civilian voices who tend to be more in tune with civilian government, but this trend is complicated by the fact that more diverse voices are heard in the pluralistic American polity.

With these caveats in mind, as well as others to be noted in the course of the analysis, it is still important to discuss the contemporary Soviet view and contrast its strategic doctrine with that of the US. The main motivation for this attempt is the all too prevalent problem of 'ethnocentrism' in strategic thinking in the West.[22] For too long now there has been a widespread tendency to see Soviet strategic thinking as somehow more 'backward' than that of the West and to assume that in time the two ways of perceiving strategic issues would 'converge' as the US educated the USSR.[23] This was a problem afflicting both 'hawks' and 'doves' in the analysis of the USSR and led to certain important distortions, for example in the understanding of the Soviet approach to SALT.[24] Therefore, in order to overcome this difficulty, we have selected pieces which deal primarily with concepts involved in strategic analysis and less with technology.[25] It is felt to be crucial to get to the root of doctrinal aspects underlying the strategic posture and to highlight important areas where there are differences between East and West.

The first area in which strategic doctrine can be discussed is the issue of general attitudes towards nuclear war. We have already dealt with many aspects of this question and it will be noted that the view of Lambeth leans more to the hawkish side of the spectrum than that of Booth. The basic question here is discerning the attitude towards war if deterrence should fail. While the fundamental US view (prior to Presidential Directive 59 in 1980) is to threaten to inflict unacceptable damage thereby preventing a total breakdown in deterrence, the USSR hopes to enhance its prospects of survival by having a more complete capability. To that end, the USSR develops forces to fight a war should it break out as well as such elements that will help it survive the military might of the opposition. Although at present this more or less represents the contrasts in strategic doctrine on this basic level, it should also be clear that this has not always been the view of the superpowers and there are signs that the US may now be moving more towards a Soviet version of 'war-fighting' capability. Far from enlightening the USSR as to the superiority of MAD, the Soviets may well be educating Washington on the subject of deterrence and defence in the strategic balance.[26]

A secondary aspect to this question is whether the USSR thinks it can win a nuclear war. As already outlined, this complex question is answered in the negative by doves and in the positive by hawks.[27] It seems on balance that the Soviets, much like the US on this matter, would like to win if they could (who wouldn't?) but see such a victory

Soviet Strategy: An Introduction

as so unlikely that this type of war ceases to serve as a practical policy tool. The superpowers also see their respective deterrence policies as being the best defence and thus Washington and Moscow believe in both deterrence and defence, although defining them in very different ways.[28]

This brings us to the second major issue in contemporary strategic doctrine: the way in which deterrence and defence are defined in the US and the USSR. Although we will cover this issue at greater length below, it is important to point out the main aspects. Soviet defence by denial is at the core of its deterrence strategy and as outlined below is based on the notion that it can deny victory to the US in a nuclear exchange. This denial strategy is composed of the Soviet ability to survive an American attack by air and civil defence as well as an ability to fight its own offensive war including the use of conventional forces. The emphasis on survivability will be stressed in the next section of our discussion.[29] US defence on the other hand is said to be guaranteed by the threat to punish the USSR even after suffering a first strike. Thus both sides have resolved the key strategic question of how to prevent strategic surprise from being decisive by very different answers.

The third major area of discussion in US and Soviet thinking is the issue of strategic stability. Much like deterrence, both powers swear by their desire to possess it, but equally both mean different things when using the term. For the US, stability means a lack of competition so as to improve the chances for coexistence, whereas for the USSR stability involves competitive coexistence. In Soviet eyes, instability is caused by quantum advances in technology by the US and therefore Moscow seeks to keep the system stable. But competition must continue as far as the USSR is concerned, if only for similar ideological factors as those which made necessary the Soviet belief in the possibility of victory in nuclear war.[30] This competition is also carried over into the field of conventional military force and whereas the US felt that stability would include a limit on superpower rivalries, say for example in the nonaligned world, this was not part of the Soviet meaning of the term. The US sought to link the strategic balance to all other aspects of the superpower relationship and suggested, for example, that if stability in Angola was upset, therefore stability in the superpowers' strategic relationship was also upset. This was a definition of *détente* never accepted in the Kremlin. Negotiations on SALT were distinct from activities in Angola and similarly in the Soviet view ratification of SALT II should be unconnected to events in Afghanistan. The Western misunderstanding of this issue, and the consequent overselling of détente, goes a long way to explaining the recent deterioration in superpower relations.

A related aspect of stability is the argument about whether the USSR seeks parity or superiority with the US. The hawks argue that Moscow does not accept stability as it seeks to be superior to the West. The doves argue (in varying degrees) that Moscow no more wants superiority than does the US (who doesn't?) and the USSR recognises that short of an unacceptable level of effort and expenditure, it cannot have it.[31] Thus parity is accepted, but within the broad confines of the term a certain important level of competition continues. Moscow does sign agreements such as SALT basically because it appreciates the economic and technological restraints preventing it from obtaining superiority, and continues to abide by these agreements because it sees the pacts as being in its own self interest.[32]

The question of stability is also concerned with technical aspects of Soviet force deployment and their significance. Those wishing to substantiate the claim that the USSR seeks superiority tend to point to the Soviet advantage in throw-weight. Those doves wishing to substantiate the claim that the USSR seeks parity, tend to offer alternate reasons for such developments. Massive advantage in throw-weight was allegedly developed due to bureaucratic and historical reasons and in any case is of far less relevance when it is considered that more accurate US warheads can achieve the same effect while requiring less weight.

A further confusing question related to stability has been raised regarding the problems of first-strike capability. Both the US and the USSR accuse each other of seeking the ability to disarm the adversary in a first blow, thereby destabilising the system, but neither power seems to have any such intention. Capability does not always equal intention.[33] The hawks in the US argue that in the early to mid-1980s the USSR will have the capability to knock out the entire US land-based ICBM force. This 'window of opportunity' for a first strike is dismissed by doves who argue that this potential exists merely because of the Soviet bureaucratic and historical inclination to concentrate on land-based forces. The US has always seen its forces as a triad so that even if the land-based component is vulnerable, the air-and sea-based units can guarantee retaliation and thereby deter war. If the USSR had the intention of a first strike then the readiness of its forces would have to be very different from what it is. Soviet missiles are not prepared to take off at a seconds notice as are the Americans, Soviet bombers spend much more time on the ground (and hence are vulnerable) than

Soviet Strategy: An Introduction 19

do those of the US, and Soviet submarines spend far more time in port (and hence are more vulnerable) than do those of the US.

The USSR does see the benefit of getting in the first blow, but not in the destabilising sense as used in the US. On the brink of war and after an escalation of tension to crisis level, the USSR, as does the US, sees that if all else has failed, striking first is of value. That is, however, a far cry from the destabilising fear of a first strike out of the blue. As part of the Soviet total war fighting capability it sees the need to strike at the hardened US ICBM force so as to prevent the US damaging the USSR. If this posture is not understood in the context of the Soviet meaning of stability and first strike, the intentions of the USSR can be easily misunderstood.

Even the meaning of the term 'strategic' in the phrase 'strategic stability' is different in Moscow and Washington. This disagreement is primarily a function of geography: for the US, as a power virtually on its own continent, strategic in the sense of strategic weapons refers to anything that can strike between continents; for the USSR, with a perceived hostile Western Europe on its continent, such an intercontinental definition of strategic weapons is not possible. For the USSR the theatre weapons of the Western alliance in Europe constitute a strategic threat, while the US sees them as distinctly non-strategic in nature. Without becoming deeply mired in weapons technology, it is clear that this conceptual problem as to what is to be deemed a strategic weapon is an important difference between the US and USSR. In a sense, the USSR wants to penalise the US for having friends in Europe and hence discussion of limitation of weapons is made more complex.[34]

The USSR is, however, not merely being obstreperous. Not only are US nuclear forces in Europe considered a threat and of strategic import, but what is Moscow to make of 'independent' French and British nuclear armed submarines? It is not surprising that the USSR should be so concerned with these and other forward-based systems in the SALT negotiations and that the negotiations on mutual and balanced force reductions in Europe should be so complicated, for the different and equally valid meanings of strategic forces are not easily overcome. Therefore, the Soviet attempts to include European forces should not be seen merely as an attempt to win in a numbers game, as their security concerns are real, and born out of their particular strategic posture and geographic position.

A related and growing concern for the USSR in the definition of what constitutes strategic forces concerns the China problem. Contrary to its attempts in the SALT process to broaden the definition of strategic weapons to include American shorter-range forces, the USSR is increasingly discovering the need to protect its own forward-based systems, especially those which are useful against China. Theatre nuclear forces, backfire bombers and SS-11's and -20s are crucial aspects to the Soviet's anti-China capability[35] and the limits on these forces being discussed with the US cause ambivalence in Moscow. As the China problem continues to grow in importance for the USSR, these difficulties in defining strategic issues are likely to increase. A full appreciation of the Soviet strategic posture will have to take these aspects into account and simplistic definitions of crucial terms will only obscure the issues.

Finally, two other important areas of discussion should be noted. Unlike the US, the Soviet Union does not discuss complex notions of bargaining and escalation in a nuclear war. For the USSR, nuclear war will not be limited. Once the crisis has gone over the brink Moscow foresees fighting a total war.[36] This, however, does not mean that the USSR does not appreciate the importance of scenarios and uncertainties of calculations in the period prior to the outbreak of war. For the Soviet Union the manipulation of these events is crucial and failure to do so may contribute to a different outcome.[37] Unless the Soviet Union is confident that it can control events to suit itself, it will be less likely to strike. Thus the USSR does not have an unsophisticated grasp of the possible variations in a nuclear confrontation, but the specific Soviet understanding is different from that of the US. Moscow's emphasis on the pre-war period rather than the US concentration on the post-outbreak-of-war period is yet another one of the contrasts in strategic thought outlined by Lambeth in this text.

4. Arms Control Issues

We have discussed several important contemporary issues only briefly, and now it will be useful to turn to a more detailed look at them and their relevance to arms control. The issues of deterrence, defence and parity in the strategic balance are all fundamental to an understanding of the Soviet attitude towards SALT and we will outline the complexities of these issues as discussed by Dennis Ross (Chapter 5).

At the root of the discussion of the USSR's attitude towards deterrence and defence lies the problem of whether the US and Soviet doctrines are the same, or at least are converging. As we have already suggested, this view of the identity or convergence of doctrine is an

Soviet Strategy: An Introduction

ethnocentric one of some Western strategists and fundamentally distorts the specific nature of Soviet strategy. In the course of Western discussions of the SALT process, the view was expressed by some that after having developed parity, a reliable second strike and having accepted a limit on ABM, that Moscow had altered its strategic doctrine and was now accepting the fundamental American theory of Mutual Assured Destruction (MAD).[38] In the first half of 1978 there emerged a series of articles debunking that myth and we have selected one of these for this book.

While the analysts suggesting Soviet acceptance of MAD tended to be of the dovish persuasion, the group denying Soviet acceptance was by no means uniform. While the hawks tended to deny the existence of a Soviet defence and deterrence doctrine altogether, the moderates suggested an intricate but valid Soviet definition of these terms.[39] These authors had largely overcome their ethnocentrism and we can best appreciate their results by concentrating on their view of the Soviet view of deterrence and defence.

Soviet thinking about deterrence and defence can be seen as being affected by several sets of factors. These factors can be divided into subjective and objective types, with three variants of the first group. Firstly, Soviet strategy is in part a result of the USSR's perception of the world through a lens of insecurity. The history of repeated invasion from East and West, the fear of Mongol hordes and German invaders, are all part of that fundamental Russian legacy.[40] This insecurity is reinforced by an ideology that perceives the West as hostile and aggressive and Soviet leaders can cite various attempts, particularly in the early days of the revolution, to quash the fledgling Communist state.[41] This sense of insecurity contributes to an unwillingness to accept a MAD notion that makes both superpowers hostage to each other. This is reinforced by the second subjective factor, the psychological and socio-cultural dimension. For example, the traditional Soviet fear of Western technological progress would mean that a doctrine of mutual hostage would make the USSR particularly vulnerable to US advances in new technology. Thus the age-old cultural responses to the West in Russia can at least in part explain a Soviet rejection of MAD. Furthermore, the traditional Soviet belief in over-insurance in defence can be seen to reinforce the tendency to overinsure in modern defence by producing massive missiles and vast numbers of them.[42]

The third subjective factor is the particular role played by the military in the formation of Soviet doctrine. Although we will discuss this issue in greater length in our next section, it is important to note the basic effect of the military mind on the issues related to arms control. MAD is unacceptable in the USSR not so much because it is an American concept, but because it is a civilian one. MAD minimises the role of the military, restricts its war fighting role, and hence its allocation of funds and position of national importance.[43] It should not be surprising that any military, but particularly one with as much influence on military doctrine as the Soviet armed forces, should reject MAD.

Having said what Soviet doctrine is not by use of these three subjective aspects, we can now say what it is. MAD is a deterrence doctrine by threat of punishment, but the Soviet view is deterrence by denial,[44] i.e. that no military advantage can be gained by striking the USSR. This doctrine meets the requirements of the three subjective aspects by guaranteeing defence and providing an important active task for all aspects of the military. The armed forces must fulfil a multiplicity of roles in this strategy in order to ensure that no attack will be successful. Thus the total Soviet commitment to a war fighting capability means that not only does the USSR possess a full range of conventional forces, but that it also has a myriad of nuclear power. This posture can be understood as having two tiers. The first provides the USSR with the ability to survive an attack and this is achieved by developing damage limitation forces of a passive and active kind. Air and civil defence constructions are seen as essential in conveying to the enemy that he cannot win, thereby strengthening defence. The second tier provides the USSR with the ability to engage in war (by proving it can fight, the USSR hopes to prevent someone from being so foolish as to attack in the first place). The Soviets ICBM force and especially its SLBM, invulnerable to Western attack, are seen as part of the Kremlin's ability to take the war to the enemy. This second tier is very similar to the MAD notions of the US, but in the USSR they are seen as part of a total war fighting capability.[45]

One of the fiercest arguments in the Western literature has centred on the importance of the first of these two tiers: passive defence. It is therefore useful at this point to analyse this issue in depth. In the Soviet Union a significant civil defence programme has existed since the 1930s[46] and in the early 1970s civil defence was given the same organisational status as the other combat services.[47] One might reasonably ask why does the Soviet posture differ so markedly from that of the West? It should be clear from the previous discussions in this introductory chapter that such an emphasis on civil defence is part and parcel of the USSR's defence and deterrence strategy.[48] In Moscow's definition of war fighting it is essential to have the ability to minimise the consequences of a nuclear attack. While Mutual Assured Destruction is in part dependent on ensuring vulnerability to nuclear attack, the Soviet doctrine does not accept this concept and seeks to show that since it cannot be successfully attacked, then war will be prevented.[49] Thus the civil defence programme lies at the heart of the differing US and Soviet strategic doctrines.

The new Soviet emphasis on civil defence, as well as its broader difference in strategy from that of the US, has provoked a fierce debate in the West on the significance of the Soviet programme. In the 1960s there were debates both within the Soviet Union on civil defence and in the West as to how real the Soviet expenditure on this effort was.[50] Following the improvement of the status of civil defence in the 1970s, the debate in the West shifted ground. Now there are few analysts who would contest that the USSR spends vast amounts on civil defence, but the debate rages as to the significance of the expenditure. The current discussion was sparked off by provocative comments by the former director of the US Defence Intelligence Agency, General George Keegan, who asserted in early 1977 that the Soviet civil defence programme had significantly altered the strategic balance.[51]

The vast majority of previous academic work on Soviet civil defence supported General Keegan in arguing that this programme was designed to protect the USSR from the US assured destruction capability and was the groundwork for a Soviet first strike.[52] They argued that the West rejected consideration of Moscow's civil defence plans merely because the US doctrine was designed to ensure vulnerability and as a consequence the USSR gained a unilateral advantage in the strategic balance. While this hawkish view has made a useful contribution by pointing to a crucial aspect of Moscow's particular strategic doctrine, it has also distorted the significance of civil defence. It is the old problem of asserting 'worst case' intentions based on 'worst case' capabilities.

Fred Kaplan has vigorously refuted both the supposed intentions and capabilities of the Soviet civil defence programme.[53] Mirroring the broader debates of Team A and Team B, Kaplan accepts that there is a large Soviet expenditure on civil defence but insists that it is ineffective. Kaplan draws on the broader aspects of the Soviet doctrine on defence and deterrence, much as contributors to this volume have done, to suggest that for both ideological and bureaucratic reasons the Soviets believe that their programme must be sustained despite its apparent flaws. The 'Barbarossa complex' stressing the need to appear to be working constructively for the defence of the homeland (and not leaving it hostage to MAD for its defence) and the purposes of internal cohesion and garrison-state mentality are only a few of the reasons cited by Kaplan for the continuation of the programme.

Thus defensive calculations rather than offensive first-strike thoughts are at the root of the Soviet civil defence programme. These calculations also apply to the use of civil defence against powers other than the US and on this aspect the question of the utility of the Soviet programme is once again raised. Kaplan accepts that the USSR may see an additional purpose in civil defence against China, the UK or some other nuclear force, but once again asserts that the Soviet programme will not provide enough protection. China with its ICBMs, and the UK with Polaris and now Trident, would all have the capability to ensure at least a minimum deterrence.[54]

The debate in the West has shifted ground once again, this time with the hawks adjusting their argument. In the face of strong evidence that the Soviet programme is not effective at present,[55] the hardliners have begun to argue a more limited use of civil defence than ensuring a first strike. One prominent analyst now suggests that the primary use of civil defence will be at the lower level of nuclear crisis. When deterrence fails, civil defence can contribute to the management of escalation, i.e. to the deterrence of coercion short of total war.[56] The hawkish argument has essentially been reduced to one of 'some civil defence is surely better than no civil defence'.[57] At least in psychological terms this is said to enhance the Soviet posture.

The essential counter-argument is that the basic economic costs still favour the offence. It is so much cheaper to develop additional offensive forces to counter the already flawed defensive measures that the vast expenditures on civil defence could be better spent elsewhere. This disagreement on 'how much is enough' is well known from other aspects of strategic debates and no clear answer is possible. The debate has, however, apparently gone against the doves. Despite articulate critics of the utility of civil defence,[58] in 1977 and 1978 large expenditures were requested by President Carter for civil defence in an explicit response to Soviet programmes.[59] Generally speaking, State Department and arms control officials opposed the spending while Defence Department and NSC officials supported it. The US was moving rapidly down the road of undermining its own MAD notion as civil defence spending was in precise contradiction to the doctrine.

Apart from such subjective aspects of the Soviet deterrence and defence doctrine as civil defence, there are also aspects that Dennis Ross (Chapter 5) calls 'objective factors'. For example, to the extent that doctrine results from available technology rather than simply being the result of some grand masterplan, it is important to understand those aspects of the USSR's political and economic system which determine the weapon systems that will be produced. Two main aspects of these objective factors can be isolated.[60] Firstly, there seems to be at least a 10 to 15 year time lag between the formulation of plans and the deployment of a system. This long lead time means that short term stimulus and response attributed to the USSR in weapons development is impossible and that in an already rigid decision making system the process is even more cumbersome. Secondly, the technology available at the time that weapons are first developed tends to be a more important factor in determining the nature of the weapon rather than being a result of a coherent and rational policy-choice among all available options, for example institutional interests are crucial in understanding why the USSR develops heavy missiles. Apart from the motive derived from traditional practice, the mere existence of an already utilised heavy rocket may have made it more likely that for a new generation of missiles the heavy rocket would be used, even though the new technology to reduce the size of warheads and make heavy missiles less necessary could also have been used. Thus intentions should not be imputed from capability as capability may well be a product of varied and institutional factors.[61]

Whereas the Western doves may be heartened by a conclusion that Soviet weapons are not necessarily the result of aggressive first-strike designs, they would be displeased with the complementary view that because of the same objective factors Soviet arms deployment is unlikely to stop growing. This raises the related question alluded to in the previous section: does the USSR seek equivalence or superiority? If we accept that the Soviet force build-up is in large part a result of momentum and permanently operating factors in the USSR, this would accord with the view expressed earlier that the USSR seeks parity not superiority.[62]

However, parity does not mean the absence of competition and consequently the arms race does not come to a halt. The USSR's meaning of the term 'essential equivalence' is more along the lines of 'equal security', thereby leaving a fair amount of room for manoeuvre. Moscow recognises strengths and weaknesses in different areas and accepts no clear point of termination such as the US does when it uses the term 'sufficiency'.[63] The ideological view of a dynamic superpower relationship only serves to reinforce this view as in the case of continuing competition in local conflict outlined in section 7.[64]

Much like the Soviet acceptance of present parity despite an ideological commitment to future victory and superiority, so in the case of SALT the USSR is able to accept an agreement that in part may be contrary to some aspects of its doctrine. The common denominator to both issues is the Soviet acceptance of the 'correlation for forces'. In the case of SALT and the Soviet acceptance of a limit on ABM (a crucial component to its damage limitation policy), the main reason was probably the relatively uneconomic cost of such defensive systems in relation to offensive penetration potential, as well as a basic appreciation that the US would benefit more by a technological competition.[65] Nevertheless, the notion of damage limitation is retained and Moscow continues to invest in new ways of solving technological problems in this sphere. Competition continues in the long run even though an agreement has been signed and abided by in the short run.

This stress on the realities of power also has relevance for those concerned with the policy-relevant problem of formulating a negotiating strategy with the USSR. Dennis Ross argues that there exists a minority in the USSR that accepts far more of the US doctrine of deterrence by punishment and that this moderate group can be encouraged. Since they perceive the US in realistic terms as a strong non-ideological power which accepts the reality of power, then the US can further the cause of these Soviet realists by pursuing its own realistic policy.[66] The alternative Western points of view are deeply flawed. The policy of the American doves who perceive convergence in doctrine where there is none will not come to grips with basic Soviet motives such as the interests of the military. Similarly, the policy of the hawks that deprecate US strength and resolve[67] will only reduce the Soviet perception of the US as strong and determined. Neither will come to grips with the essential language of the balance of power that is so important in Moscow. The pragmatic view in the USSR is that the growth of Soviet strategic power has helped shift the correlation of world forces such that the US has accepted equality and *détente*.[68] Whatever the case, this discussion of different groups and policy preferences brings us now to consider the role of the most important factor in Soviet decision-making on strategy, the armed forces.

5. The Military and Strategic Policy Making

We have already referred to the policy-making process in passing, but it would be useful to consider the subject in greater detail with particular attention paid to the role of the military. Although there is not much obvious disagreement in the West on the role of the armed forces in the decision-making process, differences do appear on the question of how serious the military is about arms control. To a great extent these differences follow the traditional hawk-dove split with those believing that the USSR is not truly interested in negotiation tending to be the same as those who see the military as not accepting any forms of arms control.[69] Raymond Garthoff (Chapter 6) looks at the role of the military in general in Soviet policy making, and more particularly the problem of SALT.

Although it is clear that the military is not a unified body, it is probably less rent by internal splits as compared with American interservice rivalry.[70] With this caveat in mind, it is possible to note the general attitude of the armed forces towards strategic issues and SALT. By and large the military is not the most enthusiastic supporter of a strategic dialogue with the US, but neither has it apparently blocked any agreement. The main concern of the military is to control American advantages, especially in new technology, while not substantially hindering its own programmes.[71] This has by and large been achieved. For example in the ABM treaty in SALT I, while the armed forces probably opposed limitation of what it considered an important component of its damage limitation policy, it recognised that the costs and inefficiency of the system were too great and the US showed every sign of deploying a superior technology. Thus pragmatic realities overrode whatever doctrinal or bureaucratic opposition there may have been.[72] The military accepts the basic aspects of Soviet strategy including deterrence, defence and parity; indeed in many ways it can be seen as the most articulate advocate of those views. What is more, the military accepts agreements and at the same time retains a belief in continuing competition in the superpower relationship. While the military may be crucial in forming doctrine as Garthoff points out, they are not doctrinaire and have implemented and monitored arms control agreements in a basically fair fashion. Especially since the SALT process has been concerned with loose control rather than savage cuts, the military has been able to focus on technical aspects and accept the agreements.[73]

As we have suggested above, it is unrealistic to look only at the conceptual issues involved in strategic posture. As we saw in Dennis Ross's article, it is necessary to look at the organisational configuration in the USSR in order to fully understand the way in which policy is made. The involvement of the military in the complex organisational pattern is not an easy issue to analyse, not the least for the paucity of hard information, but it is important to outline the framework. While this is not the place to discuss the intricacies of party-army relations in the USSR, especially since this is one area of the role of the military which is disputed by Western analysts,[74] it is important to note that the military and civilian forces in the Soviet Union have a long history of interaction. The negotiations on SALT I in particular marked the beginning of intensive military involvement in prominent aspects of Soviet foreign policy.

While not always in the conflicting manner suggested by some analysts, the pattern of involvement does show signs of disagreement and bargaining. This should not be surprising for any interest group, and especially for one as powerful and diverse as the military. It is clear that the special roots and traditions of the armed forces are not always identical to those of other interests in the state.[75] There can be no doubt then that within the framework of institutional pluralism the interests of the military are not necessarily synonymous with those of the government as a whole, and this no doubt applies to arms control issues as well.

The military is represented and involved in all levels of decision making. Arthur Alexander, in his lengthy study of the armed forces and Soviet decision making shows that the military representatives follow the flow of directives to the implementation level where on military issues it has a dominant position.[76] Decisions on strategic issues and arms control are ultimately taken in the Politburo but the key and most recent important organisational development, the Defence Council, is where the most detailed consideration of issues takes place.[77] There are various other levels of decision making, for example the state structure, the scientific community and expert academic advice.[78] Although the details are too complex to be studied here, there has developed a sizeable Western literature on these different levels affecting policy making. It has become increasingly accepted that a complete analysis of defence issues requires that account be taken of all levels of decision making and implementation, as for example was done by Karl Spielmann in his study of the SS-6 decision.[79]

The role of defence industrialists as well as military defence officials is important and, as we have already pointed out, their institutional preferences may well contribute to the more precise nature of the strategic force deployment.[80] While it is not true that the US *has* a military industrial complex and the USSR *is* a military industrial complex, nevertheless the role of these groups is clearly important in determining the Soviet force posture. It is, however, not important in the same way as it is in the US and there can be no avoidance of a detailed analysis of the specific characteristics of the Soviet complex before anything near a full conclusion can be drawn.[81]

While the military industrial complex is concerned with the point at which the civilian and military interests meet, the differing institutional preferences within the armed forces are at least equally crucial. It has been pointed out by several authors that it is important to study the specific interests of diverse military forces in order to fully understand the type of forces it uses. For example, Raymond Garthoff pointed out a long time ago that Soviet MRBM forces were deployed in an artillery-like configuration (including a re-fire capability) perhaps because the authority over the deployment of these missiles was the Main Artillery Directorate.[82]

The overall picture is one of a military dominating the decision-making process basically through control of information and expertise on military issues. Coupled with innate conservatism and incrementalism in the military and civilian leadership, the resulting synergy leads to very limited opportunity for change.[83] In order for change to occur in a dramatic fashion the civilian decision-makers must intervene, but the consensus and conservative policy-formulation process in the leadership as a whole makes such a possibility most improbable.[84] This also means of course that external pressures are not likely to have a very significant effect on policy making. Caution and conservativeness remain the key descriptions of the process in general and the role of the military in particular.

6. The Use of Military Instrument

Although some people have divided study of the Soviet use of the military instrument into internal and external dimensions, such a division is misleading. The development of military force for use beyond the borders of the USSR should be seen as part of the general Soviet conception of an all-round war fighting capability. In the Soviet view, military power must be possessed at all levels, and especially in the latter half of the post-war period, the USSR has expanded its ability to project military force beyond its frontiers. While there is very little debate in the West on whether the USSR has in fact expanded such military components, there is significant disagreement on the meaning of these developments.[85] The crucial question appears to be: will greater military capability mean a greater willingness to use it and take risks in doing so.[86] As the USSR moves closer to parity with the US, will this mean more danger or less for the West? Hannes Adomeit (in Chapter 7) approaches these issues not by dividing up the ways in which force can be used, but by studying the ways in which the USSR perceives risk and the role of Soviet capability, ideology and domestic politics. Although the role of force in internal politics and other issues such as the use of foreign military aid are of great interest, we have omitted these problems from the present analysis. It is recognised that a complete appreciation of the subject would have to take these into account.[87]

We are more concerned with the obvious growth, especially since the early 1960s, of Soviet air, naval and ground forces. The airlift capability is the most conspicuous growth area for the Soviet airforce as witnessed by operations in the Middle East in 1967 and 1973, Czechoslovakia in 1968, and most recently in Afghanistan in 1979.[88] Naval forces have also shown a significant growth especially in regard to the ability to project and sustain power at a distance from the USSR.[89] However, the counting of numbers of ships or aircraft does not in itself indicate a greater willingness to use the military instrument nor a desire to assume greater risk. Perhaps the best way to introduce this contentious subject is to look at specific areas in order to ascertain the different views as to what this force buildup signifies.[90]

There is no doubt that Soviet ground forces have increased in size, but does this mean a greater threat to the West as many have argued?[91] Between 1969 and 1978, 80 per cent of the total increase in Soviet military manpower went to the border with China. About a quarter of all Soviet military spending concerns the PRC and these costs have grown at twice the rate for the rest of the Soviet armed forces.[92] Thus higher numbers do not *necessarily* indicate greater risk for the West.

In East Europe the USSR maintains regular forces in the bloc states and has intervened massively on two occasions. Does this mean that the USSR uses military force easily and with few second thoughts in what it considers its own sphere of influence? Numerous analyses of the specific cases of the use of the military instrument in East Europe would argue to the contrary. The invasions of Hungary and

Soviet Strategy: An Introduction

Czechoslovakia were marked by much wavering and indecision in the Kremlin. The Soviet leadership apparently had no master plan for the use of force even within its own bloc and hesitated before using force.[93] Although this conclusion is not accepted as regards other areas of the world, at least in respect of East Europe even conservative commentators in the West seem to accept this point of view.[94] The constraints and the way in which they fit into the broader issues are highlighted by Adomeit in this text.

Conflict in the Middle East on the other hand has provoked much more divergent views on the uses of the Soviet military instrument. Do the Soviets have a master-plan for dominating the area, sowing conflict in the Arab-Israeli dispute, developing dependencies among local states and choking off Western access to oil? Does Moscow risk great conflict with the US by going to the brink during Arab-Israeli wars, threatening nuclear confrontation and deploying its forces in the area? Hawkish analysts in the West would answer in the affirmative,[95] although the vast majority of detailed studies of Soviet involvement in the area indicates otherwise.[96] Kremlin policy in the area has been muddled and invariably the USSR has taken advantage of other states' blunders rather than successfully masterminding events. For example, in the 1967 Arab-Israeli conflict Moscow may well have raised tensions (in order to support a weak regime in Syria) but it did not want war. In 1970 Soviet troops were engaged in combat for the first time outside the bloc, but the pattern of commitment and desire to avoid undue risk is clear. In 1972 when Soviet troops were expelled from Egypt they went quietly. In 1973 Moscow aided the Arab cause with an airlift, and only threatened to send troops in the face of imminent defeat for its allies. Adomeit pinpoints these and other aspects of the complex Soviet calculation of risk when using the military instrument.

More recent conflicts in the developing world have also been the focus of much disagreement on the use of the military instrument by the Soviet Union. Angola and Somalia were said to be cases of growing Soviet willingness to commit themselves to conflict and expand their power and influence.[97] The abrupt shift of Soviet interest from Somalia to Ethiopia left all the Western worry about bases at Berbera as a bad dream for those who warned of Soviet involvement in the non-aligned world.[98] The Soviet invasion of Afghanistan has also provoked similar disputes regarding Soviet intentions in using the military instrument. The doves suggested that Moscow acted for defensive reasons while the hawks claimed that the USSR sought to use Afghanistan as a stepping stone to the Gulf and wanted to add Kabul to its string of client states on the Soviet perimeter.[99] Whatever the outcome of the debate as to why the USSR became involved in Afghanistan and its risk calculation, it should be heartening to all concerned that Moscow is patently unable to wield its military instrument successfully against a popular uprising in a developing country. Hard questions must be asked about the utility of the military instrument. Clearly a greater quantity of armed force does not necessarily translate itself into greater power or influence.

Thus it seems clear that the Soviet willingness to use its military instrument is not merely a reflection of the USSRs capability.[100] Parity with the US leads to neither more nor less danger of military intervention as the Soviet risk calculation is dependent on too many variables to make such a simplistic judgement. The complexity of the issue, and the need to pursue a context-dependent approach, are amply highlighted by Adomeit. The subtleties of the argument also suggest that a cautious reaction is required to knee-jerk alarms regarding every use of the Soviet military instrument, for as one astute analyst has argued the historical analogy to the present problems may be more the mutual misperceptions of World War I rather than appeased aggression of World War II.[101]

7. The Use of Power

There can be no doubt, as we noted earlier, that during the 1960s and 1970s there was a rapid build-up of Soviet military strength both in quantity and quality. The problem for Western analysts has been to assess the implications of these developments in terms of Soviet military strategy.[102] As John Erickson has noted, the expansion of Soviet forces 'goes to the heart of the most critical issues in Soviet "military policy"'.[103] For many observers in the West, the implications of the Soviet build-up are clear. The Kremlin, it is argued, beyond doubt possesses too much military might for purely defensive purposes and so must be preparing to attack the West. Such a view, they argue, is reinforced not only by the importance of the ideological stance of the Soviet Union, but also by an analysis of Soviet military strategy which reveals an emphasis on surprise attack and offensive operations. These attributes (and therefore aggressive intentions), it is argued, can be clearly discerned from the study of a wide range of readily available Soviet writings on military strategy. In order to analyse this hawkish view we have selected a specific case study of Soviet naval policy,

Soviet Strategy: An Introduction 33

in terms of its role in war and peace. In this introduction, however, we will provide a broader view of some of the basic problems in analysing the capability of all three service arms of the Soviet military.[104]

7.1 The Offensive

The first major problem is how to view the question of the offensive in Soviet strategy. The stark and unambiguous picture which is often presented is far too simplistic. The formal position taken by Soviet pronouncements is that war will almost certainly be initiated by Western forces (unless of course war is seen to be unavoidable) and this will result in Soviet forces 'rolling over' as quickly as possible from the defensive to the offensive in order to administer a 'decisive rebuff' to the aggressor. As John Erickson has noted, 'this clearly does not exhaust the gamut of Soviet ideas on the form and scope of hostilities'.[105] It does, however, highlight a consistent emphasis in Soviet writings (especially the three editions of Marshal Sokolovsky on *Military Strategy*)[106] on the importance of offensive operations. Defending the Soviet Union and countering Western attacks are seen as vital objectives of Soviet military policy, but it is also the case that Soviet writers themselves stress that the predominant form of operations, particularly on land, will involve high speed and highly mobile forces striking deep into the enemy's rear.[107]

Western writers highlighting this emphasis on offensive operations as an indication of aggressive designs point to the modernisation and restructuring of Soviet forces over the past decade as an indication that Soviet leaders are preparing seriously to take the war into NATO territory.[108] They point to the range of improvements in the four basic combat branches of the ground forces which has increased their ability to operate swiftly 'off the march' to cover vast distances each day (up to 70 miles a day) and to provide for their own defence and close fire support.[109] At the same time they point to the new military hardware introduced into the three primary sectors of the air force in the 1970s, all of which has led to a broadening of the Soviet Union's concept of air power and provided greater independence in offensive operations.[110] New models have overcome the traditional limitations of range and payload which restricted Soviet aircraft to interception and limited ground support roles. Now the aircraft have the capability for a wide variety of operations, from long-range interdiction to more sustained and aggressive ground operations.

Another aspect of Soviet offensive operations is the continuing stress on the importance of the tank. Many Western observers believed that the lessons of the 1973 Arab-Israeli war, particularly in terms of the effectiveness of anti-tank missiles, would lead to a re-evaluation of the role of the tank in modern warfare. The Soviet response, however, was not to minimise the tank, but to improve its performance and tactical deployment. As one writer has noted, Soviet planners have made a concerted attempt to circumvent improved defence by innovative counter movement, unanticipated speed and imaginative advance.[111]

Without being able to foretell Soviet intentions however, it is obvious that such a profile of Soviet armed forces is not necessarily evidence that they intend to attack the West.[112] Offensive capability does not necessarily imply offensive actions. As the French demonstrated before World War I (not very successfully in their case) an *'offensive à outrance'* strategy is often designed as both a deterrent and a mode of defence to perceived enemy actions. There can be no doubt that if the West *did* intend to attack the Soviet Union, such a strategy and the present range of capability would be likely to deter such action.

This is not to argue that the military position of the West remains unchanged by the build-up and improvement of Soviet forces. Nor is it surprising that the development of such an effective offensive capability leads to worry in Western capitals and the determination to respond. Clearly, in any future war, at whatever level, the tasks of Western forces will be significantly more difficult to achieve than ten years ago. As our contributors have noted (in Chapters 4-7), it is unfortunate but necessary for the West to maintain its own defences in the light of the increases in Soviet strength.[113] The argument here is simply that the offensive emphasis of Soviet military strategy has to be viewed in the context of wartime operations. Soviet leaders recognise that war is a possibility and therefore they have to deal with the question of what war fighting capability best suits *Soviet* strategic objectives. Their conclusion, not unreasonably from a Soviet perspective, is that it is better to fight on the territory of their opponent than on their own. Many NATO commanders no doubt would wish that such a position was politically feasible for the West.

7.2 *The Resort to Nuclear Weapons*

Another controversial question in Western literature concerns whether the Soviet Union would resort automatically to nuclear, chemical and biological weapons in any conflict in Europe. This is linked to, but distinct from, the question discussed earlier of whether the USSR believes it could win a nuclear war.[114]

Soviet Strategy: An Introduction

One school of thought suggests that nuclear weapons are seen as a vital and integral part of Soviet war planning and would undoubtedly be used in any large scale conflict from the beginning.[115] Another school of thought argues that in recent years Soviet planners have gone to great lengths to provide themselves with improved conventional capabilities precisely in order to avoid the nuclear (or chemical) option. Soviet writings are themselves ambiguous on this question and reveal a debate over the employment of nuclear and conventional forces.

There is no doubt that nuclear weapons are an important part of Soviet military capability. A consistent feature of Soviet writing in the last two decades has been that, because even local conflicts 'threaten inevitably to escalate into all-inclusive nuclear war', the Soviet Union must prepare itself to fight with nuclear weapons.[116] Constant repetition is made of Marshal Malinovsky's statement in December 1962 that

> The next war, if the imperialists manage to unleash it, will be a decisive armed conflict between two opposing social systems: According to the character of weapons used, it will inevitably be a thermonuclear war, a war in which nuclear weapons will be the principal means of destruction and missiles will be the principal means of delivering weapons on target.[117]

According to Malinovsky, conflict in Europe — the main theatre of operations — would be of 'unprecedented ferocity' which would be likely to begin with initial mass nuclear strikes in great depth designed to destroy the enemy's ability to defend itself. This would involve attacks on Western nuclear launchers, supplies and communications, thus paving the way for assault by mobile forces.[118]

This stress on the primacy of nuclear weapons and the importance attached to the Strategic Rocket Forces has been balanced by Malinovsky and most other Soviet military writers with an emphasis on the continuing importance of conventional forces. Indeed during the second half of the 1960s an increasing stress was placed on the efficacy of conventional forces leading some Western writers to suggest that an important shift in Soviet thinking was underway. A favourite task of this school of thought has been to compare various editions of a Soviet military book to demonstrate the evolution of thinking towards a greater emphasis on conventional operations.[119] An example which is often used is the book *Marxism-Leninism on War and the Army*.[120] It is pointed out that the 1965 edition maintained that Soviet 'military doctrine gives the main role in defeating an aggressor to the rocket weapons. At the same time it does not deny the important significance of other kinds of weapons and means of fighting.' In contrast it is noted that the 1968 edition contained an added statement that 'the possibility existed in certain circumstances of conducting combat actions without the use of nuclear weapons'.[121] The inference often drawn is that Soviet military planners are now contemplating fighting a major conflict with conventional weapons. Those who emphasise this as a change in thinking also tend to point to the range of improvements in conventional forces which have provided the Soviet Union with many more options and much greater flexibility to conduct conventional operations.

It would, however, be misleading to conclude that such evidence provides sufficient proof that a major shift has taken place in Soviet strategy towards the kind of 'flexible response' strategy envisaged by the West. As John Erickson has pointed out, Soviet planners have for a long time remained sceptical of the view that operations can be kept at a conventional level in any major European conflict or that tactical nuclear weapons can be used in a 'selective fashion'.[122] A more detailed analysis of Soviet military writings reveals that, despite modifications, Soviet strategy continues to be centred on provision of an essentially nuclear war-fighting capability.[123] Soviet manoeuvres in recent years would also seem to confirm this view.

The problem of maintaining the threshold in Europe between nuclear and conventional war is connected to the problem of maintaining the threshold between nuclear war in Europe and a general superpower nuclear exchange.[124] The July 1980 changes in US strategic doctrine have also raised the crucial question: does the USSR accept the concept of limited nuclear war?[125] The problem has received little attention from strategic analysts,[126] but is crucial to a full understanding of the Soviet posture in Europe.

It is clear that Moscow's declaratory policy rejects the notion of limited nuclear war.[127] This is in part due to the Soviet perception that limited nuclear war is an American invention so as to overcome its basic weakness in conventional capability in Europe. The Soviet view is probably even more due to the fact that a limited nuclear war would involve the territory of the USSR and not that of the US. Therefore the USSR has insisted that it will not play by the American rules, and will not limit itself from striking at the continental US.

The USSR's actual deployment, however, suggests a more complex approach and one more in keeping with its total war-fighting doctrine.

Soviet Strategy: An Introduction

The location of limited range nuclear armed missiles and bombers in the USSR capable of striking Western Europe contains both aspects of limited and unlimited nuclear war: limited in the sense of possessing a form of response that is not automatically intercontinental; but unlimited in the sense that by basing these forces on Soviet territory rather than in East Europe Moscow encourages the US and NATO to respond by striking Soviet territory, thereby provoking Soviet retaliation on American territory. Indeed NATO's upgraded Pershing II missiles help blur the already fuzzy line of what constitutes limited nuclear war.[128] It has always been NATO's problem how to couple the fate of the US to that of Europe — a distinctly non-limited war notion — and the USSR has only facilitated the process. Given the Soviet attitude and force deployment, the limited war option for the West is in reality merely likely to ensure the rapid escalation to general nuclear war. This suits the USSR perfectly well, for it is the one that believes in unlimited war.

In sum, Soviet planners have recognised that under 'conditions of variously shaped circumstances' it is necessary to have the capability to conduct nuclear and non-nuclear operations.[129] Great stress has been placed in recent years on the use of conventional weapons in the crucial initial phases. This does not mean, however, that Soviet planners are considering a campaign fought exclusively with conventional weapons, but merely one opening in this mode. What this indicates is that an important conventional capability has been *added* to the nuclear capability (which has also been improved) rather than replacing it.

Despite the continuing importance of nuclear weapons there clearly have been modifications in Soviet strategic thinking in recent years. One of these concerns greater flexibility to cope with a range of likely contingencies, as we have already noted. Linked to this is the greater stress placed on a 'withholding strategy', especially for the Soviet navy. Traditionally Soviet attitudes towards holding back forces in a war for use at a later stage were very critical. From 1972 opinions appeared to change dramatically. In Admiral Gorshkov's articles entitled *Navies in War and Peace,* Admiral Jellico's policy of conserving forces at the battle of Jutland in 1916 was discussed favourably.[130] For the first time Soviet military planners revealed a recognition that withholding power could serve larger strategic purposes. This was accompanied by a growing scepticism in the navy of the effectiveness of anti-submarine warfare and the concern to secure the survival capacity of Soviet SLBMs. Such an emphasis on providing more protection for Soviet missile submarines clearly enhanced the wartime deterrent capability and the opportunity for the Navy to play a crucial role at a later stage in a conflict.[131]

7.3 Peacetime and Wartime Operations

Apart from growing emphasis on the importance of conserving forces in wartime, the issue of the peacetime role of the Soviet navy in the Gorshkov series of articles has also created some controversy amongst Western analysts. For some observers the Soviets had adopted a new naval policy in which the relative importance of peacetime and wartime naval roles was being significantly changed.[132] For others, interesting and illuminating as the series was, there was little evidence of 'an abrupt change in Soviet naval thinking'.[133]

Although the success of the political role of the Soviet armed forces can be exaggerated, it does appear that Soviet forces have been used more deliberately and forcefully in this capacity in recent years. Both Michael MccGwire and Robert Berman attest to this fact in their treatment of the wide variety of peacetime roles of Soviet forces.[134] Both argue that there does seem to be a progressive shift in Soviet overseas policy towards an increasing readiness to use a 'Soviet military presence' in support of foreign policy objectives.[135] Their views correspond with the emphasis given in 1972 by the Soviet writer Colonel Kulish in his book *Military Force and International Relations*. Kulish argued that greater importance was being attached both to a Soviet military presence in various far-flung conflicts as well as to an adequate level of strategic mobility by the armed forces.[136]

The question is whether this represents a major shift in Soviet thinking. Does Moscow now feel that greater gains could be made through the indirect role of armed force rather than the direct use of military force? In other words, how far is the peacetime role of the Soviet armed forces taking over from the wartime role as the primary element in Soviet strategy? As the debate tends to centre on Soviet naval developments it is this area upon which we focus our attention below.[137]

Much of the debate in the West about the implications of the build-up of Soviet naval power tends to focus on the writings of Admiral Gorshkov.[138] For some, these publications represented not only recognition of the importance of seapower in peacetime as well as in war, but also an acceptance of this view by the army-dominated military leaders and by the central political leadership. Both groups of Soviet leaders had traditionally minimised the role of the navy as being 'an expensive necessity rather than a preferred instrument of overseas policy'.[139] Such a view, it is often argued, is confirmed not only by the increasing use of naval forces to support foreign policy objectives in the 1970s, but also by the additional resources which have been allocated to naval construction. What is more, during the last decade the procurement of a powerful new range of general-purpose naval forces has significantly increased the peacetime potential of the Soviet navy and the clear shift towards a 'forward deployment' posture.

The hawkish Western analysts emphasise the importance of the peacetime roles of the Soviet navy. The burden of their argument is that these forces have been widely used for political purposes in recent years and that a significant proportion of their operations have been driven by political rather than war-related considerations.[140] This interpretation has not been accepted by all Western analysts and Michael MccGwire (in Chapter 8) questions the validity of this view. He acknowledges that there is some evidence that Soviet attitudes towards the navy and the concept of seapower have been changing and that a policy for the employment of Soviet naval forces in pursuit of peacetime objectives has been evolving in the 1970s. Nevertheless, he argues that this peacetime function is essentially a secondary concern to the Soviet navy and Soviet leaders. He also argues that much of the emerging capability to project Soviet power throughout the world is in fact largely the result of changes which have been taking place in the primary function of Soviet naval policy — that of war fighting.[141] The peacetime utility of general-purpose naval forces has reinforced more important arguments for similar forces required for essentially wartime operations.

According to MccGwire's analysis, the movement towards a 'forward deployment' strategy by the Soviet navy (which began in the early 1960s, not the 1970s) was designed initially to extend Soviet outer defence zones in the Norwegian Sea, the Eastern Mediterranean and later further afield to counter the perceived threat from Western sea-based systems. Such 'forward deployment' also afforded opportunities for some offensive actions in war including support for land-based operations. These tasks and the need to fight a long war with the traditional maritime powers necessitated a large, flexible and balanced fleet. While such forces were being procured other justifications for their use undoubtedly arose but the major functions remained that of war fighting.

To reinforce this argument, MccGwire points out that there is a great deal of evidence that the Gorshkov series was not the product of a unanimous acceptance by the military leadership of the navy's case for maritime forces for peacetime or wartime operations. Indeed, they were part of a continuing and hard fought debate by the navy to assert its position and to secure the necessary resources it felt it had been denied in the past.[142] He points out that although the debate seems to have been resolved eventually largely in the navy's favour, the argument was characterised by compromise on both sides.

Professor MccGwire also argues that although Gorshkov urged a more assertive foreign policy and advocated greater utility of naval forces in peacetime, the bulk of his subsequent book (published in 1976) dealt with war-fighting subjects. The central point being made here and throughout this discussion of Soviet military strategy is that Soviet planners are above all concerned to provide a range of military forces designed to fight as effectively as possible against the existing and projected military forces of the enemy. These forces also have increasingly important peacetime roles in support of foreign policy objectives, but it is the need to be able to fight and win a war which by and large gives rise to the particular configureation and deployment of Soviet armed forces. Soviet planners believe that such an ability makes war less likely, but if it should occur they believe that the emphasis on the provision of overall military capabilities for various contingencies will ensure the survival and triumph of the Soviet Union. John Erickson summed up this position very clearly when he said that

> The first and overriding priority is strategic defence and the protection of the 'homeland': The prime requirement is to wage (and win) a general war, should 'deterrence' fail: 'Winning' a 'long war' means diversified capabilities, for there is no 'war-winning' weapon as such: Such diversification may bring the 'spin-off' of political gain through extra-peripheral presence, but making gains of this order is a lesser priority, and in view of the tally of capability available, must remain so.[143]

8. Concluding Remarks

As this book goes to press there is much discussion among strategic analysts regarding the importance of the new American strategic doctrine. It is now more necessary than ever to understand the nature of the superpowers' strategy. We have already discussed Moscow's view in great detail and noted its basically static characteristics and, as we have already indicated, the trend towards the abandonment of MAD in Washington began some time ago. The announcement of Presidential Directive 59 altering US targeting to include more counter-force sites was yet another step down this road. US doctrine seemed to be converging somewhat more with that of the USSR, and far from Moscow learning superior strategy from the West the signs clearly indicated that it was the US who was learning the subtleties of doctrine from the USSR.

While it is too soon to determine with any precision the nature of the new American strategy, it has clearly brought US and Soviet strategic thinking closer together.[144] In retrospect the changes have been rapid, for it was not until recently that strategic analysts in the West began to appreciate the distinctive Soviet approach to defence. Principles of deterrence through denial (including civil defence) rather than deterrence through punishment, as well as concepts of stability and essential equivalence, have all been shown to have special meaning in the Soviet context. Now that US and Soviet thinking have moved closer, albeit not in the way in which it was first thought, perhaps there is room to be optimistic about the process.[145] While it may be depressing to contemplate the massive new expenditures being prepared to provide the US with a war-fighting capability, perhaps the ensuing similarity in strategic posture will allow for more simple and balanced arms control negotiations without the need to worry about asymetries in doctrine.

Notes

1. Doves and hawks were called Team A and Team B in the US government policy reassessment on the question of Soviet intent. Leading members of Team B were Paul Nitze, William Van Cleave and Richard Pipes. They also tended to be associated with the Committee on the Present Danger. On the hawk-dove continuum see also Arnold Horelick, 'The Strategic Mind-Set of the Soviet Military' *Problems of Communism,* Vol.26, No.2 (March-April 1977); Richard Foster, 'Editor's Commentary: Alternative Worldviews and Strategy Selection in US-Soviet Interaction', *Comparative Strategy,* vol.1, no.3 (1979); Alan Tonelson, 'Nitze's World', *Foreign Policy,* no. 35 (Summer 1979); and Phillip Petersen, 'American Perceptions of Soviet Military Power', *Parameters,* vol.7, no.4 (Jan.-April 1978). As will become apparent in the course of this introduction, we do not use the terms hawks and doves in any rigid categorical sense, but rather as a symbol of positions that in reality tend to be more complex. Thus our usage of the terms is meant as a shorthand for what are in fact more relative views.

2. For further reading in various aspects of the military, divided by issue and on a comparative basis, see Frank Horton (ed.), *Comparative Defense Policy* (Johns Hopkins Press, Baltimore, 1974).

3. Matthew Gallagher and Karl Spielmann Jr, *Soviet Decision-Making for Defence: A Critique of US Perspectives on the Arms Race* (Praeger, N.Y., 1972); Raymond Garthoff, 'On Estimating and Imputing Intentions', *International Security*, vol.2, no.3 (Winter 1978); Robert Jervis, *Perception and Misperception in International Relations* (Princeton University Press, Princeton, 1976); Lawrence Freedman, *US Intelligence and the Soviet Strategic Threat* (Macmillan, London, 1977); Ken Booth, *Strategy and Ethnocentrism* (Croom Helm, London 1979).

4. Morton Schwarts, *Soviet Perceptions of the United States* (University of California Press, Berkeley, 1978); Kenneth Jowitt, *Images of Detente and the Soviet Political Order.* (Institute of International Studies, University of California, Berkeley, 1977). See also Stephen Gilbert, *Soviet Images of America* (Crane, Russak and Co., N.Y., 1977) for a more hawkish line.

5. Richard Pipes, 'Why the Soviet Union Thinks it Could Fight and Win a Nuclear War', *Commentary* (July 1977) and 'Soviet Global Strategy', *Commentary* (April 1980); Joseph Douglass Jr and Amoretta Hoeber, *Soviet Strategy for Nuclear War* (Hoover Institution Press, Stanford, 1979); C.G. Jacobsen, *Soviet Strategy – Soviet Foreign Policy* (Macelhose, Glasgow, 1972); Leon Goure, Foy Kohler, Mose Harvey (eds.), *The Role of Nuclear Forces in Current Soviet Strategy* (Advanced International Studies Institute, Monographs in International Affairs, Miami, 1974); Paul Nitze, 'Assuring Strategic Stability', *Foreign Affairs*, vol.54, no.2, (January 1976); R. Judson Mitchell, 'A New Brezhnev Doctrine', *World Politics*, vol.30, no.3 (April 1978).

6. Raymond Garthoff, 'Mutual Deterrence and Strategic Arms Limitation in Soviet Policy', *International Security*, vol.3, no.1 (Summer 1978), and 'Soviet View on the Interrelation of Diplomacy and Military Strategy', *Political Science Quarterly*, vol.94, no.3 (Fall 1979); Bernard Brodie, 'The Development of Nuclear Strategy', *International Security*, vol.2, no.4 (Spring 1978). This dovish view has also appeared in the generally hawkish periodical *Orbis*, see Graham Vernon, 'Controlled Conflict; Soviet Perceptions of Peaceful Coexistence', *Orbis* (Summer 1979).

7. Karl Spielmann Jr, *Analyzing Soviet Strategic Arms Decisions* (Westview Press, Boulder, Colorado, 1978) and Part III in Erik Hoffmann and Fredrick Fleron Jr, *The Conduct of Soviet Foreign Policy* (Butterworth, London, 1971).

8. Erik Beukel, 'Soviet Views on Strategic Nuclear Weapons: Orthodoxy and Modernism', *Cooperation and Conflict*, no.4 (1979); Lawrence Caldwell, 'Soviet Attitudes to SALT', *Adelphi Papers*, no.75 (1971); Roman Kolkowicz *et al., The Soviet Union and Arms Control: A Superpower Dilemma* (Johns Hopkins Press, Baltimore, 1970); Garthoff, 'Mutual Deterrence and Strategic Arms Limitation'. The hawks tend to dismiss the notion of hawks and doves in the USSR. See for example William Scott, 'Soviet Military Doctrine and Strategy: Realities and Misunderstandings', *Strategic Review*, vol.3, no.3 (Summer 1975). The primary source material on this subject is too vast to list here, but it will be useful to cite V.D. Sokolovskiy, *Soviet Military Strategy*, (ed.) H.F. Scott (Crane, Russak and Co., N.Y., 1975) and the *Soviet Military Thought* series translated and published under the auspices of the US Air Force.

9. P.H. Vigor, *The Soviet View of War, Peace and Neutrality* (Routledge and Kegan Paul, London, 1975).

10. On Soviet ideology see for example the exchange between Richard Lowenthal, Samuel Sharp and R.N. Carew Hunt in *Problems of Communism*, vol. vol.7, no.2 (March-April 1958) and vol.7, no.3 (May-June 1958); Karen Dawisha, 'The Role of Ideology in Decision Making in the Soviet Union', *International Relations* (Nov. 1972); William Zimmerman, *Soviet Perspectives on International Relations* (Princeton University Press, Princeton, 1969).

11. On the debate see Stanley Siekiewicz, 'SALT and Soviet Nuclear Doctrine', *International Security*, vol.2, no.4 (Spring 1978) and Garthoff, 'Mutual Deterrence and Strategic Arms Limitation'.

12. Raymond Garthoff, *How Russia Makes War* (Allen and Unwin, London, 1954).

13. See generally John Erickson, *Soviet Military Power* (Royal United Services Institute, London, 1971); Raymond Garthoff, *Soviet Military Policy* (Faber and Faber, London, 1966); Thomas Wolfe, *Soviet Strategy at the Crossroads* (Harvard University Press, Cambridge, 1964); Helmut Sonnenfeldt and William Hyland, 'Soviet Perspectives on Security', *Adelphi Papers*, no.151 (Spring 1979); Kolkowicz, *Soviet Union and Arms Control;* Edward Warner III, *The Military in Contemporary Soviet Politics* (Praeger, N.Y., 1977).

14. The material on the Cold War is too vast to cover here. Probably the most judicious of the orthodox views is John L. Gaddis, *The United States and the Origins of the Cold War* (Columbia University Press, N.Y., 1972). The most balanced of the revisionists is Daniel Yergin, *Shattered Peace: The Origins of the Cold War and the National Security State* (Houghton Mifflin, Boston, 1976). The most balanced of the conservative views is Vojtech Mastny, *Russia's Road to the Cold War* (Columbia University Press, N.Y., 1979). See the latest review of the literature by Arthur Schlesinger Jr, 'The Cold War Revisited', *The New York Review of Books*, 25 Oct. 1979.

15. On this period see Andrei Sakharov, *My Country and the World* (Collins and Havrill, London, 1975) and *Soviet Diplomacy and Negotiating Behaviour*, US House, Committee on Foreign Affairs, Special Studies Series on Foreign Affairs, vol.1, 96th Congress, 1st Session (USGPO, Washington, 1979) pp206-8.

16. Herbert Dinerstein, *War and the Soviet Union* (Praeger, N.Y., 1962), Raymond Garthoff, *Soviet Strategy in the Nuclear Age* (Praeger, N.Y., 1962) and also *The Soviet Image of Future War* (Public Affairs Press, Washington, 1959).

17. Michael MccGwire, 'Naval Power and Soviet Global Strategy', *International Security*, vol.3, no.4 (Spring 1979); also Harriet F. Scott and William F. Scott, *The Armed Forces of the USSR* (Westview Press, Boulder, Colorado, 1979); Benjamin Lambeth in Chapter 4 of this volume.

18. We do not intend to argue that the arms race is a result of solely internal or external stimuli, but rather an intricate combination of the two. On the debate see for example Colin Gray. *The Soviet-American Arms Race* (Saxon House, Westmead, 1976); Spielmann, *Analyzing Soviet Decisions;* Warner, *The Military in Soviet Politics.* For a conservative view see Bernard Albert, 'The Strategic Competition with the USSR – What is it and how are We Doing', *Comparative Strategy*, vol.1, no.3 (1979).

19. For more details on these triangular factors see Gerald Segal, *The China Factor and the Strategic Balance* (Croom Helm, London, forthcoming).

20. Lawrence Freedman, 'SALT II and the Strategic Balance', *The World Today* (August 1979). Also on SALT see Thomas Wolfe, *The SALT Experience.* (Ballinger Press, Cambridge, 1979). John Newhouse, *Cold Dawn* (Harper and Row, N.Y., 1973); Strobe Talbott, *Endgame* (Harper and Row, N.Y., 1979). For a conservative view of SALT see Paul Nitze, 'SALT II and American Strategic Consideration', *Comparative Strategy*, vol2, no.1 (1980); and Foy Kohler, *SALT II: How Not to Negotiate With the Russians* (Advanced International Studies Institute, Monograph in International Affairs, Miami, 1979).

21. For a good general survey of the US see Michael Mandelbaum, *The Nuclear Question* (Cambridge University Press, Cambridge, 1979). See also note 26.

22. For an important study of these issues see Booth, *Ethnocentrism.*

23. For an obvious example see Peter King, 'Two Eyes for a Tooth: The State of Soviet Strategic Doctrine', *Survey*, vol.24, no.1 (Winter 1979).

24. Booth, *Ethnocentrism;* Fritz Ermath, 'Contrasts in American and Soviet Strategic Thought', *International Security,* vol.3, no.2 (Fall 1978); John Erickson, 'The Chimera of Mutual Deterrence', *Strategic Review,* vol.6, no.2 (Spring 1978); Jack Snyder, *The Soviet Strategic Culture: Implications for Limited Nuclear Operations* (The Rand Corp. R-2154-AF., Santa Monica, Sept. 1977).

25. In addition to our selection see Ermath, 'Contrasts in Thought' Lambeth provides a detailed review of the different meanings of the term doctrine and strategy and we share the use of the term doctrine in its less rigorous Western sense rather than the specific and narrow Soviet definition. Also on these issues too complex to study here see note 12 and Warner, *The Military in Soviet Politics* and 'The Officers Handbook; A Soviet View, *Soviet Military Thought,* no.13 (published under the auspices of the US Air Force, 1971).

26. The changes in US doctrine can be seen for example in the series of articles in *Foreign Policy,* no.39 (Summer 1980) or in R.B. Foster, 'From Assured Destruction to Assured Survival', *Comparative Strategy,* vol.2, no.1 (1980); Stephen Rosen, 'Safeguarding Deterrence', *Foreign Policy,* no.35 (Summer 1979). Those supporting this view tend to be on the hawkish side of the spectrum. Major landmarks in the evolving US strategy were the Schlesinger doctrine of targeting military rather than civilian sites so as to provide a greater war fighting capability, civil defence expenditures in 1977 and 1978 discussed in section 4 of this introduction and most recently Presidential Directive 59 of late July 1980 which sought to explicitly provide the US with limited nuclear war options as part of a more complete war fighting capability. See *The Economist*, 16 Aug., 1980.

27. For a more hawkish view see Foster, 'From Assured Destruction'; for a less hawkish view see Ermath, 'Contrasts in Thought' and Vernon, 'Controlled Conflict'.

28. See the comparisons in Robert Levgold, 'Strategic Doctrine and SALT; Soviet and American Views', *Survival,* vol.21, no.1 (Jan.-Feb., 1979) and Erickson, 'Chimera of Deterrence'.

29. Apart from Section 4 on Soviet doctrine in this volume, Ermath, 'Contrasts in Thought'.

30. For a particularly useful definition of *détente* and peaceful coexistence and the continuing peaceful competition see the appendicies as well as the text of Vernon, 'Controlled Conflict'.

31. For the hawks see Pipes, 'Why the Soviet Union' and Douglass and Hoeber, *Soviet Strategy.* For the moderates see Ermath, 'Contrasts in Thought'; Paul Nitze, 'Deterring Our Deterrent', *Foreign Policy,* no.25 (Winter 1976/77); and James Dornan Jr, 'US Strategic Concepts, SALT and the Soviet Threat: A Primer', *Comparative Strategy,* vol.1, no.3 (1979). For dovish views see Garthoff, 'Mutual Deterrence', qualified in 'Correspondence', *International Security,* vol.3, no.4 (Spring 1979).

32. On SALT see note 18 and for the moderates Marshall Shulman, 'SALT and the Soviet Union', in Mason Willrich and John Rhinelander (eds.), *SALT: The Moscow Agreements and Beyond* (Free Press, N.Y., 1974); and Raymond Garthoff, 'SALT I: An Evaluation', *World Politics,* vol.31, no.1 (Oct., 1978).

33. See note 3.

34. Ermath, 'Contrasts in Thought'.

35. Edward Warner III, 'Soviet Strategic Force Posture: Some Alternative Explanations', in Horton (ed.), *Comparative Policy;* William Garner, 'SALT II: China's Advice and Dissent', *Asian Survey,* vol.19, no.12 (Dec., 1979).

36. Benjamin Lambeth, 'The Sources of Soviet Military Doctrine', in Horton (ed.), *Comparative Policy* and Ermath, 'Contrasts in Thought'.

37. Ibid.

38. On ethnocentrism see Booth, *Ethnocentrism.* On convergence see Wolfe,

Soviet Strategy: An Introduction 45

SALT Experience. For dovish views see Alton Frye, 'Strategic Restraint, Mutual and Assured'; *Foreign Policy*, no.27 (Summer 1977) and Garthoff, 'Mutual Deterrence'. Garthoff was criticised by Donald Brennan, 'Commentary', *International Security*, vol.3, no.3 (Winter 1978) for saying that the USSR accepted MAD. Garthoff replied in no.4, clarifying his views so that they were very similar to the moderate views of Ross, for example. Garthoff claimed that the USSR accepted deterrence, parity and a balance of mutual retaliatory capability and this is not the same as MAD (a term coined by Brennan in the first place). For a more dovish view by Garthoff see our Chapter 6.

39. See for example the hawkish view in note 43 and described by Alan Tonelson in 'Nitze's World'. The moderate view is in Sienkiewicz, 'SALT and Soviet Nuclear Doctrine'; Ermath, 'Contrasts in Thought'; Levgold, 'Strategic Doctrine and SALT'; and Erikson, 'Chimera of Deterrence'.

40. For the best of the historians of Soviet foreign policy see Adam Ulam, *Expansion and Coexistence*, 2nd ed. (Praeger, N.Y., 1974) and *The Rivals* (Viking Press, N.Y., 1971). For an opposing view see Uri Ra'anan, 'The USSR and the Encirclement Fear: Logic or Western Legend', *Strategic Review*, vol.8, no.1 (Winter 1980).

41. See the beginning of our introduction and Sienkiewicz, 'SALT and Soviet Nuclear Doctrine'.

42. See also Levgold, 'Strategic Doctrine and SALT'.

43. Ibid. Sienkiewicz, 'SALT and Soviet Nuclear Doctrine'; and section 5 of our introduction. On Western strategists see Michael Howard, 'The Classical Strategists' in *Adelphi Papers*, no.54 (1969).

44. On the distinction between denial and punishment see Glenn Snyder, *Deterrence and Defense* (Princeton University Press, Princeton, 1961)

45. See Sienkiewicz, 'SALT and Soviet Nuclear Doctrine' and Levgold, 'Strategic Doctrine and SALT'. On the Soviet view see also A.A. Sidorenko, *The Offensive* (Moscow, 1970: Translated and published under the auspices of the US Air Force, 1974). As Ross suggests, the development of this second tier in Soviet strategy may be in part a result of contact with US strategic thought and especially MAD.

46. On Soviet civil defence generally see P.T. Yegorov, I.A. Shlyakhov, N.I. Alalin, *Civil Defence* (Moscow, 1970: translated and published under the auspices of the US Air Force in *Soviet Military Thought*, no.10).

47. George Kolt, 'The Soviet Civil Defence Program', *Strategic Review* (Spring 1972).

48. See the conservative views expressed most recently in Michael Deane, *The Role of Strategic Defence in Soviet Strategy* (Advanced International Studies Institute, Miami, 1980) and Jacquelyn Davis *et al. The Soviet Union and Ballistic Missile Defence* (Institute for Foreign Policy Analysis, Cambridge, 1980).

49. The Soviet view is not uniformly in favour of a shelter programme, as some moderate voices seem to suggest that 'the only real shelter today' is *détente*. See Boris Belitsky, Radio Moscow, 18 Aug. 1980 (*BBC*/SWB/SU 6502/A1/4); and Lt Gen. Mikhail Milshtein interviewed in the *International Herald Tribune*, 28 Aug. 1980.

50. Leon Goure, *The Resolution of the Soviet Controversy over Civil Defence*, 3223 – PA (The Rand Corp., Santa Monica, June 1962).

51. *The New York Times*, 3 Jan. 1977; and *Aviation Week and Space Technology*, 28 March 1977.

52. Leon Goure, *War Survival in Soviet Strategy* (University of Miami, Coral Gables, Florida, 1976) and 'Shelters in Soviet War Survival Strategy', AD-A053250/7GA (DOC NTIS, Springfield Virginia, T.K. Jones, *Industrial Survival and Recovery After Nuclear Attack* (commissioned by Boeing, submitted

to US Joint Congressional Committee on Defence Production, Nov. 1976; T.K. Jones and W. Scott Thompson; 'Central War and Civil Defence', *Orbis*, vol.22, no.3 (Fall 1978); Dallace Meehan, 'Civil Defence in the Soviet Union', *Military Review* (Nov. 1977) and Kolt, 'Soviet Civil Defence'.

53. F. Kaplan, 'The Soviet Civil Defence Myth', *The Bulletin of the Atomic Scientists*, vol.34, no. 3 and 4 (March and April 1978).

54. On the Chinese programme see Gerald Segal, 'China's Strategic Posture and the Great Power Triangle', *Pacific Affairs* (Winter 1980-1). On the minimum deterrence of other forces see Geoffrey Kemp, 'Nuclear Forces for Medium Power Powers', *Adelphi Papers*, no. 106-7 (IISS, London, 1974).

55. For example, two US government studies: *Civil Preparedness Review; Part 2: Industrial Defence and Nuclear Attack*. (Joint Defence Production Committee, 95th Congress, 1st session, April 1977) and a CIA report cited in the *International Herald Tribune*, 21 July 1978. See also a more middle ground in C.N. Donnelly, 'Civil Defence in the Soviet Union', *International Defence Review*, no.4 (1977).

56. Francis Hoeber, 'Civil Emergency Preparedness if Deterrence Fails, *Comparative Strategy*, vol. 1, no.3 (1979) and William Staudenmaier, 'Civil Defence in Soviet-American Strategy', *Military Review*, vol. 58, no. 10 (Oct. 1978).

57. Richard Foster and Francis Hoeber, 'Ideology and Economic Analysis: The Case of Soviet Civil Defence', *Comparative Strategy*, vol. 1, no. 4 (1979).

58. Arthur Broyles, Eugene Wigner, Sidney Drell, 'Civil Defence: The New Debate', *Survival* (Sept.–Oct. 1976); William Kincade, 'Repeating History: The Civil Defence Debate Renewed', *International Security* (Winter 1977-8).

59. *International Herald Tribune*, 27 April 1977, 23 June and 14 Nov. 1978, 6 Feb. 1980; *The New York Times*, 6 Dec. 1978. Congress did not respond in the quantities requested by the President.

60. Ross also discusses the role of external pressures as an objective factor in forming Soviet strategy.

61. See section 5 of this introduction and Spielmann, *Analyzing Soviet Decisions*.

62. Garthoff, 'Mutual Deterrence' and Warner, *The Military in Soviet Politics;* Benjamin Lambeth, 'The Political Potential of Soviet Equivalence', *International Security*, vol. 4, no.2 (Fall 1979). For a more recent hawkish view see Nitze, 'SALT II'.

63. Lambeth, 'Soviet Equivalence' and Edward Luttwak, 'The American Style of Warfare and the Military Balance', *Survival* (March-April 1979).

64. As noted in section 7, equivalence does not translate into more power for the USSR in non-strategic clashes as the hawks suggest, but neither does it mean that competition ceases as some doves would have it.

65. See note 27.

66. For a similar but more complete argument see Schwartz, *Soviet Perceptions*.

67. Paul Nitze for example has announced imminent Soviet advantage over the US at several junctures, e.g. in the early 1950s or the missile gap scare later in the decade: Tonelson, 'Nitze's World'.

68. Wolfe, *SALT Experience*, p.203.

69. Numerous works on these issues can be cited: see for example Warner, *The Military in Soviet Politics;* Wolfe, *The SALT Experience* and *The Military Dimension in the Making of Soviet Foreign and Defense Policy* (The Rand Corp., Santa Monica, Oct. 1977) P-6024; Marshall Brement, *Organizing Ourselves to Deal With the Soviets* (The Rand Corp., Santa Monica, June 1978) P-6123; and Spielmann, *Analyzing Soviet Decisions;* Gallagher and Spielmann, *Soviet*

Decision Making for Defence; Malcolm Mackintosh, 'The Soviet Military: Influence on Foreign Policy, *Problems of Communism*, vol.12, no.5 (Sept.-Oct. 1973); and Igor Glagolev, 'The Soviet Decision-Making Process in Arms Control Negotiation', *Orbis*, vol.21, no.4 (Winter 1978).

70. Ibid., first four citations.

71. In our Chapter 6, Garthoff argues that SALT had a more concrete effect on limiting Soviet programmes. See supporting evidence in Roger George, 'The Economics of Arms Control', *International Security* (Winter 1978/79) and Garthoff, 'SALT I'.

72. Wolfe, *SALT Experience;* Warner, *The Military in Soviet Politics;* Gallagher and Spielmann, *Soviet Decision Making for Defense;* Douglas Garthoff, 'The Soviet Military and Arms Control' *ACIS Working Paper no.10* (Center for Arms Control and International Security, UCLA, Nov. 1977).

73. D. Garthoff, 'The Soviet Military' and Warner, *The Military in Soviet Politics.*

74. On conflict in party-army relations see Roman Kolkowicz, *The Soviet Military and the Communist Party* (Princeton University Press, Princeton, 1967). On the opposite side see William Odom, 'The Party Connection', *Problems of Communism*, vol.22, no.5 (Sept.-Oct. 1973) and 'The Militarization of Soviet Society, *Problems of Communism*, vol.25, no.5 (Sept.-Oct. 1976). For the centrist view see Timothy Colton, *Commissars, Commanders, and Civilian Authority* (Harvard University Press, Cambridge, 1979) and Thomas Wolfe, 'Military Power and Soviet Policy' in William Griffith (ed.), *The Soviet Empire: Expansion and Detente* (Lexington Books, Lexington, Mass., 1976). See also, generally, Dale Herspring and Ivan Volygyes, *Civil-Military Relations in Communist Systems* (Westview Press, Boulder, Colorado, 1978).

75. Warner, *The Military in Soviet Politics;* Scott and Scott, *The Armed Forces of the USSR.*

76. Arthur Alexander, 'Decision Making in Soviet Weapons Procurement', *Adelphi Papers* no.147-8 (1978-9).

77. On organisation generally see ibid.; Wolfe, *SALT Experience*, and Spielmann, *Analyzing Soviet Decisions.*

78. More specifically see David Holloway, 'Technology, Management and the Soviet Military Establishment', *Adelphi Papers*, no.76 (April 1971).

79. Spielmann, *Analyzing Soviet Decisions.*

80. See note 72 and Karl Spielmann Jr., 'Defence Industrialists in the USSR, *Problems of Communism*, vol. 25, no.5 (Sept.-Oct. 1976).

81. Ibid.; Hanes Adomeit and Mikhail Agursky, *The Soviet Military Industrial Complex and Its Internal Mechanism* (National Security Series 1, Centre for International Relations, Kingston, Ontario, 1978). See also Strobe Talbot (trans.), *Krushchev Remembers* (Sphere Books, London, 1971) pp.474-5.

82. Cited in Gallagher and Spielmann, *Soviet Decision Making for Defense,* p.47. See also Spielmann, *Analyzing Soviet Decision;* Warner, *The Military in Soviet Politics.*

83. On general policy making see, in addition to note 67, Vladimir Petrov, 'Formation of Soviet Foreign Policy', *Orbis*, vol. 17, no. 3 (Fall 1973); Simes, *Detente and Conflict.*

84. D. Garthoff, 'The Soviet Military'.

85. Hard line views for example in Paul Nitze, 'Deterring our Deterrent', *Foreign Policy*, no.25 (Winter 1976/77) and 'Assuring Stability'; Pipes, 'Soviet Global Strategy'. For the middle view see for example Adam Ulam, 'Detente Under Soviet Eyes', *Foreign Policy*, no.24 (Fall 1976); Dimitri Simes, *Detente and Conflict: Soviet Foreign Policy 1972-1977* (Washington Papers No.44, Sage Publications, Beverly Hills and London, 1977); Helmut Sonnenfeldt,

'Russia, America and Detente', *Foreign Affairs,* vol.56, no.2 (January 1978); David Finley, 'Some Aspects of Conventional Military Capability in Soviet Foreign Relations', *ACIS Working Paper No.20* (Center for International and Strategic Affairs, UCLA, Feb. 1980). For the dovish view see Richard Barnet, *The Giants* (Simon and Shuster, N.Y., 1978); Barry Blechman and Stephan Kaplan, *Force Without War* (The Brookings Institution, Washington, 1978).

86. This problem of separating intentions and capabilities is covered in note 3. It is also similar to the level of analysis distinction made by MccGwire in our Chapter 8.

87. For example Ken Booth, *The Military Instrument in Soviet Foreign Policy 1917-1972* (Royal United Services Institute, London, 1973) and Roger Hamburg, 'Soviet Perspectives on Military Intervention' in Ellen Stern (ed.), *The Limits of Military Intervention* (Sage Publications, London, 1977). For further discussion see sections 7 and 8 of the introduction to this volume.

88. John Erickson, *Soviet Military Power* (Royal United Services Institute, London, 1971); Booth, *The Military Instrument;* Hamburg, 'Soviet Perspectives'.

89. On the various points of view on the meaning of the naval build-up see Michael MccGwire, *Soviet Naval Developments: Capability and Context* (Praeger, N.Y., 1973; Michael MccGwire, Ken Booth, John McDonnell; *Soviet Naval Policy; Objectives and Constraints* (Praeger, N.Y., 1974); Bradford Dismukes, James McConnell (eds.), *Soviet Naval Diplomacy (Pergamon Press, N.Y., 1979).*

90. Finley in 'Some Aspects of Capability' pursues a different approach by dividing the subject into the explanatory theories for Soviet conventional capability. This is particular useful in the way it highlights the strengths and weaknesses of certain explanations such as institutional forces.

91. In addition to note 19 see hawkish views from C.G. Jacobsen, *Soviet Strategic Initiatives* (Praeger, N.Y., 1979); W. Scott Thompson, 'The Projection of Soviet Power', in *Defending America* (Basic Books, N.Y., 1977); Avigdor Haselkorn, *The Evolution of Soviet Security Strategy 1965-1975* (Crane, Russak, N.Y., 1978). See a more balanced view in Alvin Rubinstein, *Soviet and Chinese Influence in the Third World* (Praeger, N.Y., 1975).

92. Data based on Testimony to the Subcommittee on Priorities and Economy in Government of the Joint Economic Committee, 95th Congress, 2nd Session, 26 June, 14 July 1970: 'Allocation of Resources in the Soviet Union and China – 1978'.

93. For the moderate view see for example Robin Remmington, *The Warsaw Pact: Case Studies in Communist Conflict Resolution* (MIT Press, Cambridge, 1971); Jiri Valenta, *The Soviet Intervention in Czechoslovakia 1968* (John Hopkins Press, Baltimore, 1979); Karen Dawisha, 'The Soviet Union and Czechoslovakia, *Jerusalem Journal of International Relations,* vol.3, nos.2-3 (1978); Edwina Moreton, *East Germany and the Warsaw Alliance* (Westview Press, Boulder, Colorado, 1978); 'Developments in Warsaw Pact Forces', *Strategic Survey 1979* (International Institute for Strategic Studies, London, 1980).

94. For example Zbigniew Brzezinski, *The Soviet Bloc: Unity and Conflict* (Harvard University Press, Cambridge, 1967); Christopher Jones, 'Autonomy and Intervention: The CPSU and the Struggle for the Czechoslovak Communist Party, 1968', *Orbis,* vol.19, no.2 (Summer 1975); Andrezej Korbonski, 'Eastern Europe and the Soviet Threat', *Proceedings of the Academy of Political Science,* vol.33, no.1 (1978); Robert Levgold, 'The Problems of European Security', *Problems of Communism,* vol.23, no.1 (Jan.-Feb. 1974); Christopher Jones, 'Just Wars and Limited Wars', *World Politics,* vol.28, no.1 (Oct. 1975).

95. Uri Ra'anan, 'Soviet Policy in the Middle East 1960-1973', *Midstream,* vol.30, no.10 (Dec. 1973); Foy Kohler, Leon Goure, Mose Harvey, *The Soviet Union and the October 1973 Middle East War* (Center for Advanced International

Studies, Monographs in International Affairs, Miami, 1974); Joseph Churba, 'The Middle East Power Balance in Transition', *Comparative Strategy*, vol.2, no.1 (1980).

96. For example Robert Freedman, *Soviet Policy Toward the Middle East Since 1970* (Praeger, N.Y., 1978); Alvin Rubinstein, *Red Star on the Nile* (Princeton University Press, Princeton, 1977); Karen Dawisha, *Soviet Foreign Policy Towards Egypt* (Macmillan, London, 1979).

97. Mordechai Abir, 'Red Sea Politics', *Adelphi Papers, no.93 (1973)*; J. Bowyer Bell, *'Strategic Implications of the Soviet Presence in Somalia', Orbis*, vol.19, no.2 (Summer 1975); Brian Crozier, 'The Soviet Presence in Somalia', *Conflict Studies*, no.54 (Institute for the Study of Conflict, London); Ian Greig, *The Communist Challenge to Africa* (Foreign Affairs Publishing Co., Richmond, Surrey, 1977); Steven David, 'Realignment in the Horn: The Soviet Advantage', *International Security*, vol.4, no.2 (Fall 1979); essays in Warren Weinstein, Thomas Henriksen (eds.), *Soviet and Chinese Aid to African Nations* (Praeger, N.Y., 1980); Walter Hahn, Alvin Cottrell, *Soviet Shadow Over Africa*. (Center for Advanced International Studies, Washington, 1977).

98. For moderate views see Hamburg, 'Soviet Perspectives'; Jiri Valenta, 'The Soviet-Cuban Intervention in Angola, 1975', *Studies in Comparative Communism*, vol.11, nos.1 and 2 (Spring/Summer 1978); Donald Zagoria, 'Into the Breach: New Soviet Alliances in the Third World', *Foreign Affairs*, vol.57, no.4 (Spring 1979); Joseph Smaldone 'Soviet and Chinese Military Aid and Arms Transfers to Africa: A Contextual Analysis', in Weinstein and Henriksen (eds.), *Soviet and Chinese Aid*.

99. On Afghanistan generally see the moderate view in Stanley Hoffmann, 'Reflections on the Present Danger', *New York Review of Books*; 6 March 1980; Leslie Gelb and Richard Ulman, 'Keeping Cool at the Khyber Pass', *Foreign Policy* no.38 (Spring 1980); Craig Whitney 'The View From the Kremlin', *New York Times Magazine*, 20 April 1980; A.G. Noorani, 'Soviet Ambitions in South Asia', *International Security*, vol.4, no.3 (Winter 1979/80). For a centrist view see Zalmay Khalizad, 'The Superpowers and the Northern Tier', *International Security*, vol.4, no.3 (Winter 1979/80); Richard Newell, 'Soviet Intervention in Afghanistan', *The World Today* (July 1980). For hawkish view see for example Edward Luttwak, 'After Afghanistan, What?', *Commentary* (April 1980).

100. See generally R.J. Vincent, 'Military Power and Political Influence: The Soviet Union and Western Europe', *Adelphi Papers*, no.119 (Autumn 1975); Jan Triska and David Finley, *Soviet Foreign Policy* (Macmillan, N.Y., 1968) Ch.9; Hannes Adomeit, *The Soviet Union and Western Europe*, National Security Series no.3. (Center for International Relations, Queens University, Kingston, Ontario, 1979).

101. Miles Khaler, 'Rumours of War: The 1914 Analogy', *Foreign Affairs*, vol.58, no.2 (Winter 1979/80).

102. Soviet military strategy has a specific meaning in Soviet writings. It is regarded as 'specific theory' which develops the basic methods and forms of armed conflict on a strategic scale and at the same time carries out the military leadership of the war: 'The Officers Handbook' p.78. See also in the *Soviet Military Thought* series translated by the US Air Force: 'Dictionary of Basic Military Terms' no.9 (Moscow, 1965). On doctrine and strategy see also Scott and Scott, *The Armed Forces of the Soviet Union*.

103. Erickson, *Soviet Military Power*, p.42.

104. For details on specific armed services see Ray Bond (ed.), *The Soviet War Machine* (Salamander Books, London, 1976). For historical details on the development of the various services see Malcolm Mackintosh, *Juggernaut: A History of the Soviet Armed Forces* (Secker and Warburg, London, 1967); Jeffrey

Record, *Sizing up the Soviet Army* (The Brookings Institution, Washington, 1976); Asher Lee, *The Soviet Air Force* (Duckworth, London, 1961); Robert Kilmarx, *A History of Soviet Air Power* (Faber, London, 1962); Alexander Boyd, *The Soviet Air Force* (Macdonald and Jane's, London, 1977); Donald Mitchell, *A History of Russian and Soviet Sea Power* (Andre Deutsch, London, 1974); Michael MccGwire (ed.), *Soviet Naval Developments* (Praeger, N.Y., 1973); Eric Morris, *The Russian Navy: Myth and Reality* (Hamish Hamilton, London, 1977).

105. Erickson, *Soviet Military Power*, p.67.

106. Sokolovsky, *Military Strategy* (editions of 1962, 1963, 1968).

107. John Despres, Lilita Dzirkals and Barton Whaley, *Timely Lessons of History: The Manchurian Model for Soviet Strategy*, R-1825-NA (The Rand Corp., Santa Monica, 1976).

108. Other than the material already cited see Dismukes and McConnell, *Soviet Naval Policy;* Sir John Hackett et al., *The Third World War* (Sphere Books, London, 1979); William Schneider Jr., 'Soviet General Purpose Forces', *Orbis*, vol.21, no.1 (Spring 1977). For the moderate view see note 29.

109. Erickson, *Soviet Military Power.*

110. Robert Berman, *Soviet Air Power in Transition* (The Brookings Institution, Washington, 1978).

111. Jacobsen, *Soviet Strategic Initiatives.*

112. See for example the question of the already mentioned anti-tank weapons debate: C.N. Donnelly, 'Soviet Tactics for Overcoming NATO Anti-Tank Defences', *International Defence Review* no.7 (1979); Phillip Karber, 'The Soviet Anti-Tank Debate', *Survival* (May-June 1976).

113. See Berman, *Soviet Air Power,* and MccGwire in this volume. Soviet forces, even if in an offensive posture, still have serious problems that at least for the present make the offensive use of weapons less likely. The continuing problem of combined arms operations is a case in point. See John Erickson, 'The Ground Forces in Soviet Military Policy', *Strategic Review*, vol.6, no.1 (Winter 1978), 'Soviet Breakthrough Operations: Resources and Restraints', *RUSI*, vol.121, no.3 (Sept. 1976) and 'Trends in the Soviet Combined Arms Concept', *Strategic Review*, vol.5, no.1 (Winter 1977); C.N. Donnelly, 'Tactical Problems Facing the Soviet Army', *International Defence Review*, no.9 (1978); Peter Vigor, 'Doubts and Difficulties Confronting a Would-Be Soviet Attacker', *RUSI*, Vol.125, no.2 (June 1980).

114. See section 1 of this introduction.

115. Scott and Scott, *The Armed Forces of the USSR.*

116. R. Ya Malinovsky, *Vigilantly Stand Guard Over the Peace* .

117. Ibid.

118. Berman, *Soviet Air Power* and Erickson, 'Trends in Combined Arms'. Generally on West Europe in the Soviet view see Vincent, 'Military Power and Political Influence' and Adomeit, *The Soviet Union and Western Europe.*

119. Scott and Scott, *The Armed Forces of the USSR.*

120. N. Ya Sushko and SA Tyushkevich (eds.), *Marxism Leninism on War and the Army* (Moscow, 1965 and 1968). See also Harriet Scott, *Soviet Military Doctrine* (Stanford Research Institute, California, 1971) p.59.

121. Ibid.

122. Erickson, *Soviet Military Power.*

123. Scott and Scott, *The Armed Forces of the USSR,* pp.54-6.

124. See section 3 of this introduction.

125 On PD 59 see *The Economist,* 16 August 1980.

126. Benjamin Lambeth, *Selective Nuclear Operations and Soviet Strategy*, P-5506 (The Rand Corp., Santa Monica, Sept. 1975); Snyder in *The Soviet Strategic Culture* argues that the USSR does not accept limited nuclear war. For a

more hawkish view suggesting that the USSR does accept limited nuclear war see Joseph Douglas Jr, 'Soviet Nuclear Strategy in Europe: A Selective Targeting Doctrine', *Strategic Review*, vol.5, no.4 (Fall 1977).

127. Lambeth, *Selective Nuclear Operation*.

128. In a certain very limited sense of limited nuclear war the USSR does seem to accept the validity of the concept. As regards a lesser, more tactical use of nuclear weapons by the USSR, the fact that these forces are based on non-Soviet territory would seem to mean that a response by the West would not necessarily involve Soviet territory. While Soviet territory is not affected, then US territory can also be spared. This equality makes it more likely that a limited tactical use of nuclear weapons is possible, even if it far less likely on a theatre level.

129. Grechko in Scott and Scott, *The Armed Forces of the USSR*, p.55. The Soviet hope would be to capture Europe and its economic structure intact and thus would be likely to adopt the least damaging strategy.

130. *Survival* (March-April 1975).

131. Jacobsen, *Soviet Strategic Initiatives*.

132. James McConnell in *Survival* (March-April 1975).

133. Michael MccGwire in ibid.

134. MccGwire in this volume. Also, generally, Michael MccGwire, Ken Booth, John McDonnell (eds.), *Soviet Naval Policy* (Praeger, N.Y., 1975); Michael MccGwire and John McDonnell (eds.), *Soviet Naval Influence* (Praeger, N.Y., 1977); Dismukes and McConnell, *Soviet Naval Diplomacy;* Berman, *Soviet Air Power*.

135. Ibid.

136. Moscow, 1972.

137. The debate is also concerned with such issues as the airlift capability. See Boyd, *The Soviet Air Force*.

138. On the debate see *Survival* (March-April 1975) and see also S.G. Gorshkov, *The Sea Power of the State* (Pergamon, N.Y., 1979): reprinting the 1976 Russian language edition).

139. MccGwire in this volume.

140. Dismukes and McConnell, *Soviet Naval Diplomacy*.

141. It is also in part a reaction to technological and bureaucratic factors which in general affect weapons procurement. See sections 4 and 5 in this introduction.

142. MccGwire in this volume as well as his contribution in the three Praeger volumes on naval strategy cited in notes 90 and 120.

143. Erickson, *Soviet Military Power*, p.50.

144. It is important to note that in the Soviet reaction to PD 59 they have assumed a more MAD posture than the US in arguing that PD 59 is wrong in thinking that civilians can be isolated from military conflict. See note 133 and Tass comment by A. Krasikov 8 August 1980 (*BBC*/SWB/SU/6494/A1/1).

145. Among other things, such convergence would increase the likelihood of success for the 'missions' approach suggested by Christoph Bertram, 'The Future of Arms Control: Part II: Arms Control and Technological Change', *Adelphi Papers*, no.146 (Summer 1978).

PART ONE:

THE EVOLUTION OF SOVIET STRATEGY

2 SOVIET ATTITUDES TOWARDS NUCLEAR WAR: DO THEY REALLY THINK THEY CAN WIN?

Robert L. Arnett

Can the Soviet Union win and survive a nuclear war? Until recently few people would have taken this question seriously because the United States has long had the advantage in strategic nuclear weapons. The massive Soviet build-up of strategic nuclear weapons over the past decade and their emphasis on civil defence in the past five years, however, have led Westerners to re-examine estimates of the Soviet capability to win and survive a nuclear war. The US government's current official position is that the Soviet Union does not have such a capability,[1] but some people disagree; among the sceptics are those who contend that the Soviet Union has the capability to win and survive a nuclear war or at least that the Soviet leaders believe they have such a capability. Retired Major-General George Keegan, retired General Daniel Graham, T.K. Jones, Eugene Wigner, Foy Kohler and others, in fact, contend that the Soviets have the capability, or believe they have the capability, to come out of a nuclear war with fewer population losses than they suffered in World War II.[2] To support these conclusions, two types of evidence are used: (1) analyses of the relative nuclear capabilities (offensive and defensive) of the United States and the Soviet Union, and (2) analyses of Soviet attitudes on nuclear war derived from Soviet open source publications.

Both types of analysis are essential in studying this question, but the there are two reasons why more attention should be given to attitudinal analysis. Firstly, while there have been many studies in recent years which are based upon assessments of US and Soviet capabilities, there has been little systematic, in-depth research on Soviet attitudes towards the consequences of a nuclear war.[3] Secondly, our ability to deter the Soviet Union from launching a nuclear strike is not solely based upon objective strategic capabilities, but is also based upon their leadership's perceptions of these capabilities. Thus while analyses of capabilities are crucial for determining our war-fighting capability, analyses of Soviet attitudes are crucial for determining the credibility of the American deterrent capability.

Knowledge of Soviet views towards the US nuclear deterrent is essential to evaluate our strategic nuclear weapons needs, our strategic civil defence needs, our targeting doctrine and the effectiveness of our deterrent strategy. To understand what the Soviets think about nuclear war and the strategic capability of the United States, it is necessary to review what they have said about: (1) nuclear war as an instrument of policy, (2) victory in a nuclear war, and (3) the consequences of such a war.[4]

Soviet Views on Nuclear War as an Instrument of Policy

To understand Soviet attitudes towards the use of nuclear war as an instrument of policy, we must make certain crucial distinctions. Firstly, when they espouse the dictum that war is a continuation of politics even in the nuclear era, does it mean that they believe nuclear war is an effective instrument of policy? Furthermore, when they refer to war as being an instrument of policy, do they mean it can be used as a practical means for obtaining a political objective or only that it is conceivable that someone, someday, might use nuclear weapons? In addition, when the Soviets talk of war as an instrument of policy, are they referring to nuclear or conventional war or both? The following discussion will consider these questions in analysing what the Soviets have said about nuclear war as a practical instrument of policy.

Some Western analysts conclude that the Soviet advocacy of war as a continuation of politics means that the Soviets believe that war, even nuclear war, can still be used as a practical instrument of policy. Richard Pipes, for example, states that the Soviets believe 'thermonuclear war is not suicidal, it can be fought and won and thus resort to war must not be ruled out'. To support his claim, Pipes cites Marshal Sokolovsky's book *Voyennaya Strategiya* (Military Strategy) which stated, 'It is well known that the essential nature of war as a continuation of politics does not change with changing technology and armament.' Pipes also states that, 'As long as the Russians persist in adhering to the Clausewitzian maxim on the function of war, mutual deterrence does not really exist.'[5] Other Westerners also interpret the continuing advocacy of the dictum 'war is a continuation of politics' to mean that the Soviets believe that nuclear war can serve as a practical instrument of policy.[6]

A review of Soviet writings, however, suggests that such an inference is incorrect. To the Soviets, there is an important difference between defending the thesis that 'war is a continuation of politics' and arguing that 'war is an instrument of policy'. They continue to argue that war is a continuation of politics because it is a basic tenet of Marxism-Leninism which helps to explain their theory of the causes, nature and essence of war. A 1972 article in *Voyenno-Istoricheskiy Zhurnal* (Military Historical Journal), for example, referred to the dictum as 'the most fundamental one (tenet) in understanding the essence of war'.[7] An editorial in *Krasnaya Zvezda* (Red Star) made a similar claim,

> This formula serves as a methodological starting point which enables us to detect what is most important in war, to discover its class nature and to establish the subordination of its targets, means and methods to the economic and political interests of states and classes involved in it.[8]

These statements illustrate that the concept of war as a continuation of politics is fundamental to the Soviet theory of war. That theory, in brief, contends that wars do not just happen. Wars are caused by the existence of classes within a nation pursuing by violent means (war) certain political objectives which they could not achieve by peaceful means. Thus, every war is a continuation of politics. The Soviets avidly defend the dictum because they believe 'it is impossible to understand the essence of war without first studying its connections with the politics which were formed long before the war'.[9] In this context, it is evident that when the Soviets defend the dictum as being valid even in the nuclear age, they are not suggesting, as some Westerners contend they do, that nuclear weapons can be used as practical instruments of policy. Instead, the Soviet spokesmen are arguing that the Marxist-Leninist theory of war is still valid and that if a nuclear war does start, it too will occur because certain classes within a nation are pursuing a policy by violent means.

The Soviets have been pointing out for over a decade that to argue that 'war is a continuation of politics even in the nuclear era' is not the same as to argue that nuclear war can serve as a practical instrument of policy.[10] The 1972 edition of *Marxism-Leninism on War and the Army* states explicitly that,

> Western sociologists and authors on military subjects confuse two closely interconnected yet different questions, namely, the theoretical question of the essence (content and character) of nuclear war and the practical question of whether it can serve as an effective instrument of policy-making.[11]

In addition, LTC Ye. Rybkin pointed out in *Kommunist Vooruzhennykh Sil* (Communist of the Armed Forces) in 1965 that, 'War is always the continuation of politics, but it cannot always serve as its weapon.'[12]

Soviet criticisms of Western interpretations of Soviet writings, however, are not necessarily valid. With this in mind, I examined the texts of numerous Soviet articles which cite the dictum 'war is a continuation of politics'.[13] This review provides corroboration that the Soviets cite the dictum to explain the theory of war and to defend the theory from attacks by the West and the Chinese. It is improper, therefore, to infer that the Soviet usage of this dictum means they believe that nuclear war can serve as a practical instrument of policy or to conclude, as Pipes has done, that 'as long as the Russians persist in adhering to the Clausewitzian maxim on the function of war, mutual deterrence does not really exist'.[14]

The fact is that Soviet spokesmen emphatically deny that nuclear war can serve as a practical instrument of policy.[15] Colonel Ye. Rybkin, for example, wrote that 'a total nuclear war is not acceptable as a means of achieving a political goal'. Nuclear weapons, he argues, have made such an endeavour unfeasible.[16] The same view was expressed by a civilian spokesman who, in discussing the possibility of a nuclear war, claimed that, 'The practice of past centuries when armed force and war were used as instruments of foreign policy is totally unacceptable in our epoch.'[17] A nuclear war, he contends, would have fatal consequences for the entire world.

Thus, Soviet spokesmen believe that their Marxist-Leninism theory of war is still valid in the nuclear era — war remains a continuation of politics. At the same time, they explicitly state that nuclear war is not a practical instrument to achieve political objectives.

Soviet Attitudes Towards the Possibility of Victory in a Nuclear War

Soviet spokesmen frequently refer to the possibility of victory in a nuclear war. They insist that socialism (the USSR) will emerge from such a conflict victorious and imperialism (the US) will be crushed. In addition, certain Soviet spokesmen who have argued that victory is not possible in a nuclear war have been denounced by certain other Soviet spokesmen. As a result, some Western analysts conclude that the Soviet leaders believe they would be victorious in a nuclear war. This conclusion, however, is based upon a superficial examination of Soviet views on the subject and ignores three very important questions: (1) Why do the Soviet spokesmen talk of victory in a nuclear war? (2) What kind of victory are they referring to? (3) Are their statements about victory consistent with what they have said about the consequences of a nuclear war?

Soviet spokesmen have mentioned several reasons why statements about the possibility of victory are important. One reason is that such statements are required by their ideology, or at least some ideologues believe that such statements should be required in discussions of nuclear war. According to Marxism-Leninism, the fates of capitalism and socialism are historically predetermined and cannot be changed. Thus even if the United States initiated a nuclear war to try to reverse the trend of history, the Soviet Union would prevail because it is the superior system. The former Chief of the Strategic Rocket Forces, Marshal of the Soviet Union N. I. Krylov, for example, wrote in 1969 that,

> The imperialists are trying to lull the vigilance of the world's people by having recourse to propaganda devices to effect that there will be no victor in a future nuclear war. *These false affirmations contradict the objective laws of history* . . . Victory in war, if the imperialists succeed in starting it, will be on the side of world socialism and all progressive mankind.[18]

Thus certain Soviets believe that to deny the possibility of a Soviet victory in any war, including a nuclear war, is to challenge, even if not intentionally, Marxist-Leninist ideology and the laws of history which are expressed by that ideology.

This perspective helps to explain why Soviet spokesmen can talk of the dire consequences of a nuclear war and yet still assert that socialism will emerge victorious. They may not be contradicting themselves as it appears they are doing but merely expressing their assessment of the consequences of such a war while maintaining the proper ideological position on the outcome of the conflict.

Soviet statements on the possibility of victory in a nuclear war are also considered important for maintaining the morale of the military and the civilian population.[19] One Soviet military writer stated explicitly that,

> . . . the dubious theoretical concepts whose adherents deny the possibility of a victory in armed struggle involving the use of nuclear missiles are capable of sowing seeds of pessimism among the fighting men and weakening the combat abilities of the armed forces.[20]

In addition to ignoring what Soviet spokesmen have said about why victory statements are important, certain Westerners have also ignored the fact that there are many kinds of victory. At one extreme there is absolute victory in which one nation totally defeats another and incurs no damage. At the other extreme is a victory in the sense of just barely coming out ahead of a totally defeated enemy. Between these extremes, there are many degrees of victory. Thus, it is important to remember that a Soviet statement on victory, by itself, does not tell us what kind of victory they might perceive as being possible.

In analysing Soviet statements about victory, one must also guard against confusing statements of goals with statements of realistic expectations. Certain spokesmen may believe that the Soviet Union should try to win and survive a nuclear war, if it occurs, but this does not necessarily mean that they believe such an objective is possible now or in the forseeable future. In such cases we must analyse what else the they are saying in order to determine how close they perceive they are to achieving such a goal.

Because the word 'victory' is vague, by itself, and because Soviet spokesmen can have various motives for talking about victory does not necessarily mean that they, or at least some of them, do not actually believe in such a possibility. In the 1972 edition of *Marxism-Leninism on War and the Army,* for example, the authors not only talk about victory which they say is determined by the objective laws of history but also about the balance of forces which they suggest now favours the Soviet Union.[21] Thus there is some indication that the authors actually believe victory is possible in such a conflict. In the same work, however, the authors talk about the dire consequences of a nuclear war and state that there would be unprecedented destruction.[22] Such a juxtaposition leads us to question (1) whether the authors really believe victory is possible, and (2) what kind of victory they are referring to?

Thus, Western assertions that 'the Soviet leaders believe in victory' are too vague to be of any real value. A Soviet decision to go to war, if they have the choice, will be based upon their perceptions of the available alternative in conjunction not only with their estimates of whether or not they will be victorious, but more importantly on what kind of victory they would obtain. A belief in a meaningful victory may be an encouragement to start such a conflict, while perceptions of a pyrrhic victory will inhibit rational leaders from initiating a war. Thus, it is necessary to examine what Soviet spokesmen have been saying about the consequences of a nuclear war to determine if they believe victory is possible, and if so, what kind of victory they expect.

Soviet Attitudes Towards the Consequences of a Nuclear War

Westerners who argue that the Soviet view of nuclear war survival differs radically from the view held in the United States have ignored or down-played Soviet statements about the consequences of a nuclear war. A detailed examination of what Soviet spokesmen have said on this subject, in fact, indicates that their assessments of the consequences of such a war are similar to Western estimates.

Politburo Views

Members of the Politburo rarely make their views public regarding the consequences of a nuclear war, but those who have addressed this subject seem to be in agreement as to what would happen. Brezhnev's references to the consequences of a nuclear war suggest that although he may not endorse a mutual assured destruction (MAD) strategy as a basis for national security, he does recognise the reality of MAD. For example, in a speech in October 1973, he stated that existing nuclear stockpiles were 'capable of blowing up the entire planet'. He also recalled the destruction of World War I and World War II and last concluded that World War III would be 'a tragedy the like of which has not been seen in the history of mankind'.[23]

Other Politburo members seem to concur with Brezhnev's assessment. Andrey Gromyko, the Foreign Minister, stated in a 19 January 1974 speech in Yerevan, Armenia, that World War III '... would have the most tragic consequences for all countries and nations'.[24] Mazurov declared that such a war would be a '... horrible disaster for all mankind'.[25] Kirilenko has noted that enough weapons have been stockpiled to annihilate the whole of mankind,[26] while Kosygin has stated that World War III would be even more horrible than previous wars and could be disastrous for mankind.[27] The head of the KGB, Andropov, claimed in a speech in Moscow in 1976 that nuclear weapons '... make the consequences of a nuclear war truly catastrophic'.[28] Finally, Grechko, the late Politburo member, Minister of Defence and Marshal of the Soviet Union, wrote in 1975 that in the event of a nuclear war hundreds of millions would die, the earth's surface would be contaminated, entire countries would be destroyed, and basically that it would be an enormous disaster for mankind.[29]

These members of the Politburo, therefore, do not seem to have any illusions about their nation being able to survive or win a nuclear war in any meaningful sense of the terms. They do seem to believe that the US can still inflict vast damage upon their nation. And while it is true that we cannot be sure what they consider to be 'unacceptable' damage, their statements that the consequences of a nuclear war would be worse than experienced in World War II, truly catastrophic, and threatening the existence of mankind, indicate they still believe the US has an assured destruction capability.[30]

Civilian Spokesmen

Among civilian spokesmen, other than Politburo members, there is a general consensus that the Soviets could not avoid unacceptable damages, nor obtain a meaningful victory, in a nuclear war. V. G. Dolgin, a deputy chief of an unidentified department of the CPSU Central Committee, has warned that one, several or many nuclear devices will wipe from the face of the earth cities, and even entire states, turn our planet into a chaos of chain reactions, global disasters and undermine the conditions of the existence of mankind.[31]

Statements in the daily newspaper of the Soviet government *Izvestiya* (News) express a similar view. V. Matveyev, an *Izvestiya* political commentator, has written that a nuclear war '... would mean the destruction of hundreds of millions of people and the turning of world civilization and culture into ruins and ashes'.[32] A. Bovin, another political observer for *Izvestiya*, wrote that a nuclear war would cause '... inestimable misfortunes to mankind. The aggressor would be crushed. But at what cost?'[33]

Another dire estimate of the consequences of a nuclear war was made in *Izvestiya* in 1976 by an Academician — Ye. Fedorov. He wrote,

> Modern knowledge enables us to evaluate what might happen to our planet and mankind in the event of a world conflict involving the use of the current store of nuclear and other weapons, but it is difficult for the imagination to envisage such a picture.[34]

The predictions made in *Izvestiya* have also been made in *Pravda*, the daily newspaper of the CPSU Central Committee.[35] For example, in February 1977, Sh. Sanakoyev wrote that a nuclear war would be a 'catastrophe on a colossal scale'.[36]

Other public utterances also illustrate Soviet awareness of the devastating consequences of nuclear war.[37] In a 1972 brochure on the nature of a future nuclear missile war, Zh. Dyusheyev wrote, 'The devastation and losses in civilian population which occurred in past wars cannot be compared to the great losses in the civilian population or the tremendous amount of destruction that will occur if a nuclear missile war is unleashed.'[38] Strong statements in this regard have been made by members of the two prestigious foreign affairs research institutes of the USSR Academy of Sciences — The Institute of World Economy and International Affairs (IMEMO) and the Institute for the Study of the USA and Canada.[39] One such statement was made by V. M. Berezhkov, editor of *SSCA,* the journal of the USA Institute, who argued that the nuclear arsenals of the United States and the Soviet Union are so powerful that nuclear war could not serve as a practical instrument of policy, and that neither side can expect to survive such a conflict in any meaningful sense of the word. In 1977 he wrote,

> Whereas in previous eras whole peoples were sometimes exterminated and great civilizations perished as a result of wars, at that time the aggressor, having prepared his attack well, could count on his country having a chance of surviving even after a very destructive war, in the event of victory. In our time there is no such chance.[40]

This review of what civilian spokesmen have been saying about the consequences of a nuclear war indicates that there is a general consensus of opinion. They do not believe that their country could avoid unprecedented destruction in such a conflict.

Military Views

Those in the West who argue that the Soviets believe they could win and survive a nuclear war generally cite statements made by military spokesmen. Indeed, in recent years some military spokesmen have attacked those who argue that a nuclear war will result in the death of civilisation and that there can be no victor. In 1972, Colonel V. F. Khalipov quoted Lenin who said 'no destruction can make civilisation disappear'.[41] In 1973, General-Major A. Milovidov attacked those v ho concluded that no victory is possible in a nuclear war. Milovidov argued that these authors had made errors in calculating the consequences of a nuclear war because they relied strictly on quantitative analyses which resulted in an exaggeration of its destructiveness.[42] Eight months later, Rear Admiral Shelyag also argued that certain authors erred in calculating the consequences of a nuclear war because '. . . they do strictly quantitative analyses'.[43] It is interesting to note that Khalipov, Milovidov and Shelyag are all from the Lenin Military Political Academy.[44]

Statements, such as those made by these military spokesmen, have been presented as evidence by some Western analysts that the Soviet military leaders believe they can win and survive a nuclear war, and therefore that they do not believe the US has an assured destruction capability. In evaluating such declarations by Soviet military spokesmen, however, several factors must be taken into consideration. Firstly, stating that civilisation will not be destroyed in a nuclear war is not the same as arguing that unacceptable damages could be avoided. What it does mean, which Shelyag points out, is that they do not believe that all mankind would be destroyed.[45] In reality, such an assertion is not very profound. The fact is that Western estimates of the consequences of such a war have reached the same conclusion.

In addition, there are strong ideological reasons, especially for members of the Military Political Academy, to argue against statements suggesting that in a nuclear war victory would not be possible and that fatalities would be unacceptably high. It is the job of political officers to ensure that military writings contain the proper ideological positions and to ensure high morale is maintained within the armed forces. The view that victory is not possible in a nuclear war is not considered to be ideologically proper, at least by the idealogues.[46] According to Marxism-Leninism the tide of history cannot be changed even if the West, in frustration, unleashed a nuclear war; the socialist countries are bound to prevail. Thus those who question the possibility of victory, challenge, even if not intentionally, the Marxist-Leninist ideology. Thus it is not surprising to find members of the Military Political Academy attacking such thinking. Likewise, to keep up morale, political officers can be expected to criticise those who talk of high casualty rates, the death of civilisation, or the impossibility of obtaining victory in a nuclear war.

In evaluating the statements of Khalipov, Milovidov and Shelyag, we must also guard against confusing statements of goals from statements of realistic expectations. They might believe that the Soviet Union should try to win and survive a nuclear war, but this does not necessarily mean that they believe such an objective is possible under current conditions.[47]

In fact, Khalipov and Shelyag have expressed doubts about their chances for meaningful victory and survival in such a war. Khalipov states that such a war '. . . can lead to unprecedented destruction to entire countries and can destroy entire peoples' and '. . . it can inhibit the advance of the revolutionary process'. He also admits that losses may be extremely high, but claims that this '. . . depends on the activeness of the masses'.[48] Shelyag wrote that the proper 'Marxist-Leninist view is not one of futility and pessimism' although he admits that a nuclear war would be extraordinarily dangerous.[49] Thus, a re-examination of the views expressed by Khalipov, Milovidov and Shelyag provides no evidence to support the view that they believe nuclear war is a practical instrument of policy or that they believe the Soviet Union could avoid unprecedented damages in a nuclear war.

More important is the fact that, contrary to the impression which some Western writers have presented, most Soviet military spokesmen who discuss the consequences of a nuclear war appear to have little doubt that the United States has the capability to inflict unacceptable damage upon the Soviet Union. The strongest statements on this subject have been made by General-Lieutenant P. A. Zhilin, the Chief of the Institute of Military History of the Ministry of Defence. Zhilin's writings suggest that he believes that both the United States and the Soviet Union have an assured destruction capability. In 1973, he wrote, 'The contemporary revolution in means of conducting war .. has led to a situation where both combatants can not only destroy each other, but can also considerably undermine the conditions for the existence of mankind.'[50] He made similar statements in 1975 and 1976.[51] General Zhilin's view does not appear to be the exception. Another member of the Institute of Military History, Colonel Ye. Rybkin, wrote that the rejection of nuclear war is dictated by the realities of the era. He cited Brezhnev's statement that enough weapons had been stockpiled to destroy all life several times over.[52]

Another military spokesman who has given a dire assessment of the capabilities of the nuclear arsenals of the United States and the Soviet Union is General-Major R. G. Simonyan. While arguing that adding weapons could not give either side a military or political advantage, he stated, 'both sides possess weapons which are capable of annihilating all life on earth many times over'.[53]

Other military writers have commented on the consequences of a nuclear war in the prestigious journal of the Main Political Directorate of the Soviet armed forces, *Kommunist Vooruzhennykh Sil* (Communist of the Armed Forces). In 1972, Colonel T. R. Kondratkov wrote that a nuclear war would have 'exceptionally dangerous consequences'. After mentioning the tremendous human and material losses suffered in World War I and World War II, he states that World War III 'will wreak unprecedented destruction on entire countries'.[54] In July 1975, Colonel A. Dmitriyev wrote that '... a nuclear war will bring immeasurable disasters and suffering to the masses of working people and make it more difficult to achieve the goals of socialist building'.[55]

Several months later, Colonel S. Tyushkevich, from the Institute of Military History, wrote that World War III would result in much greater losses and destruction than had been suffered in World War I and World War II combined. He said, 'The two World Wars took over 70 million human lives and wiped out thousands of prosperous cities and villages off the face of the earth. A World War involving the use of nuclear missile weapons would lead to even greater losses.'[56]

Another pessimistic assessment of the consequences of a nuclear war was made in the 1972 edition of a book writen 'for the attention of Soviet officers, generals, and admirals'. The book, *Marxism-Leninism on War and the Army,* written by faculty members of Soviet military-educational institutions, stated that a nuclear war would cause unprecedented destruction, kill hundreds of millions of people, lay entire countries to waste, inflict irretrievable losses on material and spiritual culture and throw mankind back many decades.[57]

When Soviet military spokesmen consider the possibility of an attack by US strategic nuclear forces, they vigorously proclaim that the imperialist forces would be crushed and the socialist nations would emerge victorious. When they discuss the practical consequences of a nuclear war, however, they admit that there would be unprecedented destruction. Thus, Soviet military spokesmen seem to expect that, at best, in a nuclear war they could only obtain a pyrrhic victory.

Conclusion

What Soviet spokesmen have been saying about nuclear war does not support the claims of various Western analysts who argue that the Soviets believe they can win and survive a nuclear war — especially the notion that they can survive such a war with fewer losses than they incurred in World War II. The Soviet usage of the dictum 'war is a continuation of politics' is a basic tenet of Marxist-Leninist theory explaining the causes of war and is not an expression of their views on survival or victory in a nuclear war. Soviet statements proclaiming that victory is possible in such a war seem to tell us little about actual Soviet thinking on the subject. This conclusion is based upon the fact that these statements are necessary to keep up morale and are required by Marxist-Leninist ideology. In addition, these declarations about victory are contradicted by their statements made on the usefulness of nuclear war as a practical instrument of policy, and by their estimates of the probable consequences of such a conflict.

Soviet spokesmen in publications written for internal consumption contend that nuclear war cannot serve as a practical instrument of policy and they continually talk about the dire consequences of such a war. Spokesmen at all levels, in different forums, generally agree that nuclear war would cause unprecedented damage. Thus, the Soviets seem to be acutely aware of the destructive capability of the US nuclear arsenal and there seems to be little doubt that the US has the capability to inflict unacceptable damages [58] upon the Soviet Union.

Notes

1. Department of Defense. *Annual Defense Report Fiscal Year 1979*, (2 February 1978), pp. 4–6, 60; US Arms Control and Disarmament Agency, *US and Soviet Strategic Capability Through the Mid-1980s: A Comparative Analysis*, August 1978; CIA, *Soviet Civil Defense*, NI–78–10003 (July 1978); Richard Burt, 'Secret Carter Study of Soviet Threat'. *The Washington Star* (6 January 1978), pp. A1, A6.
2. Retired Major General George J. Keegan cited in 'Can the US Survive a Nuclear Exchange', *The American Intelligence Journal* (Fall 1977, pp. 20–2; Foy D. Kohler in Leon Goure, *War Survival in Soviet Strategy* (Center for Advanced International Studies, University of Miami, Miami, 1976), p. xiii; Retired General Daniel Graham, cited in 'Civil Defense Seen as a Fading Program', *New York Times*, (20 February 1977), p. 35. Also see Leon Goure, Foy D. Kohler, Mose L. Harvey, *The Role of Nuclear Forces in Current Soviet Strategy* (Center for Advanced International Studies, University of Miami, Miami, 1974); Richard Pipes, 'Why The Soviet Union Thinks It Cound Fight and Win a Nuclear War, *Commentary*, vol. 64, no. 1 (July 1977), pp. 21–34; T. K. Jones and W. Scott Thompson, 'Central War and Civil Defense', *Orbis*, vol. 22, no. 3 (Fall 1978).
3. A notable exception is the recent article by Raymond Garthoff, 'Mutual Deterrence and Strategic Arms Limitation in Soviet Policy', *International Security* (Summer 1978), pp. 112–47. For an analysis of Soviet writings which arrives at different conclusions than those presented in Garthoff's article and in this article see Leon Goure *et al.*, *The Role of Nuclear Forces in Current Soviet Studies*, (Center for Advanced International Studies, University of Miami, Miami, 1974).
4. I agree with Richard Pipes that 'Buried in the flood of meaningless verbiage (of Soviet writings), nuggets of precious information on Soviet perceptions and intentions can more often than not be unearthed by a trained reader'. Pipes, 'Why the Soviet Union Thinks It Could Fight and Win a Nuclear War', p. 27.
5. Ibid., pp. 30, 34.
6. Another evaluation of Soviet attitudes regarding nuclear war by Carl Gustaf Stroehm makes even stronger statements in this regard. Stroehm notes that Army General Viktor Kulikov, the then newly appointed Chief of the Warsaw Pact, wrote an article defending the thesis that war is the continuation of politics by other means in which he stated that no weapon can change the interrelationship between politics and military strategy. Stroehm argues that Kulikov's statements have a 'strategic foreign significance' because they mean that the Warsaw Pact Chief believes nuclear war can serve as a practical instrument of policy. Stroehm claims, 'In contrast to Khrushchev, who at least in his last years . . . said that a nuclear war would bring a general ruin with it, Kulikov is of the opinion that even this "ultimate weapon" may be used as the continuation of politics and thus as a political tool.' '. . . this marshal is ready to think beyond the point where thought stops among Western military men: acceptance of a nuclear inferno': Carl Gustaf Stroehm, *Die Zeit* (8 February 1977), p. 5, cited in JPRS *Translations on USSR Military Affairs*, 69026, no. 1272, (2 May 1977) pp. 1–4.
Also see *The Strategic Intentions of The Soviet Union: Fallacies in Western Assessment*, Report of A Study Group of the Institute for The Study of Conflict (Eastern Press, London and Reading, March 1978) pp. 5, 8, 24, 28.
7. *Voyenno-Istoricheskiy Zhurnal* (Military Historical Journal), book review,

no. 4, (April 1972), pp. 105–10, cited in JPRS 56087, *Translations on USSR Military Affairs*, no. 810 (May 24 1972), p. 32.

8. 'Theory, Politics, Ideology on the Essence of War,' *Krasnaya Zvezda* (24 January 1967), cited in FBIS, *Daily Report: Soviet Union*, no. 20 (30 January 1967), p. bb 19.

9. *Spravochnik Ofitsera* (Officer's Handbook) (Voyenizdat, Moscow, 1971), USAF translation, Soviet Military Thought Series no. 13 (GPO, Washington, D.C.), p. 41.

10. See LTC Ye. Rybkin, 'On The Nature of a Nuclear Missile War,' *Kommunist Vooruzhennukh Sil*, no. 17 (September 1965). Colonel Rybkin wrote in October 1973 that, 'Those individuals who deny this (dictum) are confusing the causes, essence, and social nature of the phenomenon with the expediency of using it as a means of achieving a political goal. Although inseparable, these two represent two different aspects of the matter.' Ye. Rybkin, 'The Leninist Conception of Contemporary War', *Kommunist, Vooruzhennykh Sil*, no. 20 (October 1973), pp. 21-8, cited in JPRS 60667, *Translation on USSR Military Affairs*, no. 987, pp. 8–9. Several months later, another prominent military writer made the same distinction,: 'Considering the essence of a possible nuclear war, Marxist-Leninists do not confuse it with another question of the admissibility of nuclear war.' Colonel T. R. Kondratkov, 'War as a Continuation of Politics', *Soviet Military Review* (February 1974), p. 7. In July 1975, Colonel Dmitriyev argued that certain Western and some Soviet authors had failed to '. . . distinguish the question of the nature and substance of a war from the question of its possible consequences, of its effectiveness as an instrument of policy'. (see note 13) Colonel A. Dmitriyev, 'The Marxist-Leninist Doctrine of War and the Army is an Important Element of the Scientific World Outlook of Military Cadres', *Kommunist Voorzhennykh Sil*, no. 13 (July 1975) pp. 9–17, cited in JPRS 65480, *Translations on USSR Military Affairs* (18 August 1975), pp. 1–12.

11. Colonel B. Byely *et al.*, *Marksizm-Leninizm o Voyne i Armii* (Marxism-Leninism on War and the Army) (Moscow, 1972), USAF translation, Soviet Military Thought Series no. 2 (GPO, Washington, D.C.), p. 28.

12. LTC Ye. Rybkin, 'On The Nature of a Nuclear Missile War', cited in William R. Kintner and Harriet Fast Scott, *The Nuclear Revolution in Soviet Military Affairs* (University of Oklahoma Press, Norman, 1968), p. 109.

13. An article by Colonel T. Kondratkov entitled 'War as a Continuation of Policy' *(Soviet Military Review,* February 1974, pp. 7–9) is typical of Soviet usage of the dictum. Kondratkov discusses the Marxist-Leninist theory of the causes of war. War, he argues, is a political phenomenon inherent in a society divided into antagonistic classes. The contradictory interests and aims of these classes eventually lead to war which is a continuation of the policies pursued by the classes during peace. Kondratkov then states that one 'cannot understand the character of a war correctly without defining what policy has given rise to it, and what policy it continues'. He goes on to attack those who do not believe war is a continuation of politics in the nuclear era. He states that nuclear war 'cannot arise out of nothing, out of a vacuum'. It would be caused by a nation (and thus the classes within the nation) pursuing a political objective by use of force. Kondratkov's usage of the dictum, therefore, is to explain and defend the Marxist-Leninist theory of the causes of war. He does not suggest that nuclear war can be a practical instrument of policy. He explicitly states that, 'Considering the essence of a possible nuclear war, Marxist-Leninists do not confuse it with another question, close but not identical with it – concerning the admissibility or inadmissibility of nuclear war as a means of politics.' Among the many other publications reviewed were: Byely *et al.*, *Marxism-Leninism on War and the Army Army*, pp. 6–10, 21–31; Colonel V. Izmaylov, 'The Nature and Features of Modern Wars', *Kommunist Vooruzhennykh Sil*, no. 6 (March 1975), pp. 67–75, cited in JPRS 64665, *Translations on USSR Military Affairs*, no. 1137 (30 April

1975), p. 38.

14. Pipes, 'Why the Soviet Union Thinks It Could Fight and Win a Nuclear War', p. 34.

15. G. Arbatov, Chief of the Institute of the USA and Canada in Moscow, wrote, '. . . with the emergence of nuclear missiles any correspondence between the political ends of war and the means was lost, since no policy can have the objective of destroying the enemy at the cost of complete self-annihilation', G. A. Arbatov, 'The Impasse of the Policy of Force', *Problemy Mira I Sotsializma* (Problems of Peace and Socialism), no. 2 (February 1974), cited in FBIS *Daily Report: Soviet Union* no. 35, (20 February, 1974), p. B2. In August 1975, the editor of the journal of the Institute of the USA and Canada, V. M. Berezhkov, made a similar argument. He states that, 'Universal war can no longer be regarded as a means of policy because of the destructiveness of the weapons', V. M. Berezhkov, 'Detente Prospects and Soviet-American Relations', *SShA: Ekonomika, Politika i Ideologiya* (USA: Economics, Politics, and Ideology) hereafter referred to as *SShA*. no. 9 (21 August 1975), pp. 3–14, cited in FBIS *Daily Report: Soviet Union* (9 October 1975), p. A7.

16. Colonel Ye. Rybkin, 'The Leninist Conception of Contemporary War', *Kommunist Vooruzhennykh Sil*, no. 20 (October 1973), pp. 21–8, as cited in JPRS 60667, *Translations on USSR Military Affairs*, no. 987, pp. 8–9.

17. V. M. Berezhkov, 'Basic Principles of Soviet-US Relations', *SShA*, no. 4, (1977), pp. 3–11.

18. Marshal N. I. Krylov, 'The Instructive Lessons of History', *Sovetskaya Rossiya* (Soviet Russia), (30 August 1969), cited in FBIS *Daily Report: Soviet Union*, (2 September 1969), p. A20.

19. Raymond Garthoff argues that the standard military statements implying Soviet victory in nuclear world war are predominantly intended for indoctrination and morale-boosting of the armed forces and the public. Raymond L. Garthoff, 'SALT and the Soviet Military', *Problems of Communism* (January/February 1975), p. 33.

20. LTC N. Tabunov, 'New Weapons and the Moral Factor', *Kommunist Vooruzhennykh Sil*, no. 2 (January 1969), pp. 25–32, as cited in JPRS 47667, *Translations on USSR Military Affairs*, no. 509 (18 March 1969), p. 6.

21. 'In the new war, if it should be allowed to happen, victory will be with the countries of the world socialist system . . . because the balance of forces between the two systems, the logic of history, its objective laws prescribing that the new social development is invincible – all this predicts such an outcome'. Byely *et al.*, *Marxism-Leninism on War and the Army*, p. 30.

22. Ibid., pp. 30, 73.

23. Leonid Brezhnev, speech at Moscow World Peace Congress, cited in FBIS *Daily Report: Soviet Union* Supplement no. 40. (29 October 1973), pp. 9, 14. Nine months later, he noted that there were enough nuclear weapons in the world 'to destroy everything on earth several times over'. Then, in November 1976, he declared that in a nuclear war, 'mankind might be wholly destroyed'. (See note 30.) Leonid Brezhnev, speech to Polish Sejm, (21 July 1974), cited in FBIS *Daily Report: Soviet Union*, no. 141 (22 July 1974), p. D17. Leonid Brezhnev, speech at Soviet-Romanian Friendship rally in Bucharest, (24 November 1976), cited in FBIS *Daily Report: Soviet Union*, no. 228 (24 November 1976), p. D5.

24. A. A. Gromyko, 19 January 1974, speech in Yerevan, Armenia, cited in FBIS *Daily Report: Soviet Union*, no. 16, (23 January 1974), p. R9.

25. K. Mazurov, 21 February 1972, speech to Syrian People's Assembly in Damascus, cited in FBIS *Daily Report: Soviet Union* (25 February 1972), p. F1.

26. A. P. Kirilenko, speech at 21 March 1975 meeting in Bologna, Italy, cited in FBIS *Daily Report: Soviet Union*, no. 64 (2 April 1975), p. E12.

27. A. N. Kosygin, speech for Libyan Prime Minister in Libya, 13 May 1975, cited in FBIS *Daily Report: Soviet Union* (15 May 1975), p. F3.

28. Yu. V. Andropov, 22 April 1976 speech at Lenin Birthday Anniversary meeting in Moscow, cited in FBIS *Daily Report: Soviet Union* (23 April 1976), p. R10.

29. Marshal of the Soviet Union A. A. Grechko, *The Armed Forces of the Soviet State* (1975), USAF translation, Soviet Military Thought Series no. 12, pp. 84, 164. He expressed these same views in two other publications several years earlier. He wrote in *Kommunist* (Communist) that a nuclear war '... will assume a particularly destructive nature', and in *Pravda* that it would be a '... deadly threat to the future of mankind'. MSU A. A. Grechko, *Kommunist*, no. 15 (October 1972), cited in FBIS *Daily Report: Soviet Union* (21 November 1972), p. M3, MSU A. A. Grechko, 29 September 1972 speech to the Presidium of the USSR Supreme Soviet, cited in FBIS *Daily Report: Soviet Union* (30 October 1972), p. H6.

30. Some Westerners claim that after a Soviet first strike against the US strategic forces, the President would be 'self-deterred' from launching a retaliatory strike. The reasoning is that the President would realise that the Soviet Union could absorb a retaliatory strike and still wipe out the major cities in the US. A discussion of the self-deterrence argument depends on an assessment of US and Soviet strategic capabilities and upon an assessment of whether or not the President would push the button. Such assessments are outside the scope of this paper. It should be noted however, that Soviet views of the consequences of a nuclear war, cited in this paper, give no indication that they have any confidence that the US might be self-deterred.

31. V. G. Dolgin, 'Peaceful Coexistence and the Factors Contributing to its Intensification and Development', *Voprosy Filosofi* (Problems of Philosophy), no. 1 (January 1974), cited in Edward L. Warner, III, *The Military in Contemporary Soviet Politics, An Institutional Analysis* (Praeger Publishers, New York/London, 1977), p.253.

32. V. Matveyev, 'Struggle for the Most Important Thing', *Izvestiya*, 10 June 1972, p. 4, cited in FBIS *Daily Report: Soviet Union*, no. 115, (13 June 1972), p. H1. He made the same comment in A. Artamonov, V. Matveyev and N. Polyanov, 'A Historic Day and a Historic Document', *Izvestiya*, 24 June 1973, pp. 1, 3, cited in FBIS *Daily Report: Soviet Union*, no. 125, (28 June 1973), pp. AA8–11. In the June 1973 article he also stated that '... only madmen can see anything in nuclear war except disaster for our planet', and in August 1973 he argued that 'no responsibile statesman can ignore the consequences of such a conflict'. In 1974, in another publication, Matveyev repeated Brezhnev's pronouncement that the available nuclear arsenals could blow apart the entire planet. Finally, in December 1976, he talked of a nuclear war 'whose consequences for mankind and our planet would be unimaginable'. V. Matveyev, 'In the Interests of All People', *Izvestiya*, 7 August 1973, p. 2, cited in FBIS *Daily Report: Soviet Union*, no. 156, (13 August 1973), p. H1; V. Matveyev, 'The Realities and Demands of the Nuclear Age', *Mezhdunarofnaya Zhizn* (International Affairs), no. 3 (1974), pp. 81–94, cited in FBIS *Daily Report: Soviet Union*, no. 63, (1 April 1974), pp. AA6; V. Matveyev, 'New Limits of The Peaceful Offensive', *Izvestiya*, 7 December 1976, p. 4, cited in FBIS *Daily Report: Soviet Union* (14 December 1976), p. BB1.

33. A. Bovin, 'Peace and Social Progress', *Izvestiya*, 11 September 1973, cited in FBIS *Daily Report: Soviet Union*, no. 179, (13 September 1973), p. A4.

34. Ye. Fedorov, 'To Stop the Arms Race', *Izvestiya*, 21 September 1973, cited in FBIS *Daily Report: Soviet Union* (29 September 1976), p. AA4.

35. In May 1977, an article in *Pravda* criticised the Chinese view of the desirability of a nuclear conflict. The article which was signed I. Aleksandrov – a pseudonym for authoritative Kremlin statements – warned that, 'If the world thermonuclear holocaust, which the Maoists are provoking, were to break out, it would cause incalculable disaster for all the earth's peoples without sparing the Chinese people'. I. Aleksandrov, 'Peking: A Course Towards Wrecking

International Detente Under the Guise of Anti-Sovietism', *Pravda*, 14 May 1977, pp. 4–5, cited in FBIS *Daily Report: Soviet Union*, no. 94 (16 May 1977), pp. C6.

36 Sh. Sanakoyev, 'Real Preconditions', *Pravda*, 24 February 1977, p. 4, cited in FBIS *Daily Report: Soviet Union* (1 March 1977), pp. AA3.

37. An article in *Krasnaya Zvezda* in July 1973 by D. Tomashevskiy argued that, 'Unless it is averted, a new world war can threaten the very existence of entire countries and peoples and lead to grave disasters for mankind'. D. Tomashevskiy, 'The Leninist Principles of Foreign Policy in Action', *Krasnaya Zvezda*, 4 July 1973, pp. 2, 3, cited in FBIS *Daily Report: Soviet Union*, no. 135, (13 July 1974), p. A3.

In September 1976, V. Karenov wrote in *Novoye Vremya* (New Times) that a nuclear war would cause '. . . colossal damage to mankind'. V. Karenov, 'Real Paths to Disarmament', *Novoye Vremya*, no. 39 (September 1976), pp. 4–6, cited in FBIS *Daily Report: Soviet Union*, no. 194 (5 October 1976), pp. AA5. Several months later, in the same publication, V. Kuznetsov, in arguing that the continuing military build-up was senseless, noted that 'both sides already possess weapons capable of killing everything on earth several times over'. V. Kuznetsov, 'According to the Laws of Detente', *Novoye Vremya*, no. 5, (28 January 1977), pp. 4–5, cited in FBIS *Daily Report: Soviet Union*, no. 21, (1 February 1977), p. A4.

38. Zh. Dyusheyev, *Samopomoshch i Vzaimopomoshch Pri Primenii Oruzhiya Massovogo Porazheniya i Pri Neschastnykh Sluchayak* (Self Help and Mutual Assistance When Mass Destruction Weapons are Being Employed and During Accidents) (1972), cited in JPRS 59294, *Translation on USSR Military Affairs*, no. 925, p. 22.

39. The head of IMEMO, N. N. Inozemtsev, who is a candidate member of the Central Committee and is reported to have access to certain Politburo and Secretariat members, wrote in 1972 that a nuclear war would be '. . . suicide for whomever unleashed it'. N. Inozemtsev, 'The Principle-Mindedness and Effectiveness of Soviet Foreign Policy', *Pravda*, 9 June 1972, pp. 4–5, cited in FBIS *Daily Report: Soviet Union*, no. 14, (12 June 1972), p. A8. More recently, a staff member of IMEMO, D. Proektor, a retired colonel, argued that a nuclear war could lead to the destruction of civilisation. Writing in *Kommunist,* the bi-weekly journal of the CPSU Central Committee, in May 1977, he concluded that, 'In our time, when unlike the situation in the past, the threat of a new world war, unless blocked, could lead to the destruction of civilisation, problems of international security have come to the fore with unparalleled urgency . . . Today the risk (of war) has become excessive and the failure of detente may mean a step toward universal destruction.' D. Proektor, 'Socialism and International Security', *Kommunist*, no. 7 (1977), pp. 109. Members of the Institute of the USA and Canada have also made predictions about the dire consequences of a nuclear war. For example, the head of the Institute, G. A. Arbatov, is a candidate member of the CPSU Central Committee who is reported to have access to Brezhnev's staff and perhaps Brezhnev himself. Arbatov stated in an interview in Hungary in 1973 that, 'The prevention of nuclear war equally serves the interests of the United States and the USSR since nuclear war would be suicide to both'. Gl Arbatov, 5 August 1973, interview for Budapest Domestic Television, cited in FBIS *Daily Report: Soviet Union* (7 August 1973), p. A15.

Another member of the Institute expressed his concern in a 1976 monograph. G. A. Trofimenko, the head of the Department for the Study of US Foreign Policy, wrote that, '. . . the stakes in a nuclear conflict are now so colossal'. In another publication the same year, he quoted Brezhnev's assessment that current nuclear weapon inventories could blow up the entire planet. G. A. Trofimenko, *SShA: Politika, Voyna, Ideologiya* (The US: Policies, War and Ideology), (Izdatel'stvo Mysl', Moscow, 1976) in forward, G. A. Trofimenko, 'The Logic of Detente Dictates', *Za Rubezhom* (Abroad), no. 48 (25 November 1976), pp.

9–10, cited in FBIS *Daily Report: Soviet Union* (2 December 1976), pp. AA1.
Two senior analysts at the Institute of the USA and Canada, M. A. Mil'shteyn, a retired General-Lieutenant, and L. S. Semeyko, a retired colonel, have written about both the short-term and the long-term effects of nuclear war. They state that 'the latest research (a US Academy of Science study) once again reminds us of the catastrophic consequences which might result from a nuclear conflict'. Citing the findings of the study, the authors note that there would be a sharp reduction in the concentration of the ozone layer in the atmosphere which would drastically increase solar radiation and could lead to climatic changes. Harvest yields would diminish causing famines in many parts of the world. The mortality rate would rise and 'solar radiation would give rise to genetic diseases . . . in more than thirty generations of people'. 'Epidemics would rage in the world for a long time.' M. A. Milshteyn and L. S. Semeyko, 'The US and the Question of New Types of Mass Destruction Weapons'. *SShA: Ekonomika, Politika i Ideologiya*, no. 5 (1976), pp. 33–4.

40. V. M. Berezhkov, 'Basic Principles of Soviet-US Relations', *SShA: Ekonomika, Politika i Ideologiya*, no. 4 (1977), p. 8. In 1975, he wrote, 'Universal war can no longer be regarded as a means of policy because of the destructiveness of the weapons'. V. M. Berezhkov, 'Detente, Prospects and Soviet-American Relations', *SShA: Ekonomika, Politika, i Ideologiya*, no. 9 (21 August 1975), pp. 3–14, cited in FBIS *Daily Report: Soviet Union* (9 October 1975), p. A7.

41. V. F. Khalipov in *The Philosophical Heritage of V. I. Lenin and the Problems of Contemporary War* (Progress Publishers, Moscow, 1972) USAF translation, Soviet Military Thought Series no. 5 (GPO, Washington, D.C.), p. 16. (Note: the book, published in 1972, does not identify who V. F. Khalipov is. A 1974 source, however, identifies Colonel Vyacheslav Filippovich Khalipov, Doctor of Philosophy, head of the Scientific Research Department of the Military Political Academy. It states that he is a prolific writer. Because of the nature and authorship of the 1972 book, it is very likely that these are the same individuals. *Znamenosets* (Banner), no. 11 (1974), p. 34).

42. General-Major A. Milovidov, 'A Philosophical Analysis of Military Thought', *Krasnaya Zvezda* (17 May 1973), pp. 2–3, cited in FBIS *Daily Report: Soviet Union* (23 May 1973), p. M2.

43. Rear Admiral V. V. Shelyag, 'Two World Outlooks – Two Views on War', *Krasnaya Zvezda* (7 February 1974), cited in FBIS *Daily Report: Soviet Union* (12 February 1974), pp. A1–A5.

44. Shelyag was Deputy Chief of the Academy (*Krasnaya Zvezda*), 7 February 1974. Milovidov was listed as being on the Academy faculty *(Krasnaya Zvezda)*, 17 May 1973, pp. 2–3. For Khalipov, see explanation in note 41.

45. Shelyag, 'Two World Outlooks – Two views on War', in FBIS p. A5.

46. To avoid criticism from the ideologues, Soviet spokesmen preface their views about the dire consequences of a nuclear war with a statement that 'imperialism will be destroyed in such a conflict'.

47. It may be argued that the pursuit of such a goal (to win and survive a nuclear war) is not consistent with stable mutual deterrence. Such an argument is valid if it is feasible to attain the goal. On the other hand, if the Soviets cannot attain the ability to achieve a meaningful victory, then the pursuit of such a goal will not upset the reality of mutual deterrence.

48. V. F. Khalipov in *The Philosophical Heritage of V. I. Lenin and Problems of Contemporary War* (1972), USAF translation, Soviet Military Thought Series no. 5 (GPO, Washington D.C.), pp. 15–17.

49. Shelyag, 'Two World Outlooks – Two Views on War', cited in FBIS, p. A4.

50. General-Lieutenant P. Zhilin, 'Characteristics of Current World Development', *Mezhdunarodnaya Zhizn*, no. 11, pp. 31–4, cited in JPRS 60729,

Translations on USSR Political and Sociological Affairs, no. 469 (10 December 1973), p. 19.

51. In a book written for officers and generals of the armed forces, Zhilin wrote, '... such a mass of lethal weapons has been accumulated making it possible to destroy every living thing on the world several times over ... ' General-Lieutenant P. Zhilin, *Problemy Voyennoy Istorii* (Problems of Military History) (Voyenizdat, Moscow, 1975). He repeated his argument in *Krasnaya Zvezda* in 1976. 'This task (explaining the causes of war) is especially topical in the epoch of nuclear missile weapons capable not only of inflicting incalculable disasters and suffering on peoples but also of destroying the conditions for the existence of mankind.' General-Lieutenant P. Zhilin, 'The Truth of History is Irrefutable', *Krasnaya Zveda*, 1 September 1976, cited in FBIS *Daily Report: Soviet Union* (17 September 1976), p. A4.

52. Colonel Ye. Rybkin, 'The 25th CPSU Congress and the Problem of Peaceful Coexistence Between Socialism and Capitalism', *Voyenno-Istoricheskiy Zhurnal*, no. 1 (January 1977), pp. 3–9. (Note: Rybkin apparently moved from the Lenin Military Political Academy to the Institute of Military History of the Ministry of Defence sometime in the early 1970s. In 1975, he is definitely identified as being at the Institute of Military History. See interview with General-Lieutenant Zhilin in *Krasnaya Zvezda*, 11 April 1975, p. 2.) Several years earlier, in a book written for military personnel, Rybkin cited Brezhnev's view that in a nuclear war hundreds of millions would be destroyed, and the earth's surface and atmosphere would be contaminated (by radiation). Colonel Ye. Rybkin, in USAF Translation of *The Philosophical Heritage of V. I. Lenin and Problems of Contemporary War* (Moscow, 1972), USAF translation, Soviet Military Thought Series no. 5 (GPO, Washington, D.C.), p. 36.

53. General-Major F. G. Simonyan, Moscow Domestic Service in Russian 1400 GMT, 17 June 1977, cited in FBIS *Daily Report: Soviet Union* (21 June 1977), p. A8.

54. Colonel T. Kondratkov, 'Social Character of Modern War', *Kommunist Vooruzhennykh Sil*, no. 21 (November 1972), pp. 9–16, cited in JPRS 57930, *Translations on USSR Military Affairs*, no. 880, p. 39.

55. Colonel A. Dmitriyev, 'The Marxist-Leninist Doctrine of War and Army is an Important Element of the Scientific World Outlook of Military Cadres', *Kommunist Vooruzhennykh Sil*, (July 1975), pp. 9–17, cited in JPRS 65480, *Translations on USSR Military Affairs* (18 August 1975), pp. 1–12.

56. Colonel S. Tyushkevich, 'The Development of the Doctrine on War and the Army on the Basis of the Great Patriotic War', *Kommunist Vooruzhennykh Sil*, no. 22, (November 1975), pp. 9–16, cited in FBIS *Daily Report: Soviet Union* (18 December 1975), p. A6. (Note: Tyushkevich is listed as being at the Instutute of Military History. *Krasnaya Zvezda*, 11 April 1975, p. 2)

57. *Marxism-Leninism on War and the Army*, Byely *et al.* p. 73 in USAF translation.

58. Some Westerners argue that we do not know what the Soviets consider to be 'unacceptable damages'. True, we can never be positive about exactly how much is enough. But Soviet statements which contend that nuclear war would cause unprecedented damage, or that the results are unimaginable, or many other statements about the dire consequences of such a war which have been presented in this paper seem to be good indications that they perceive that the US can still inflict what *they* consider to be unacceptable damages upon the Soviet Union.

Othern Westerners argue that the Soviet view of what would be unacceptable damages is different from the US view. The argument is that since the Soviets killed so many of their own people in the purges and held up under such devastating losses in World War II, the level of damages which they would consider to be unacceptable will be much higher than the level the US would consider to be unacceptable (for example, see Pipes, 'Why the Soviet Union

Thinks It Could Fight and Win a Nuclear War', pp. 29, 34.). Just as likely, however, the opposite conclusion may be true. Because the Soviets have suffered so much, and are so aware of the consequences of severe destruction on their own territory, their threshold of what is considered to be unacceptable may be lower than that of the US. An article in *Kommunist Vooruzhennykh Sil,* for example, stated, 'Having lost 20 million of its sons and daughters during the last war, the Soviet people know how to appreciate the blessings of peace.' *(Kommunist Vooruzhennykh Sil,* no. 20. October 1973, pp. 3–8, cited in JPRS 60667, 30 November 1973, *Translations on USSR Military Affairs,* no. 987, p. 19)

Another important factor to consider is that a calculated Soviet decision to initiate, or threaten to initiate, a nuclear war will be made for a specific purpose – i.e. to obtain a political objective. The level of damage that is considered to be unacceptable will vary depending upon the importance of the political objective desired. We must then consider the benefits to outweigh the costs which would result from a nuclear war. For the current Soviet leadership, there seems to be only one instance in which they would make a calculated decision to use nuclear war as an instrument of policy – that would be if they believed the US was about to launch a nuclear attack against the Soviet Union.

3 THE MILITARY INSTRUMENT IN SOVIET FOREIGN POLICY

Ken Booth

The security of the homeland against external threat is a primary obligation of all states, whatever the political philosophy of their prevailing group. From a Western viewpoint Soviet military power has been conceived primarily in terms of deterring their enemies, dealing with the outside world from a position of strength, and the successful defence of the homeland should deterrence fail.[1] This definition of the constituents of strategic policy is a universal one, and should be viewed in the light of Crankshaw's useful reminder that:

> One of our difficulties when it comes to understanding foreign countries is that we think of them almost exclusively in terms of foreign policy, whereas they are thinking of themselves much more in terms of domestic policy. It means, for example, that the Soviet Union is seen by us always in relation to our problems and hardly at all in relation to its own. To hear people talk, to read the Western newspapers, one would think that the Soviet Government devotes nine-tenths of its energies and ingenuity to making trouble for us, whereas in fact it is spending most of its time in trying to make the Soviet Union work.[2]

Maximising the security of the USSR has always been the basic foundation of Soviet strategy. The pursuit of this goal has been the overriding task of the Soviet armed forces since 1917. It is a task which has always been irreducible, emotive, worrying and difficult. For most of the first 55 years of its existence, the Soviet Union has been, both objectively and in the eyes of its leaders, in a chronic state of relative military weakness. In such circumstances, the building up of military power for deterrence, together with a variety of diplomatic ploys to engineer a 'breathing space', have been pressing aims in policy. On several occasions, observers in the West have mistaken an image of Soviet aggressiveness (often deliberately and carefully contrived) for real military strength. The susceptibility of states in the West during the period of Stalin's bellicosity in the late 1940s, and to Khrushchev's in the late 1950s, helped to obscure Soviet strategic weakness. Western preconceptions about Soviet aggressiveness helped to confirm rather than expose Soviet military posturing.

Military vulnerability, in fact, has been a characteristic feature of Russian history. Czarist expansion has been interpreted by some writers as having been not so much a simple lust for imperial power, but as a reaction to military vulnerability in a hostile environment.[3] The result of this was a search for secure frontiers, and an effort to spread as much territory as possible between potential enemies and the 'huddled defensive community' in the national heartland.[4] Such a single-factor explanation of the expansionist impulse is misleading; there are clearly other interpretations to consider.[5] Nevertheless, the part played by this feeling of weakness and the consequent 'defensive expansion' remain important, particularly with reference to Soviet policy in certain strategically vulnerable areas, such as the approaches from Central Europe, the borderlands with China, and some of the approaches from the Near East.

1. From the Revolution to the victory in the Great Patriotic War

For the first few years of the Soviet period, the Bolshevik leadership was not only on the strategic defensive, but was actually in a most critical military position. They had to end the war with Germany. They were involved in the life or death struggle against the counter-revolutionary forces in the civil war. They faced the intervention by British, French, Japanese and US forces. And in 1920 their troubles were compounded by the outbreak of war with a resurrected Poland, whose military vigour, for a short time, looked overwhelming. At the very birth of the first Soviet republic, the actions of the interventionist powers confirmed the ideological and national perceptions of the Bolshevik leaders.

In the most pressing of circumstances, the Bolsheviks survived. In the histories of Western nations, the events of 1917—20 are minor and largely obscure: in Soviet history, however, they are of decisive legendary and ideological significance. In part, the events of these years are important because they seemed to verify ideological precepts about the inevitability of war.[6] In the Marxist—Leninist formulation, war was a phenomenon of class society, and was innate in the capitalist system; as long as capitalism existed, war would be inevitable, for the capitalist states would attempt to use it to gain colonies, to gain ascendancy over their rivals, and to resist communism. War would cease to exist only when capitalism was totally destroyed and replaced by communism. Such precepts were stongly held; their elaborations cannot be dismissed easily as merely hortatory. The position was summarised by Lenin in 1919; in a famous passage, he wrote

> We are living not merely in a state but in a *system of states* and the existence of the Soviet Republic side by side with the imperialist states for a long time is unthinkable. One or the other must triumph in the end. And before that end supervenes, a series of frightening collisions between the Soviet Republic and the bourgeois states will be inevitable. That means that if the ruling class, the proletariat, wants to hold sway, it must prove its capacity to do so by its military organisation.[7]

The belief in 'frightening collisions' was deep: the ideological prognosis, which was confirmed and developed by the conditions of 1917–20, continued to play an important part in the image and behaviour of the Bolshevik leaders.[8]

The proletariat, led by the Bolsheviks (and helped by the failings of their enemies) did prove their capacity for military organisation. By 1921 the Soviet state had emerged from its worst crisis, victory had been achieved in the civil war, the foreign intervention had fallen apart, and the Polish invasion had been thrown back and terms agreed. Despite these successes, however, the Bolshevik leaders did not believe that they were secure; militarily, economically, and politically, they saw themselves as weak and vulnerable. Events in Central Europe demonstrated to them that security would not be forthcoming through immediate world revolution, and a transformation to a communist order, but through 'peace' with the capitalist states; this would allow the consolidation of internal control, the foundation of the new political system, and the building up of strength for future contingencies. With perceptions of 'capitalist encirclement' and 'inevitable war', the Soviet leaders conceived the 'relation of forces' and 'the present historical period' as demanding temporary peaceful coexistence. In 1921 the New Economic Policy was inaugurated to build a strong Soviet state, and within a few years this merged into the period of 'socialism in one country'.[9] The aim during this period was to build up the Soviet state into an industrially vigorous and militarily powerful socialist base. Although Stalin no doubt exaggerated and manipulated the capitalist threat to serve a number of his own personal domestic interests, the threats perceived by the leadership cannot simply be dismissed as tactical, and they were undoubtedly intensified by such warnings as that in 1924 from M. V. Frunze, Trotsky's successor as Commissar of War, that: 'The situation of our Red Army is especially serious and we cannot consider the army fit for combat.'[10] The implication for Soviet foreign policy was clear: the aim must be to avoid war as long as possible, but if it became unavoidable, the aim, said Stalin, should be 'to enter last. And we must enter in order to throw the decisive weight onto the scales, the weight which can tip the scales.'[11] Militarily, the Soviet state was weak: externally, its policy had to be circumspect; internally, it had to create the foundations for real strategic power. The 'revolutionary' element in Soviet policy was confined to the activities of the Comintern.

By the end of the 1920s, Soviet exertions had constructed a strong foundation for the further consolidation of military power.[12] Through the gravest difficulties, the industrial base for a modern armaments industry had been created, and the doctrine and organisation of the new forces had slowly evolved, partly with the assistance of the Reichswehr.[13] The extent of rebuilding was such that it was possible to channel offensivism into the rather more positively left-wing policy of the late 1920s.[14]

The perception of strategic vulnerability in the face of 'capitalist encirclement' remained powerful. After 1933 these fears were intensified by the rise to power of Hitler, who confronted the Soviet leaders with a resurgent and stridently anti-Bolshevik Germany. Against this mounting threat, 'world communism' was sacrificed for, or had to work towards, the direct security interests of its Russian base. During this anxious period it was axiomatic that the aim of Soviet policy must be to postpone the 'inevitable' war as long as possible. The outcome was a mixture of peace propaganda, respectable diplomacy, disarmament proposals, attempts to build up 'fronts', efforts to exploit the tensions and contradictions within the capitalist world, and the building up in the background of economic and military strength. Foreign policy was unprovocative; the Comintern, despite its ostensible mission, was no longer the international bogeyman of the early 1920s.

Soviet foreign policy was a compound of immediate tactical expediency and longer term strategic planning. The Soviet problem was illustrated by its relations with Japan in a rather extreme form. In the first half of the 1930s, Soviet policy was one of obvious appeasement towards the rise of Japanese military expansion on the East Asian mainland. At the same time, though, this occured against the background of a considerable Soviet effort to build a powerful military capability in the Far East; this involved the reorganisation and strengthening of local forces, increasing the capacity of the Trans-Siberian Railway and giving priority in the supply of submarines to the Soviet Pacific fleet.[15] Isolated, and facing a hostile Japan in the

The Military Instrument in Soviet Foreign Policy 79

east and a hostile Germany in the West, Soviet foreign policy had to be circumspect, while its military policy had to be geared to meeting the exhausting requirements for adequate deterrence and to defend the homeland. In such circumstances the use of military force for projecting power would have been highly 'adventuristic'.

From the end of the civil war the Soviet Union was granted, and worked for, 20 years of peace, if not real security; this juxtaposition of the two conditions was epitomised by the Nazi-Soviet Pact of 1939–1941. During this long breathing space, when the military instrument played little part in advancing Soviet power, internal communist rule was consolidated, often brutally, and, paradoxically (as the great purges showed), sometimes to the detriment of the state's steadily growing military power.[16] Nevertheless, considering the decimation of senior officers during the purges, the capabilities of the Soviet forces in the late 1930s emerged, though significantly depleted, surprisingly intact.

In its role as defender of the homeland, the military instrument was used without caution or squeamishness, but with characteristic heroism and endurance. Between the end of the foreign intervention in 1920 and Hitler's invasion of the Soviet Union in 1941, the only overt military pressure exercised against the Soviet Union came from Japan. Throughout the 1930s there were numerous border incidents arising along the Soviet frontier with the Japanese puppet state of Manchukuo. The incidents were a symptom of a deep conflict of interests which resulted in frequent talk of war. The prudence of both governments averted major war, but two serious military clashes did occur at the end of the 1930s. Neither side was free of responsibility for starting them. Between July and August 1938 there was a clash at Changkufeng (Khasan), and between May and September in the following year there was a local war in the Nomonhan (Khalkin-Gol) region. The fighting was bitter: tanks, motorised groups, and aircraft were deployed on a large scale; force levels were high; and casualties were large on both sides. Despite the effects of the purges, the Soviet forces stood their ground, restored the *status quo ante,* and gave Japanese expansionists a warning that circumspection must not be mistaken for passivity, and that any intruders on Soviet territory would be dealt with violently.[17]

Between 1922 and 1941 the building up of military power for deterrence had been a keystone of Soviet exertions; and, when called upon, the defensive use of military force had been uninhibited. These efforts faced their greatest test after June 1941, when Soviet diplomacy and military power were no longer able to deter Hitler's ambitions. In the event, not only did the deterrent effort fail, but also the defensive preparations revealed many shortcomings. For the second time in a generation, the Red Armies had to fight a life and death struggle of the bitterest intensity. Despite Soviet incantations about inevitable war, and despite all the sacrifices of the previous years, their defensive perimeter was not able to contain the expanding torrent of German forces; for two years the future of the Soviet system west of the Urals was in doubt. During this critical period, the urgent need to strengthen the armed forces absorbed all Soviet efforts. With the checking of the German military thrust at the start of 1943, however, the strategic situation changed radically. As the momentum of the successful counter-offensive gathered speed, new opportunities arose for the expansion of Soviet power. From then and for the next five years, in the territory occupied between Stalingrad and the Elbe, the military instrument played a central part in the advancement of Soviet policy.

2. From victory over Germany to the Cold War

With the defeat of the Axis in 1945, a less troubled era seemed assured for the Soviet Union. Although the suffering had been terrible, and many sectors of national life badly weakened, the Soviet Union had emerged from the war as the second power in world affairs. A new strategic frontier had been gained across the decisive bridgehead connecting western Russia to Central Europe. Germany and Japan, the two main threats of the pre-war years, had been crushed and demilitarised. The great colonial powers of Western Europe had been exhausted. The Western great powers were steadily demobilising their vast wartime armies.[18] From one perspective, the outlook for Soviet security appeared satisfactory. However, what developed was not an era of peaceful reconstruction, but a bitter and dangerous period of neither war nor peace, in which the conflict of interests between the USSR and its former allies became exacerbated by a cycle of interreacting policies into the matrix of the Cold War. However one appraises the origins of, and blame for, the Cold War, it cannot be doubted that Soviet planners, basing their projections on a compound of ideological and national outlooks, and well-established worst-case strategic forecasting, perceived that the post-war world would not (and could not) be trouble-free. In fact, the situation contained a number of highly worrying characteristics.

From the viewpoint of a Soviet planner, the immediate future promised peace, but not a satisfactory long-term security position.

Domestic problems in the USSR were perplexing, with twenty million dead and a battered economy. In foreign affairs the leadership was confronted by a booming United States which had demonstrated, and was developing, strategic airpower of devastating new potential. However powerful the image created by the performance of the Red Armies during the war, the Soviet Union was undeniably vulnerable to atomic attack by a United States which was being drawn increasingly into the organisation of the post-war world. However benevolent, however war-weary, however weakened, and however non-aggressive the Western powers themselves have felt, the subjective feeling of insecurity on the part of Soviet leaders persisted.

Stalin faced a series of most difficult problems.[19] Internally, he had to revive a pulverised state, and maintain his own position. Externally, he was faced by two impulses: on the one hand, his own desire not to betray his 'hour of destiny' encouraged probing, bellicosity, and the furthering of communism; on the other hand there were the sobering capabilities of US strategic power, which dictated prudence and the avoidance of extreme provocation. Even if the 'relation of forces' did not permit wide hopes of further expansion, at the least, as Stalin said in private conversation towards the end of the war,

> This war is not as in the past; whoever occupies a territory also imposes on it his own social system. Everyone imposes his own social system as far as his army has power to do so. It cannot be otherwise.[20]

While the Soviet leaders attempted to pursue their various internal and external interests in the immediate post-war years, it was axiomatic that the maintenance of significant deterrent and defensive power must remain a primary aim of policy. The evidence for this is plentiful. After allowing his people only the briefest of respites, Stalin in February 1946 called for a new internal drive to build up Soviet strength.[21] Although demobilisation took place, formidable forces still remained.[22] These were years of a hard routine of training and indoctrination for the conscripts and officers of the Soviet forces, and exceptionally strict discipline.[23] Large-scale reorganisation took place, which indicated the importance attached to trying to meet the threat represented by the US strategic capability.[24] Finally, while Soviet military doctrine often appeared to be stagnating, constricted by Stalinist orthodoxy, in reality the assimilation of the military-technical revolution was proceeding rapidly: there was an impressive programme of research and development, which resulted, within a surprisingly short time, in atomic and thermonuclear weapons, a variety of mass-produced equipment, including submarines, tactical aircraft, a variety of air defence systems, a long-range air force and an early start on the development of long-range missiles.[25] Whatever Stalin's long-term intentions might have been, his minimum requirements for the deterrence and defence of the homeland, given his perception of his strategic environment, had to be expansive and modern.

The Cold War was the product of a conflict of irreconcilable interests between the wartime allies, raised to higher levels of hostility by the mood of the time and the logic of events. Increasingly, the chief adversaries tended to concentrate on the purely military aspects of the confrontation, until it developed its own momentum. The appetite for military strength grew by what it fed upon.

Undoubtedly the misperceptions, predispositions, inconsistencies, failings and prudence of the Western powers contributed to the deterioration of relations with the USSR and the confirmation of mutual hostility. The initial catalyst,[26] though, appears to have been the understandable determination of the Soviet Union to hold the ground it had occupied in defeating Germany, and thereby to secure a position which was of vital defensive value, which was thought to be theirs by seignorial right and which the Western powers had implicitly or explicitly accepted in wartime conferences.[27] Given the world view of the Soviet leadership, and 'worst case' planning, the Soviet penetration of Eastern Europe, their great suspicion of Western actions, and their concentraion on heavy industry and armaments were understandable responses to their situation in 1945–46. Equally, for the Western powers, on the basis of their own world view and 'worst case' planning, the Truman Doctrine of March 1947, the Marshall Plan of June 1947, and the articulation of the containment doctrine were equally understandable responses to their situation in 1946–7. The Soviet reply to such moves was the *Zhdanovshchina* of 1947–8. This period was one of internal control and external militancy, and was market by the total domination of Eastern Europe (including the establishment of the Cominform and the *coup* in Czechoslovakia), and by aggressiveness towards the West (including the Berlin blockade). Whether the period of the *Zhdanovshchina* was objectively one of militant probing, or simply bellicosity to shroud weakness, Western officials certainly interpreted it as the former. In response, the Western powers moved towards the formation of NATO, the unification of the zones of occupation in Germany and, with the outbreak of war in Korea, a new period of rearmament which soon involved the decision to rearm West Germany. The latter decision, less than 10 years after the Nazi excesses, stabbed at an open nerve in the Russian psyche.[28] By the early 1950s the spiral had become complete. Whether or not the Soviet Union intended to invade western Europe,[29] the Western powers had sufficient evidence for anxiety and therefore new military preparations. From 1945 onwards, actions which both sides had hoped would enhance their security, only brought a hardening of the lines, crises, and the nearness of war. Conflicting ideological and national perceptions and 'worse case' strategic forecasting in a fluid situation produced the Cold War. Inevitably, these years enhanced the significance of the deterrent and defence role of the military instrument in the postures of the chief adversaries.

Despite many alarms, and with Europe sharply divided into two hostile systems orbiting around dominant superpowers, a bipolar balance emerged and structured Soviet–US relations. This balance was given its stability by 'asymmetrical deterrence', with US superiority in air power being countered by the massive imbalance created by the deployment of Soviet conventional forces in Eastern Europe. In addition to the role of occupation troops and first line of defence, Soviet forces in Eastern Europe also came to be seen as serving a directly deterrent role by holding Western Europe 'hostage' in the event of a US attack.[30] As long as the homeland of the United States remained invulnerable to Soviet power, the threat of a preventive nuclear attack remained the datum line of Soviet strategic planning. Although the period of the US atomic monopoly passed safely, Soviet anxieties about a surprise attack did not decline in the mid-1950s. The tactical and ritual nature of Soviet declarations on the subject of surprise attack should not be underestimated. In the eyes of the Soviet leaders their strategic position remained alarming. They appreciated the terrifying destructive power of the US nuclear strike forces, the creation and expansion of NATO, the development of British nuclear power, the relative invulnerability of the US homeland until the late 1950s, the growth of tactical nuclear forces in Europe, the revival of German military power and the complete encirclement of the USSR by a ring of US bases and a series of hostile military alliances. There was even talk about roll back and the liberation of Eastern Europe. All this maintained the spectre of surprise nuclear attack on the Soviet Union as a possible if increasingly improbable scenario.

A major preoccupation of the Soviet leaders throughout the 1950s was to avoid nuclear war. After Stalin's death the interplay of the new defence debate amongst the Soviet leaders revealed the problems involved in the increasingly complex business of nuclear-age military policy, and the absence of clear guidelines on optimal deployments, weapons systems, targeting preferences, mixes of forces, troop levels, and tactical and strategic doctrines.[31] The policy which emerged from the debate had three major aspects. In the background there was the continued development of inter-continental strategic systems, the consolidation of general strength, and the adaptation of the forces in the primary European theatre for nuclear war conditions. Secondly, in military procurement, the development of air defence received a special and traditional Russian attention, although it is extremely doubtful whether Soviet planners have ever been very satisfied that they could cope with the threat from the air, even after the waning of their immediate fears of a US surprise attack.[32] Soviet concern with the threat of a surprise nuclear attack by the United States can be deduced from the deployments and characteristics of Soviet naval building,[33] and from the details of Soviet disarmament and partial measures proposals in the 1950s.[34] There were indications that the Soviet leaders perceived the usefulness of flexible diplomacy to improve their strategic position. The aim was to reduce dangerous tensions while exploiting (when this was compatible) enemy weaknesses.[35] This effort was a mixture, which in practice was not always well directed, and which was sometimes contradictory, of politico-strategic policies. On the one hand there was the promulgation of the peaceful coexistence doctrine,[36] the generation of the 'spirit of Geneva' and the 'spirit of Camp David' and the general manipulation of the atmosphere of international relations as seen in the Stockholm Peace Appeal, the signing of the Austrian State Treaty and in various arms control proposals. On the other hand, this period also witnessed the consolidation of Soviet military control over Eastern Europe through the instrument of the Warsaw Pact, the attempt to solve the Berlin and German questions by intimidation, by preliminary diplomatic and propaganda efforts to prise the United States out of Europe, the attempt to forestall moves towards European integration, such as the European Defence Community, and the attempt to loosen NATO's cohesion by more flexible policies towards its diverse members. By the middle and late 1950s, Soviet military and political leaders must have considered themselves successful; to the extent they believed that NATO, led by the United States, was hostile and aggressive, they had reason to believe that their deterrent efforts had, in fact, deterred.

Despite the depth of the ideological and national confrontation between the superpowers, war was averted. The image of nuclear war imposed a distinctive rationality on their decision-makers. As a mark of this, Khrushchev in 1956 revised Lenin's doctrine about the fatalistic inevitability of war: he said that

There is, of course, a Marxist-Leninist precept that wars are inevitable as long as imperialism exists . . . But war is not fatalistically inevitable. Today there are mighty social and political forces possessing formidable means to prevent the imperialists from unleashing war.[37]

This was a bold move, although a shift from the rigidity of the 'two camp' image of the *Zhdanovishchina* had been foreshadowed in 1952 by Stalin himself.[38] Khrushchev's revision, while encouraging to Western observers, was none the less not inspired by a sudden conversion to a benevolent interpretation of Western policies. War was no longer fatalistically inevitable, he argued, not because of some profound change in the capitalist system, but because of the continuing strength of the Soviet bloc. Such was the deterrent power of the Soviet military instrument by the mid-1950s that their leaders were confident that it would impose rationality even on the class enemies. This position has, with some refinements, been held since that time. The further refinements, elaborated during the polemics with China, have stressed the destructiveness of modern war to all concerned. A statement in *Kommunist,* in September 1960, argued that a world war

> would cause the complete destruction of the main centres of civilisation and the annihilation of whole peoples. It would bring untold suffering to all mankind. Only madmen could want such a catastrophe to happen . . . The working class does not think of creating a Communist civilisation on the ruins of the centres of world culture . . .[39]

The reasonableness and rationality of the Soviet position was stressed partly as a tactic to discredit the apparently less reasonable Chinese. Nevertheless, the genuineness of the underlying belief cannot be doubted. The position basically remains as M. Suslov stated in February 1964:

> The task of averting war has become especially urgent because the most destructive weapons in the history of mankind have been created, and stocks of them have been accumulated which could bring incalculable disaster upon all peoples.[40]

These changes in Soviet thinking about the inevitability and utility of war expressed a fundamental truth about the impact of nuclear weapons. They signified the determination of the Soviet leaders to possess a credible deterrent, and the fact that, like their US counterparts, they had learned to live with their adversary's growing nuclear arsenal.

3. Nuclear proliferation and the problem of China

The Soviet Union achieved at least a minimally satisfactory strategic relationship with its most powerful enemy by the end of the 1950s. However, it still faced many considerable military problems. One particularly worrying threat to Soviet planners was that of a nuclear armed People's Republic of China and Federal Republic of Germany. As a result of such fears, shared by many in the West, the Soviet leadership supported a range of proposals, from atom-free zones in Central Europe and the Far East in the 1950s, to non-proliferation exercises in the 1960s, which eventually led to the steering with the United States of a Non-Proliferation Treaty in 1968. The latter, however, only partly solved the overall problem, and did nothing at all to constrict the already developing capability of China. The original Soviet decision to give assistance to China in modern military technology was probably their most 'bitterly regretted' decision since 1945.[41] The prevention of a nuclear armed and independent Federal Republic of Germany was a key theme in Khrushchev's politico-strategic policy, and was probably given a priority which many Western observers have underestimated.[42] Although the urgency of the nuclear proliferation issue has subsided since the Chinese acquisition, and the ratification of the Non-Proliferation Treaty by many states, the basic problem remains. It is in the foreground as a result of China's developing nuclear arsenal and delivery systems, and in the background as a result of the non-signature or non-ratification of the Treaty (which in any case is not a tight one) by a significant section of potential nuclear powers. In their desire to inhibit, if not completely prevent, the rise of independent sources of nuclear power, the Soviet Union and the United States share an important common interest.

Through the 1960s Soviet leaders have continued, with changes of emphasis, the development of the deterrent and defence postures laid down in the late 1950s. From the anxieties of the early 1960s, when the Kennedy–McNamara defence effort resulted in the creation of a 'missile gap' which was very much to the advantage of the United States States,[43] the Soviet strategic relationship with the United States moved steadily towards a recognised 'parity' in the nuclear numbers game for the first time; in terms of the political reality of deterrence, though, 'parity' had existed since at least the mid-1950s. Because of the lead times involved, the strengthening of the Soviet military posture in the second half of the 1960s was clearly the result of decisions taken several years earlier, and must largely have been in response to the impact of qualitative and quantitative improvements in US military power during the Kennedy—McNamara period.[44] The growth of Soviet strategic power during the second half of the 1960s was impressive.[45] The development of intercontinental strategic forces proceeded at an increasing pace. New attention was given to the modernisation, integration, and strengthening of the Warsaw Pact in the still primary European theatre. Continued efforts were directed towards improving air defence, including considerable attention to the costly and baffling problem of ballistic missile defence. These efforts towards creating a powerful and credible capability were matched by a foreign policy which, after the Cuban crisis, eschewed adventurism. Instead, there were continuing efforts to reduce tensions, or to exploit weaknesses amongst adversaries. The manipulation of the atmosphere of *détente* was a characteristic feature of Soviet policy through the 1960s, with arms control proposals playing an important role. In addition, there were diplomatic and propaganda efforts to weaken US relations with Europe, serious attempts to loosen NATO's cohesion as its twentieth anniversary approached, and hopes of weakening the movement towards European economic unity. The means of achieving such aims have included the encouragement of European nationalism, and the supporting of vague but fine-sounding proposals for a European security conference. The atmosphere, if not the reality, of *détente* was maintained throughout most of the 1960s, despite such obstacles as the war in Vietnam and the invasion of Czechoslovakia. The nuclear predicament imposes major constraints; it moulded a dynamic and dangerous superpower confrontation into an effectively stable competitive relationship.

A minimally satisfactory balance of deterrence has therefore emerged out of the Cold War. The equilibrium of the present superpower relationship, which has been felicitously described as a 'limited adversary' one,[46] cannot be easily upset, though it is proper to exaggerate its 'delicacy'. Although both powers press on with military research and development, this stability is likely to continue, provided of course that they remain roughly in step. As long as both sides have the capability of assured destruction, as long as the efficiency of damage limitation or counter measures remains low, and, above all, while both sides recognise the irrationality of nuclear war, a determination to avoid the use of nuclear weapons is likely to remain the basis of relations between the United States and the Soviet Union.

Through the 1960s Soviet strategic relations with the United States became increasingly tolerable. The most urgent challenge for the Soviet Union came, paradoxically, from her former Communist ally, the People's Republic of China; by the end of the 1960s the deterioration in their relations had taken on a military as well as an ideological and nationalist dimension.[47] While the United States remained the ultimate threat in terms of capabilities, the most troublesome and immediate military challenge to the Soviet Union's position came from China, a Communist power with a limited but growing nuclear potential, a population in excess of 800 million, an ideological rival for leadership of the socialist inclined states, a national rival over disputed borderlands and with a government, in Soviet eyes, controlled by anti-Russian megalomaniacs.

At the end of the 1960s Soviet relations with China were strained and obsessional. In 1969 there was much talk of war between the two states,[48] but how much was serious and how much was declaratory for bargaining purposes or internal manipulation it is impossible to know. If a showdown had been decided upon, the military initiative lay with the Soviet Union, but the attraction of the option of preventive war could be seen as having only short-term benefit. This, apparently, was the advice of at least one senior member of the Soviet military establishment.[49] Irrespective of whether the Soviet leaders claimed military victory in a limited war against China, the likelihood would be a protracted war with the most populous country in the world. A 'surgical strike' is a beguiling medical metaphor: the operation, in reality, is always likely to be much more messy than expected.

4. Towards strategic parity with the United States

At the end of 1972 the Sino-Soviet confrontation remained serious. Its impact on the Soviet Union's position was indicated by the fact that Soviet manpower deployed on the border with China had risen spectacularly, from 15 divisions in 1968 to 44 divisions in 1972.[50] With this trebling of the Soviet deployment, nearly one-third of the Soviet Army's 'active formations' were now committed in this area. During the Soviet build-up, the threat represented by Chinese capabilities had also increased with the modernisation of its military equipment, including nuclear weapons and their associated delivery systems. Furthermore, China's international status had risen with its admission into the United Nations in October 1971, and the *rapprochement* with the United States in the following year.

Clearly, the threat from and competition with China would remain with the Soviet Union for the immediate future. During 1972 the verbal clashes between them continued more or less unabated.[51] More seriously, in December, the Soviet Union reported that military clashes had broken out on the border, after 3 years of relative calm.[52] In their competition to expand influence through diplomacy and military aid, the two states were in opposition both amongst the countries of South and South-East Asia, and the Far East, and amongst the socialist-inclined states and various revolutionary movements.[53] During 1971 and 1972 the international politics of the Asian rimlands were in flux, and influence in such important countries as Japan, India, Pakistan, Bangladesh, Afghanistan and North Vietnam was a tempting prize in the diplomatic struggle between the chief Communist powers. Soviet diplomacy was partly based upon the search for a collective security system in Asia. While this tactic in its containment policy won no adherents, Soviet diplomacy did make some important incremental gains, especially in the Indian sub-continent, although the limits as well as the opportunities for penetration were visible.[54] In addition to the vigorous regional competition, the uncertainty of global international politics during the challenging period of what President Nixon called the 'new era of multilateral diplomacy'[55] added further strains to their relationship. In particular, from the Soviet viewpoint, the *rapprochement* between the United States and the People's Republic of China, which had been marked by President Nixon's well-staged visit to Peking in February, must have perturbed the Soviet leaders, despite Mr Nixon's subsequent visit to Moscow in May. However wary the minuet between China and the United States, the anxiety felt by any adversary of both partners is not difficult to imagine.[56] With all these international developments, full of prizes, dangers and problems, relations between the Soviet Union and China remained a taut preoccupation for both sets of leaders, especially at a time when important domestic concerns needed attention.

The possibility of war between the USSR and China cannot be ruled out, especially while the Soviet Union has something approaching a first-strike capability. As time passes, though, and the costs of any war increase even further, it seems likely that major war will not be a chosen instrument of policy. Nevertheless, even if the Soviet leaders continue to reject the idea of preventive war, the importance of the military instrument in Soviet relations with China will remain considerable. The threat of swift and massive military action, for active deterrence and possibly coercive bargaining, will continue to have an important role in the range of Soviet tools in the confrontation. At the minimum, local military superiority can be expected to ensure Soviet success in any further border clashes (however they are started, and by whom). Militarily and politically, it may be argued that it will be to the advantage of the Soviet Union that the present Chinese government feels a degree of vulnerability.

Against a background of military superiority, the Soviet leaders will be able to wait for better times. Depending upon the predispositions of particular Soviet leaderships, 'better times' might be the emergence of stable deterrence with a powerful China, or the decline of China as a significant international actor because of internal stress, or the revival of the former Communist partnership (albeit on a more equal footing than before) through the emergence in China of a government whose view of the world is more akin to that of the Soviet leaders. While both states have obvious incentives for improving their relations, many basic issues divide them. By the early 1970s a far-reaching Sino—Soviet *rapprochement* seemed to most observers as remote a possibility as had a *rapprochement* between the United States and either of the chief Communist powers 20 years earlier.

The immediate and possibly long-lasting (but not inevitable) strategic confrontation with China will ensure that the Soviet Union will maintain very high levels of military manpower, will be disposed constantly to modernise its military equipment, and will remain wedded to thinking of security very much in military terms.

Whatever additional roles are given to the Soviet military instrument, deterrence and defence of the homeland will remain the primary and irreducible requirement. In practice, though, from the viewpoint of the Soviet Union's potential adversaries the important operational questions concern the ways in which the Soviet Union will choose to manifest its primary strategic aim of deterring, of dealing with the world from strength and of preparing to defend. Since 1945, these aims have been pursued as logically and as consistently as the inherent nuclear predicament and the particular predicaments of the Soviet state have allowed. In this some observers have noted a tendency for Soviet governments (like the Czarist governments before them) to overinsure in military affairs.[57] The Soviet leaders are said to support the 'rather simple concept that the more military power the country has the better' — a lesson drummed into them by a long and bitter history. It is a tendency we can detect in the decisions made at the start of the 1960s or before, which have resulted in the massive build up in Soviet strategic nuclear forces since 1965. This argument has weight and is useful. It is also consistent with the present thesis about the primacy of deterrence and defence, and the high level of minimum requirements these demand. However, the impulse to overinsure does not explain everything. Several further observations should be made. Firstly, the desire to overinsure is an inherent one amongst major powers in a world of independent states, and is by no means peculiar to the USSR. Until the very late 1960s, the United States held tenaciously to the doctrine of superiority.[58] Overinsurance is an inevitable outcome of strategic planning based on very bad or worst-case assumptions. It is not difficult to imagine the anxiety felt, and consequently the action recommended, by Soviet planners to even fairly bad assumptions fed into their interpretation of the Kennedy–McNamara thrust in US strategic policy at the start of the 1960s. Secondly, interpretation of Soviet force structures, postures and levels should not be confined simply to elucidating their rational calculations of their strategic options, or to discovering historically derived impulses. An additional set of analytical tools should be fashioned by research into Soviet organisational processes and bureaucratic politics. Research in this field is difficult; it is none the less highly important. Certainly, both Russian value-systems and the rational selection of choices do play a part in the evolution of Soviet military policy. But it is at least likely that the outputs of organisational processes and the outcomes of bureaucratic politics have also played a very important role in the shape of the overall effort. Awareness of the possible impact of such processes is therefore necessary in any analysis of the weight and emphasis of hardware procurement.[59]

It can never be assumed that policy is simply the result of the rational deliberations of a value-maximising unitary decision-making group. By basing analysis on a strict model of Soviet rationality, it was possible, with some justification at least, to interpret the performance characteristics of the SS-9 missile system as a step towards a first-strike posture. Mr Laird, the US Secretary of Defence, argued as much in 1969.[60] By looking at other evidence, including Soviet national interests, value-systems, organisational processes, bureaucratic politics, and the impressive and diverse capabilities of the US deterrent posture, the picture becomes very blurred.[61] While the deployment of the SS-9 must be closely monitored, it is far from being the main or only evidence of Soviet intentions. Superpower deterrence is inherently stable, and nuclear war remains 'unthinkable' in Clausewitzian terms, if not those of Herman Kahn. Wide analysis, assuming the continuation of the existing strategic environment, must always reject a first-strike hypothesis, except as a very improbable contingency. Rational choice, however, clearly has had an impact on Soviet procurement.

Interpretations of Soviet calculations behind the missile build-up vary, but the following one is widely held. Throughout the 1960s, the United States had a tremendous lead in the amount of deliverable nuclear power. Some observers in the West expected the Soviet Union to accept a permanent inferiority as the basis for stable deterrence (for example, halting its procurement at one-half of the US strength).[62] It is not surprising that this expectation did not materialise; instead, Soviet strategic power has grown until it is now fully recognised as having achieved parity. If inferiority is not acceptable to one superpower, as it has clearly not been to the United States, then there is no reason why it should have been acceptable to the other. The USSR has certainly been 'overinsuring', but it has been doing no more (in the nuclear field anyway) than following the lead set by the United States. Premeditated first strikes (assuming that there are no radical technological breakthroughs, and out of the context of a pre-emptive strike, when one or other superpower thinks war is inevitable) remain unthinkable methods of securing reasonable political objectives. Rather than the Soviet Union moving to a first-strike position, or even massive superiority (which would trigger a US reaction), the major rational impulse behind the Soviet effort was probably, as Mackintosh has argued, to seek a 'numerical superiority over the US at the highest level which will not spark off another major round in the strategic arms race'.[63] Thus having reached a position satisfactory for a superpower, the Soviet Union entered the Strategic Arms Limitation Talks to freeze it.

The first round of the SALT talks, which were finally begun in Helsinki in November 1969, were ceremonially concluded during President Nixon's visit to Moscow in May 1972. A bundle of agreements was reached. Most important, there were the strategic arms limitation accords themselves. These consisted of a treaty limiting anti-ballistic missile systems (which was of unlimited duration, but subject to five-yearly reviews), an interim agreement limiting offensive strategic missiles (up to five years), and a protocol defining the effect of the latter upon submarine-launched missiles. A memorandum containing 'interpretations' and 'understandings' was also initialled. The areas covered by the additional agreements were the prevention of naval incidents, scientific and technological cooperation, joint space exploration, medical research cooperation, joint environmental studies, the establishment of a Joint Commercial Commission to negotiate trade treaties and a declaration of the 'Basic Principles of Relations'. In the latter the intention was expressed of avoiding confrontations which might lead to nuclear war, and of exercising restraint in their mutual relations.⁶⁴ Almost all observers have been agreed upon the possible significance of these agreements, which encompassed strategic, political, economic and scientific aspects of their relationships, and which included their first major bilateral arms control agreements. However, when the precise nature of the significance is discussed, there is scope for wide disagreement.

In the United States in particular, the question 'Who won SALT 1?' was the subject of an important and multi-faceted debate in the months after the agreements were signed.⁶⁵ Was it the world through the progress in arms control, as the Administration and its supporters and some (but not all) arms control enthusiasts claimed? Was it the Soviet Union, as was argued by some conservative critics, because of the freezing of Soviet numerical superiorities, while areas of US technological superiority were left free for competition? Was it the United States, as was claimed by those who feared that without the checks of an agreement the Soviet Union might have drawn distinctly ahead in the arms race? Or did everybody lose, as was asserted by the proponents of more 'defensive emphasis', and by the critics of the now crystallised MAD (Mutual Assured Destruction) deterrent strategy? Or were, in fact, the achievements and significance of SALT I greatly exaggerated — 'more apparent than real' — as was argued by those who pointed to the continuing momentum of superpower strategic arms competition?⁶⁶ With such a short perspective and with so many variables to consider the wide differences of opinion amongst Western observers are not surprising. The agreements of SALT I were of apparent consequence, but it will be necessary to wait a good many years before their consequences can be assessed.

From the immediate Soviet viewpoint however, the outcome seems clear. There are a number of reasons for supposing that the Soviet leaders should have been very satisfied by the agreements, in terms of the substantive accords which were reached, the atmosphere and images which were generated and the institutionalised relationships which were established. On balance, the Soviet Union probably gained more from the agreements than the United States: this is not to say that the United States 'lost'.

The list of the aims which the Soviet leaders and their advisers may have set themselves — and mostly achieved — in SALT I was a long one. As a result of the agreements the Soviet leaders might feel that the expensive and dangerous arms race of the previous 25 years had been brought to a new and safer stage in which the danger of nuclear war had been perceptibly reduced. With the new constraints on missile deployment the massive Soviet strategic build-up since the mid-1960s would quantitatively, if not qualitatively, cease; scarce economic resources might therefore be released for allocation to some of the Soviet Union's other pressing needs. With the completion of the agreement near the climax of the Soviet build-up, the Soviet numerical superiority in fixed land-based ICBM and SLBM launchers and in 'throw weight' was frozen. While this Soviet numerical lead was frozen, there was no agreement about MIRV technology, in which the United States had a clear lead. The Soviet Union was therefore free, if it wished, to devote attention to eliminating this area of inferiority. Furthermore, the ABM agreement effectively prevented the United States from capitalising on its generally admitted technological lead in this field. In addition, while the United States remained free to improve its existing submarine force, the Soviet Union would be able, if it chose, to achieve numerical superiority in SLBMs under the protocol allowing the conversion of obsolete ICBMs and obsolete SLBMs into Polaris-type SLBMs. In the general field of arms control, several Soviet interests might have been served. To the extent that the Soviet leaders put a value on communication between the two bureaucracies in exchanging strategic ideas, an important beginning was made. Specifically, the opportunity was created for the sounding out of informal and tacit restraints. From the Soviet (as well as the US) viewpoint, an institutionalised strategic relationship is likely to be less dangerous. Politically, the agreements crystallised (for some) the impression that the United States, after years of clear strategic superiority, has been matched and in some cases overtaken. The impression has become current that parity has been achieved by the Soviet Union on by no means unfavourable terms. To the extent that the Soviet leaders value the formalisation of superpower strategic parity, therefore, the agreements were more than successful.

In addition to these results, the process of negotiation itself apparently contributed to improving mutual confidence between the two leaderships. Taken together the bundle of agreements helped to institutionalise a special bilateral superpower relationship. By their joint readiness to talk and agree in some fields, *détente* took on a slightly stronger meaning. The resulting improvement in the atmosphere of their relations was expecially important to the USSR, in view of Soviet anxieties about the United States–China *rapprochement,* its desire to achieve a number of objectives in Europe (focusing on the idea of a security conference), and its wish for access to the technical expertise and financial and other resources of the United States and Western Europe. Important Soviet objectives in these fields could only be achieved through better relations with the United States. Apart from any strategic payoffs, therefore, SALT I was also potentially instrumental for a wide range of Soviet foreign policy objectives.

Against these solid achievements, the Soviet Union faced few disadvantages. Certainly, the existing US advantages in strategic bombers, MIRV technology, and forward-based systems remained, but the opportunity of eliminating them was not closed. Secondly, the ABM freeze contributed to the continued nuclear viability of China, the United Kingdom and France, which would have been at least partially undermined had the alleged advantages of a defensive option been left open. Here was a loss, but the Soviet delegation must have considered that it was more than outweighed by the various advantages contained in the agreements as a whole. Thirdly, the agreements meant that the Soviet Union was denied the possibility of further increasing its numerical lead in strategic offensive missiles. However, this theoretical disadvantage can be disregarded for other reasons — economic and political, as well as the irrelevance of more overkill. The freezing of a small numerical lead was preferable to the costs of another round in the quantitative arms race. Compared with the advantages, these disadvantages were few. For a range of political and military reasons, therefore, the Soviet Union had reason to be pleased with the outcome of SALT I.

When compared with the strategic inferiority complex of the Soviet Union only ten years before, as exposed by the Cuban missile crisis, the position by mid-1972 was one of real strength and confidence. This change had been made possible by the strategic build-up in the second half of the 1960s. By 1972, military might had been translated into political power so effectively that the image of 1962 had been expunged. To the extent, therefore, that the Soviet political and military leadership is satisfied with deterrence based upon Mutual Assured Destruction (even if they do not regard the situation in that particular Western way) they have every reason to have been satisfied by the political outcome of their strategic exertions over the previous ten years.

Six months after the Moscow agreements, SALT II began in Geneva. Most observers considered that any further agreements would be increasingly difficult to reach. In a sense, the easy areas had been dealt with first; secondly, the very process of negotiation had encouraged the parties to provide themselves with powerful bargaining positions; and thirdly, the qualitative aspects of the arms race are always less amenable to agreement, because of problems of definition, inspection, and the more complex issue of assessing symmetry. Many issues were open for inclusion on the agenda. The main ones were a reduction in the numbers of strategic offensive systems, mobile ICBMs, strategic bombers, forward-based systems, MIRV technology, control of megatonnage and payload, the transfer of technology between allies, the control of strategic research and development, air-to-surface missiles, anti-aircraft and anti-submarine warfare systems.[67] In some of these categories, the Soviet Union is in a position to aim for favourable changes. However, relative gains will be far from easy since, in the aftermath of SALT I, the US Administration has been stiffened by both Houses of Congress to ensure that exact symmetry is achieved in the next round.

Whatever the results of SALT II, – if any – both superpowers will still emerge with secure second-strike assured destruction capabilities. The central balance will not be easily tipped. However, incremental changes in matters such as forward-based systems or technology-transfer might have political and military repercussions in particular regions (such as Europe) or on third-party images of the central balance (which in turn might have political consequences). Few would deny the potential value of the negotiations but the arms race will nevertheless go on; it might be constrained but it will not be abandoned. Applying SALT to the present superpower nuclear confrontation might make the future concoction more tolerable: short of a radical change in the chemistry of politics, it will not presently turn it into ambrosia.

The dynamics of modern technological innovation and the imperatives of a superpower confrontation therefore undermine the idea of totally freezing deterrent and defence situations. Soviet strategic thinking, policy and posture may be seen to have moved on from the particular 'cross-roads' described by Wolfe in the middle 1960s,[68] but the result has only been to reach another set further on. Cross-roads are the inescapable habitat of strategic thinking: and not only is there no one clear route towards security, but – and this is perhaps the hardest lesson of all – whichever route is chosen, there is no final destination, only an infinity of cross-roads. As long as the international system remains as it is, this prospect is the same for both the Soviet Union and the United States, although, of course, the ideology of the former does promise an eventual and satisfying resting place.

Notes

1. This is J. M. Mackintosh's definition of 'strategic policy' from the Soviet viewpoint, in his 'Soviet Strategic Policy', *The World Today,* vol. 26, no. 7 (July 1970), p. 272.
2. E. Crankshaw, *Khrushchev's Russia* (Penguin Books, Harmondsworth, revised edition, 1962), Foreword.
3. Variations on this theme can be found, for example, in G. B. Cressey, *The Basis of Soviet Strength* (McGraw-Hill Book Co., New York, 1945); B. Moore, *Soviet Politics – The Dilemma of Power* (Harvard University Press, Cambridge, Mass., 1950); F. L. Schuman, *Government in the Soviet Union* (Thomas Y. Crowell Co., New York, 1961); R. J. Kerner, *The Urge to the Sea* (University of California Press, Berkeley and Los Angeles, Calif., 1942); L. J. Halle, *The Cold War as History* (Chatto and Windus, London, 1967); R. Strausz-Hupe, 'The Western Frontiers of Russia', in H. W. Weigert (ed.), *New Compass of the World* (The Macmillan Co., New York, 1949), pp. 150–61.
4. The phrase in Halle's *The Cold War as History,* Chapter II, 'The Behaviour of Moscow as a Reflection of Russia's Historic Experience'.
5. For Example: Pan Slavism, traditional imperialism, missionary zeal, the initiatives of local Russian officers and officials, and balance of power considerations.
6. Amongst the many analyses of the doctrine of inevitable war, see F. S. Burin 'The Communist Doctrine of the Inevitability of War', *The American Political Science Review* (June 1963), pp. 334–54; T. W. Wolfe, *Communist Outlook on War* (The Rand Corporation, P-3640, August 1967).
7. Quoted by Stalin, *Problems of Leninism* (Foreign Language Publishing House, Moscow, 1947), p. 160.
8. In 1956 the prognosis was reformulated by Khrushchev.
9. 'Socialism in one country' is summarised in I. Deutscher, *Stalin: A Political Biography* (Oxford University Press, London 1949), pp. 281–93.
10. Quoted in J. Erickson, *The Soviet High Command 1918–41: A Military–Political History* (Macmillan & Co. Ltd London, 1962), p. 111.
11. In a speech to the Central Committee in 1925; quoted in R. L. Garthoff, *Soviet Military Policy. A Historical Analysis* (Faber & Faber, London 1966), p. 14.
12. See, for example, Erickson, *The Soviet High Command 1918–41,* pp. 113–322; J. M. Mackintosh, *Juggernaut: A History of the Soviet Armed Forces* (Secker & Warburg, London, 1967), pp. 52–67; and M. Garder, *A History of the Soviet Army* (Pall Mall Press, London, 1966), pp. 70–82.
13. See, for example, Erickson, *The Soviet High Command 1918–41,* pp. 144–163, 247–82; G. Freund, *Unholy Alliance: Russian–German Relations from the Treaty of Brest Litovsk to the Treaty of Berlin* (Chatto & Windus, London, 1957), pp. 112–3, 124–6, 201–12, 246–7.
14. Use will occasionally be made of the idea of swings in Soviet foreign policy, between right and left policies. For definitions, analytical explanations and problems, see M. D. Shulman, *Stalin's Foreign Policy Reappraised* (Harvard U.P., Cambridge, Mass., 1963), Chapter I.
15. I am grateful to M. K. MccGwire for the corroborating evidence from Soviet naval policy. By 1935 submarine strength in the Pacific fleet was greater than that in the three other Soviet fleets.
16. Amongst many discussions of the purges and the armed forces, see Erickson, *The Soviet High Command 1918–41,* pp. 449–509; Mackintosh, *Juggernaut: A History of the Soviet Armed Forces,* pp. 84–110.
17. At Khalkin-Gol, for example, the Soviet effort included 498 tanks, 346

armoured cars, and 500 aircraft. Estimates of Soviet deaths in the border conflicts of these years are as high as 30,000. Erickson, *The Soviet High Command 1918–41*, pp. 494–9, 532–7; C. W. Tinch, 'Quasi-War between Japan and the USSR, 1937–1939', *World Politics*, vol. III (Jan. 1951), pp. 174–99; M. Blumenson, 'The Soviet Power Play at Changkufeng', *World Politics*, vol. XII (Jan. 1960), pp. 249–63.

18. It is likely that Stalin's thinking at the end of the war was affected by Roosevelt's famous comment at Yalta that he did not believe that US forces would stay in Europe 'much more than two years'. Quoted in H. Feis, *Churchill, Roosevelt, Stalin: the war they waged and the peace they sought* (Princeton University Press, Princeton, 1957), p. 531.

19. Stalin's precise motivations defy definitive analysis. The balance in his thinking between the ideologist and the realist have been dealt with by many authors. One congenial interpretation is that of A. Schlesinger, Jnr, who has argued that, while the role of ideology can easily be exaggerated, 'Nothing the United States could have done in 1944–45 would have abolished . . . (Soviet) mistrust, required and sanctified as it was by Marxist gospel.' *Foreign Affairs*, vol. 46 (October 1967), 'Origins of the Cold War', p. 47. Such an interpretation does not necessarily involve acceptance of the idea that Stalin had a 'blueprint' for Communist expansion. There is reason to believe that he did not, even on the critical question of the future of Germany. See, for example, W. Z. Laqueur, *Russia and Germany: A Century of Conflict* (Weidenfeld and Nicholson, London, 1965), pp. 271, 274–5; M. Djilas, *Conversations with Stalin* (Penguin Books, Harmondsworth, 1963), p. 199, recorded his and Soviet puzzlement over the future of Germany.

20. Djilas, *Conversations with Stalin*, p. 90.

21. *Pravda*, 10 February 1946, quoted by Garthoff, *Soviet Military Policy*, p. 20.

22. T. W. Wolfe, *Soviet Power and Europe 1945–70* (The Johns Hopkins Press, Blatimore, 1970), pp. 9–12.

23. Mackintosh *Juggernaut: A History of the Soviet Armed Forces*, chapter 13.

24. Ibid., p. 273.

25. Ibid., pp. 272–5.

26. This view, of course, has been strongly challenged by the 'revisionist school' of cold war historians, who place most, or major, responsibility for post-war troubles on US policy. The major revisionist works are: G. Alperovitz, *Atomic Diplomacy: Hiroshima and Potsdam* (Vintage Books, New York, 1967); D. F. Fleming, *The Cold War and its Origins, 1917–60*, 2 vols. (Doubleday and Co., Garden City, N.Y., 1961); D. Horowitz, *The Free World Colossus: A Critique of American Foreign Policy in the Cold War* (Hill and Wing, New York, 1965); W. A. Williams, *The Tragedy of American Diplomacy* (World Publishers, Cleveland, Ohio, 1959).

27. Churchill's 'spheres of influence' bargain was perhaps the most famous example. See W. W. Rostow, *The United States in the World Arena* (Harper and Brothers, New York, 1960), pp. 101–8.

28. The crucial importance of Germany in Soviet policy calculations should never be underestimated. Even when Germany was weak, Soviet leaders were still sensitive to the latent threat. See, for example, Stalin's *Economic Problems of Socialism in the USSR* (International Publishers, New York, 1952), pp. 29–30, in which he predicted the revival of German power, and consequent aggressiveness.

29. Reasons for thinking that this was not the Soviet intention can be found in A. B. Ulam, *Expansion and Coexistence. The History of Soviet Foreign Policy, 1917–67* (Secker and Warburg, London, 1967), pp. 378–455.

30. It can be argued that the hostage role of Western Europe was implicit from

the late 1940s, before being articulated by Khrushchev. See, for example, Wolfe *Soviet Power and Europe,* pp. 32–5, 152–4.

31. See H. S. Dinerstein, *War and the Soviet Union. Nuclear Weapons and the Revolution in Soviet Military and Political Thinking* (Praeger, London, revised edition, 1962), Chapters I–VI.

32. For an interesting survey of the Soviet air defence mentality, with special reference to ballistic missile defence, see J. R. Thomas, 'The Role of Missile Defence in Soviet Strategy and Foreign Policy' in J. Erickson (ed.) *The Military–Technical Revolution* (Pall Mall, London, 1966), pp. 187–218.

33. M. K. McGwire, 'The Background to Russian Naval Policy', *Brassey's Annual 1968* (Wm. Clowes and Sons, London, 1968), pp. 141–58, especially pp. 149–51.

34. See, for example, Mackintosh's analysis of the Soviet proposal of 10 May 1955. *Strategy and Tactics of Soviet Foreign Policy* (Oxford University Press, London, 1962), pp. 97–102. For a discussion of changing Soviet attitudes to surprise attack, see T. W. Wolfe, *Soviet Military Theory: An Additional Source of Insight into its Development* (The Rand Corporation, P-3258, November 1965), pp. 15–21.

35. On Malenkov's hope to reduce international tension see Dinerstein, *War and the Soviet Union,* pp. 65–90.

36. Of the considerable literature on peaceful co-existence, see M. P. Gehlen, *The Politics of Coexistence – Soviet Methods and Motives* (Indiana University Press, Bloomington, 1967); W. W. Kulski, *Peaceful Coexistence* (Regnery Company, Chicago, 1959); and R. C. Tucker, *The Soviet Political Mind* (Frederick A. Praeger, New York, 1963), especially pp. 201–22.

37. Khrushchev's speech to the 20th Party Congress, 15 February 1956. See Burin, *The Communist Doctrine of the Inevitability of War,* pp. 334, 343–8; Dinerstein, *War and the Soviet Union,* pp. 80–4; Garthoff, *Soviet Military Policy,* pp. 191–206; and T. W. Wolfe, *Soviet Strategy at the Crossroads* (Harvard University Press, Cambridge, Mass., 1963), pp. 18–25, 70–8, 110–17.

38. In his *Economic Problems of Socialism in the USSR,* Stalin had shifted to the position that war between the USSR and the capitalist powers was less likely than new wars amongst the capitalist powers themselves (pp. 28–29). Just after Stalin's death, this was taken a step further by an obscure writer, M. Gus, presumably with the support of Malenkov and others, who questioned the inevitability of war. Dinerstein, *War and the Soviet Union,* pp. 66–9.

39. *Kommunist,* no. 13 (September 1960), pp. 15–16. Quoted by Garthoff, *Soviet Military Policy,* p. 194.

40. Ibid. Report to Central Committee Plenum, 14 February 1964.

41. *Ulam,* Expansion and Coexistence, p. 611.

42. Ulam, is an exception, ibid., pp. 610–11, 620–1, 661–2, 680–2.

43. For example, see A. L. Horelick and M. R. Rush, *Strategic Power and Soviet Foreign Policy* (Chicago University Press, Chicago, 1966), especially chapters 11 and 12.

44. Secretary of Defence Mr McNamara later stated that this was his belief. See his speech delivered before the editors of the United Press International, 18 September 1967. Quoted by R. J. Art and K. N. Waltz (eds.), *The Use of Force, International Politics and Foreign Policy* (Little, Brown and Co., Boston, 1971), pp. 503–16, especially p. 508. Soviet planners must have been particularly impressed by President Kennedy's striking statement in the *Saturday Evening Post,* 31 March 1962, in which he said that in certain circumstances he would initiate the use of nuclear weapons. See Horelick and Rush, *Strategic Power and Soviet Foreign Policy,* especially pp. 83–102.

45. Of the many analyses of this development, Wolfe, *Soviet Power and Europe,* and J. Erickson, *Soviet Military Power* (Royal United Services Institute, London, 1971) are particularly useful.

46. The phrase is M. D. Shulman's. See his 'Relations with the Soviet Union', in K. Gordon (ed.), *Agenda for the Nation* (Brookings Institution, Washington, 1968), p. 374.

47. For a background to the problem, see F. L. Garthoff, *Sino—Soviet Military Relations* (Praeger, London, 1966).

48. See, for example, H. Salisbury, *The Coming War Between Russia and China* (Secker and Warburg, London, 1969).

49. The Chief of the General Staff, Marshal Zakharov. See Erickson, *Soviet Military Power*, p. 27.

50. *The Military Balance 1968—1969*, p. 6; ibid. *1972—73*, p. 7.

51. One of the most interesting developments occurred on 21 December 1972, when Mr Brezhnev alleged that the Chinese government had refused in 1971 to sign a treaty outlawing the use of military force in their mutual relations. He took this opportunity to make this 'disclosure' from their secret talks in a major policy speech to mark the fiftieth anniversary of the founding of the Soviet State. See *The Times*, 22 December 1972. On its part, the Soviet Union (like the United States) has not accepted a long-standing Chinese proposal for a no-first-use agreement on nuclear weapons.

52. *Strategic Survey 1972*, pp. 3, 85.

53. For a breakdown of the current orientation of the major and minor Communist parties of the world, and various 'extremist movements', see the *Annual of Power and Conflict 1972—73* (The Institute for the Study of Conflicts, London, 1973) especially p. 162.

54. For example, while India agreed in September 1972 to establish a Commission on Economic, Scientific and Technical Cooperation, the idea that it might be associated with COMECON was rejected.

55. *U.S. Foreign Policy for the 1970s: Building for Peace.* A Report to the Congress (US Government Printing Office, 1971), p. 4,

56. As is always possible in fluid circumstances, moods can change quickly. In the middle of 1973, after Mr Brezhnev's visit to the United States and the apparent success of his theatrical western policy, it is likely that the Chinese leaders felt neglected. However, President Nixon was in a relatively favourable position to provide them with some reassurance. See *The Economist*, 7 July 1973. Of these three major powers, the United States, for the time being, was in the most flexible position.

57. For example, see Mackintosh, 'Soviet Strategic Policy', p. 270.

58. See, for example, Louis Heren, 'Sanctity of American Nuclear Superiority', *The Times*, 7 July 1967.

59. A major contribution to thinking about such improved bases for explanation is G. T. Allison, 'Conceptual Models and the Cuban Missile Crisis', *The American Political Science Review*, LXIII (September 1969), pp. 689—718.

60. Laird asserted: 'the Soviets are going for a first-strike capability, and there's no question about it'. *New York Times*, 22 March 1969.

61. See Erickson's arguments on this subject in his *Soviet Military Power*, especially pp. 41—52.

62. Some US officials expected that the Soviet Union would be satisfied with a 1 : 2 missile inferiority since (in US eyes) this would provide the USSR with a fully credible second-strike capability. Not for the first time, Soviet logic was different. Not surprisingly, President Johnson's proposed 'freeze' in 1964 was rejected.

63. Mackintosh, 'Soviet Strategic Policy', p. 273. There has been much discussion in recent years of the 'parity', 'superiority', 'inferiority', 'sufficiency' conundrum. Of particular value are *Soviet—American Relations and World Order: Arms Limitations and Policy* Adelphi Paper no. 65 (ISS, London, February 1970), especially J. J. Holst, 'Parity, Superiority or Sufficiency? Some Remarks on the Nature and Future of the Soviet—American Strategic Relationship', pp. 25—39;

R. Kolkowicz, *The Dilemma of Superpower: Soviet Policy and Strategy in Transition* (Institute for Defence Analyses, Arlington, Virginia, October 1967) and 'Strategic Parity and Beyond. Soviet Perspectives', *World Politics*, vol. 23, no. 3 (April 1971), pp. 431–51; and W. Slocombe, *The Political Implications of Strategic Parity*, Adelphi Paper no. 67 (ISS, London, May 1971).

64. *The Times*, 27 and 30 May 1972.

65. There is an abundance of material on this subject. See, for example, *Military Implications of the Treaty on the Limitation of Anti-Ballistic Missile Systems and the Interim Agreement on Limitation of Strategic Offensive Arms*, US Senate Committee on Armed Services, 92nd Congress, 2nd Session (USGOP, Washington, DC., 1972); *Strategic Arms Limitation Agreements*, US Senate Committee on Foreign Relations, 92nd Congress, 2nd Session (USGOP, Washington, DC., 1972). For a summary of the achievements, significance and prospects for SALT from the US Administration's viewpoint, see *U.S. Foreign Policy for the 1970s. Shaping a Durable Peace*, A Report To The Congress by Richard Nixon, President of the United States, 3 May 1973. A useful range of sceptical analysis, from differing viewpoints, is given by C. S. Gray, 'Of bargaining chips and building blocks: arms control and defence policy', *International Journal* (Spring 1973), pp. 266–90; and W. R. Kintner and R. L. Pfaltzgraff, 'Assessing the Moscow SALT Agreements', *Orbis*, XVI (Summer 1972), pp. 341–60. The various military 'balances' reached are concisely discussed in *The Military Balance 1972–1973* (IISS, London, 1972), pp. 83–6.

66. In the short run at least, there was plenty of evidence to support such a position. Since the negotiations began in November 1969 the research, development, procurement and deployment of ever more costly and usually destructive weaponry has gone on apace. The most spectacular systems have been the continuing development of the *Trident* submarine system by the United States, and the continuing development of a MIRV capability by the Soviet Union. The successful testing of the latter was announced in Washington in August 1973. See the *Guardian*, 20 August 1973. The pressures for innovation will not be easily controlled.

67. A balanced discussion of some of the problems relating to the securing of agreement in most of these fields can be found in *Strategic Survey 1972* (IISS, London, 1973), pp. 14–19.

68. Wolfe, *Soviet Strategy at the Crossroads*, especially pp. 1–17, 259–62.

PART TWO:

CONTEMPORARY ISSUES

4 HOW TO THINK ABOUT SOVIET MILITARY DOCTRINE

Benjamin S. Lambeth*

Throughout most of the past two decades, Western analysis of Soviet military doctrine was largely the esoteric preoccupation of a relatively small body of area specialists in Soviet strategic affairs. Since the emergence of SALT and the ambitious Soviet military build-up that first became apparent during the late 1960s, however, Soviet doctrine has increasingly become a topic of widespread discussion throughout the Western defence research community as a whole. Moreover, with the mounting popular disenchantment over *détente* and the rising concern over what many regard as a disturbing trend in Soviet weapons development and modernisation, Soviet military philosophy — with its avowed emphasis on war-fighting — has additionally surfaced as a touchstone of growing attention and controversy among journalistic commentators and the public at large. With major new US procurement programmes at stake (most notably M-X and the cruise missile), sharpening disagreement over the nature of the East-West nuclear predicament and its implications for US security planning, and the imminent prospect of a highly controversial SALT II agreement, the stage-setting may be under way for the most acute debate over US defence requirements and Soviet strategic intentions that has occurred since the ABM controversy of 1969.

This resurgent concern among American defence analysts and opinion elites over what the Soviets are up to and what the United States should do about it is a healthy trend in US strategic policymaking. For years, the US defence community remained substantially oblivious of the content and nuances of Soviet military thought, relying primarily on Western strategic logic and what were widely held to be 'objective' principles of nuclear strategy as the guiding criteria for US strategic planning and force structure design. As long as the United States enjoyed a commanding lead in military technology and a position of clear numerical preeminence in the strategic balance, that was an approach which — however misguided or inappropriate — we could afford to employ with little operational consequence. Today, however, with the Soviet posture roughly equivalent to our own in size and capability, it has become far more difficult to ignore the enunciated principles of Soviet doctrine with equanimity.

In an era in which the past asymmetries between US and Soviet forces have largely been eradicated and 'essential equivalence' has become a declared goal of both superpowers' defence policies and SALT strategies, the respective force employment concepts of the two sides have risen markedly in importance as factors affecting each country's overall strategic prowess. It is almost an axiom of military practice that in any confrontation between matched opponents, the side that commands the more astute array of strategic concepts is the side more likely to dominate in crises and war. The Soviets are keenly attentive to developments in US strategic policy and are fond of intimating publicly that, in their view, the USSR possesses a superior military strategy. Whether or not that is the case, there is little denying that doctrinal adroitness and the operational effectiveness of war plans can make a great deal of difference in the outcome of confrontations between otherwise equal opponents. Soviet military doctrine, in marked contrast to prevailing US strategic orthodoxy, is highly systematic in formulation, unambiguously martial in tone, and explicitly geared to a belief that should deterrence fail, some recognisable form of victory is theoretically attainable through the skilful exploitation of initiative, surprise and shock. Coupled with the dramatic Soviet force expansion and modernisation effort that has been steadily under way since the mid-1960s, this robust Soviet image of nuclear war and the seemingly confident belief in the military utility of strategic weaponry that informs and permeates it warrant legitimate Western concern about Soviet intentions and serious attention to what the Soviets have to say about deterrence and war.

At the extremes, one finds two opposing views on the significance of Soviet doctrine prevalent in contemporary American strategic discourse. The first view holds that the essentials of official Soviet thought on deterrence and war are abundantly evident in a large body of translated Soviet military writings which are readily available to any observer willing to take the time to read them. Those of this persuasion argue that the Soviets say what they mean and mean what they say, that their declared views on the importance of being able to fight and win a nuclear war are inseparably linked to their ongoing strategic force improvement programme, and that simple prudence required US decisionmakers to heed Soviet doctrine not only as a valid indicator of underlying Soviet strategic beliefs and expectations, but also as an important baseline from which US strategic force planning should be conducted.

At the opposite end of the spectrum, there is the school of thought which maintains that whatever Soviet military doctrine may superficially say, it should not be taken at face value because it emanates solely from professional military men and, as such, cannot reflect the real beliefs and views of those authoritative civilians on the Politburo who are ultimately responsible for Soviet strategic programmes, policies and behaviour. Those espousing this viewpoint maintain that the Soviet weapons acquisition process is not driven primarily by *a priori* doctrinal imperatives, but by such institutional factors as programme momentum, bureaucratic politics, technological determinism and reactions to perceived external threats, factors which, by and large, shape the defence policies of all modern industrial powers, the United States not excluded. Moreover, they assert, the principles of doctrine represent, at best, merely a reflection of desiderata that Soviet military leaders regard as optimum warfare and a wish-list for parochial use in budgetary infighting rather than any codification of actual Soviet military expectations or rigid body of rules the Soviet leadership would feel compelled to follow in a real contest of wills with the United States. As exemplified both by the ABM Treaty and the traditional pattern of Soviet circumspection in past crises, this school argues, Soviet political leaders, at bottom, accept mutual deterrence as the only solution to the East-West nuclear dilemma, notwithstanding the militancy and bombast of Soviet doctrinal writings.

It is not the purpose of this essay to adjudicate these countervailing arguments or to take sides in the debate, although as it will become clear presently the tone of the following discussion will tend to treat the former view somewhat more sympathetically than the latter. Nor is it to reconstruct in detail the specific axioms and principles already in the academic literature and are by now generally familiar to most attentive students of strategic affairs. Rather, its objective is to highlight the key themes and propositions of Soviet doctrine and to offer some perspectives on how — and with what reservations — they should be used as a basis for understanding broader Soviet strategic programmes and behaviour. Protagonists on both sides of the debate may well bridle at the dichotomy of views etched out above and maintain that it unfairly reduces their highly nuanced arguments into easily demolishable straw men. While there is doubtless ample room for such criticism, the device none the less has its uses in defining the boundaries of contention on the issue. In fact, it is the thesis of this essay that both points of view contain important elements of truth and that reality consists of a complex amalgam of the two. It is a further argument of this essay that there is much we do not know — and cannot know — about Soviet objectives and motivations, either from formal doctrine or from other observables such as Soviet forces and deployment rates, and that all analyses of Soviet intentions based on these incomplete and frequently ephemeral indicators should be advanced with a seemly measure of diffidence and caution. The essential argument here is that while Soviet military doctrine tells us far less than we need to know about the motive forces behind Soviet behaviour (and can be dangerously misleading if read out of context as a 'master plan' of Soviet strategic goals), it none the less reveals a great deal about the general mind-set of the Soviet leadership regarding the preconditions of deterrence, the technical requirements for maintaining it, and the military responsibilities that would be energised in the event of its catastrophic failure.

Key Themes in Soviet Doctrine

In the formal taxonomy of Soviet military thought, military doctrine is typically defined as

> the sum total of scientifically-based views accepted by the country and by its armed forces on the nature of contemporary wars which might be unleashed by the imperialists against the Soviet Union, on the goals and missions of the armed forces in such a war, on the methods of waging it, and also on the demands, which flow from such views, for the preparation of the country and the armed forces for war.

This conception of doctrine constitutes the central component of a complex system of military thought which is stimulated by the inputs of military science (the lessons derived from reflection on past wars and the opportunities provided by modern weapons technology) and, in turn, provides inspiration and guidance for the development of military art (the actual strategy and tactics of wartime force application). Were one to delve deeply into the scholastic disquisitions of Soviet writers on the specific content and purposes of these interconnected categories of thought and attempt to uncover the precise interaction and feedback relationships among them, one would quickly become snared in a philosophical Byzantium and lose sight of the more practical question of what it is that constitutes the mainstream of Soviet thinking on war and peace. For the purposes of this discussion, it is sufficient to note that official Soviet views on deterrence and war are highly formulaic and systemised, aimed at providing broad criteria for peacetime weapons acquisition and wartime force employment. These views are continuously worked out and refined by theoreticians in the senior service academies, the Main Political Administration of the armed forces, and the Main Operations Directorate of the General Staff, and are integrated into finished doctrine at the Ministry of Defence level for review and formal approval by the Party leadership.

Reduced to its essentials, Soviet doctrine accords closely with the Clausewitzian dictum that war is simply a violent extension of politics and must be constantly conducted with sensitivity to the political objectives at stake. Soviet military writers fully appreciate that modern weapons technology, with its vast destructive potential, has dramatically altered the traditional *character* of war and has elevated deterrence to a level of unprecedented importance in the Soviet hierarchy of national objectives. They steadfastly deny, however, that nuclear weapons have in any way altered the *essence* of war as a political event or the long-standing responsibility of the Party leadership to take every practicable measure for assuring the survival of the Soviet state should it occur. From the vast body of published Soviet writings on military doctrine, one can extract the following propositions as constituting perhaps the most fundamental tenets of declared Soviet strategic thought.

The Best Deterrent is an Effective War-fighting Capability

During the past fifteen years, American defence policy has increasingly come to rest on the belief that nuclear war is both irrational and unwinnable in any meaningful sense, and to adopt as its principal standard the maintenance of a survivable 'assured destruction' capability so as to guarantee that any Soviet nuclear attack against the United States would cost a prompt retaliation that would visit unacceptable damage on Soviet society. In effect, this policy has placed abiding faith in the durability of deterrence and in the assumption that the Soviet leadership would always remain circumspect under duress. In doing so, it has concentrated (indeed counted) on the preservation of deterrence and has tended to pay less heed, by comparison, to the concepts, capabilities, and strategies that might be required to cope successfully in the event of a deterrence failure. It has also led to the adoption of a fairly explicit set of 'sufficiency' criteria, stipulating that an arsenal which projects an image of 'equivalence' with Soviet forces and guarantees the capacity to inflict a specified level of retaliatory damage following the worst imaginable Soviet attack is adequate for underwriting US national security.

There is nothing in known Soviet military thought that even approximates this American pattern of logic. Soviet strategic pronouncements typically maintain that the only acceptable deterrent is one that rests on the intrinsic capabilities of Soviet forces rather than on the rationality and good will of the enemy. In practical terms, this reduces to a doctrinal requirement for an inventory of forces and battle management infrastructure that could rapidly generate to a level of high readiness in a crisis, carry out the necessary actions dictated by the circumstances of the crisis, and retain control of the situation throughout the period of hostilities, blunting the enemy's military initiatives and exerting every possible effort to assure the Soviet Union's emergence from the crisis in a position of net advantage.

The principal difference between this strategic orientation and that of the United States is that American deterrence theory places primary stress on the required measures for preventing war in the first place, whereas Soviet thinking concentrates largely on the requirements for responding effectively and surviving in the event deterrence fails. This fixation of Soviet doctrine can be seen reflected across a wide range of observable features in the current Soviet strategic posture. It is also apparent in the absence of any discernible criteria of strategic 'sufficiency' in Soviet force structure development. Soviet military planning adheres to no known yardsticks of strategic adequacy in any way comparable to the American 'assured destruction' concept. Instead, it allows for an open-ended process of arms accumulation constrained only by domestic economic and technological resources, US forbearance, and the formal protocols of negotiated arms limitation agreements. It would probably not be overly facetious to suggest that for Soviet military planners the favoured measure of strategic sufficiency is the notion that 'too much is not enough'. This is not to say, of course, that the Soviet leaders have inexorably committed themselves to the achievement of strategic superiority over the United States whatever the cost. They well understand the obstacles that would confront any such policy commitment and doubtless appreciate that by precipitously galvanising American fears and provoking an American reaction in kind, they could well find themselves ultimately worse off in the strategic balance than they might have been otherwise.

On the other hand, the Soviet leadership has given every indication — both at SALT and elsewhere — that it is determined to test the United States at every step to see what the traffic will bear and to acquire the most expansive and diversified inventory of weapons that US tolerance and Soviet resources will permit. Whether or not this behaviour pattern is directly driven by Soviet military doctrine it certainly accords with the basic injunctions of that doctrine, which holds that nuclear war — however gruesome to contemplate — is not impossible, that its occurrence would place great demands on Soviet capabilities, and that the best way to prevent it is to exert every practicable effort to prepare for it.

Victory is Possible

Naturally associated with this doctrinal emphasis on the need for a credible war-waging posture is the conviction that some meaningful form of victory, even in high-intensity nuclear war, is theoretically attainable if the proper military actions are executed in a timely fashion. To be sure, two important qualifications must be immediately attached to this statement. Firstly, the fact that Soviet doctrine stipulates a requirement for the capability to wage nuclear war and insists that it would be irresponsible not to assume that Soviet victory is theoretically achievable does not mean that the Soviet military leadership *ipso facto* prefers war to peace or places any less emphasis than their American counterparts on the overriding importance of deterrence. It does attest, however, to a Soviet recognition that deterrence can fail despite the best efforts of both sides to prevent it, and that in such a circumstance the Soviet armed forces have an obligation to do more than simply absorb the initial attacks of the enemy passively and then retaliate indiscriminately with their surviving forces in a consummation of their deterrent threat for no political ends other than to inflict a punitive reprisal for the enemy's transgression. Instead, they have a perceived duty to make the best they can out of an inherently bad situation by recognising the situation for what it is, seizing the initiative, and doing everything possible to prevent an already dismal state of affairs from devolving into something even worse. Secondly, the Soviet doctrinal belief in the possibility of victory is in no way an expression of sublime confidence in the minds of Soviet military planners that victory would be an automatic and natural consequence of their compliance with the dictates of Soviet nuclear strategy in an emergency. It merely indicates that the Soviet High Command — and presumably the Party leadership — regards victory as an objective to be consciously striven for with every reasonable effort, ranging from determined investment in adequate strategic forces and other war survival measures during peacetime to bold and assertive strategic operations should deterrence come under imminent and unambiguous risk.

The Soviet civil defence programme provides a fitting illustration of this perspective. There has been much heated debate in the United States recently over the extent of Soviet efforts in this area and the degree to which they have provided the Soviets with a real capability for protecting their population in wartime. A strong case can ade, however, that the most significant aspect of the Soviet civil defence programme is not its precise capacity to minimise Soviet population fatalities in a nuclear war (which even the Soviet leaders themselves can not know with confidence) but what it indicates about the general Soviet attitude toward nuclear war.

One frequently finds declarations in Soviet military commentary such as this statement made several years ago by the last Minister of Defence, Marshal Grechko, that in the event of a new world war, 'we are firmly convinced that victory in this war would go to us'. Such remarks are far more reflective of exhortation than serious strategic analysis, and it is a considerable overstatement to suggest categorically that 'the Soviet Union thinks it could fight and win a nuclear war'. In all probability, Soviet military men are not fundamentally different from most other professional soldiers the world over: knowing more intimately than anyone else what the real rigours and agonies of combat are like, they are the last to seek a fight, the least convinced things will go easily, and the most acutely sensitive to the fact that one can never be sufficiently prepared.

On the other hand, one also occasionally encounters remarks in the Soviet literature to the effect that 'any *a priori* rejection of the possibility of victory is harmful because it leads to moral disarmament, to a disbelief in victory, and to fatalism and passivity. It is necessary to wage a struggle against such views.' Statements of this genre are another matter altogether and deserve the most serious consideration of Western military planners. While they bespeak no confident expectation that Soviet victory in war is foreordained, they strongly suggest that the Soviets are fully committed to confronting the spectre of nuclear war with their eyes wide open.

It Pays to Strike First

Surprise, initiative, mass, shock and momentum have been among the most recurrent themes in Soviet military writings during the past decade and a half. Occasionally one can even find direct assertions in those writings that 'preemption in launching a nuclear strike is the decisive condition for the attainment of superiority over [the enemy] and the seizure and retention of the initiative'. The sources of this Soviet fixation on the need for being able to 'frustrate' and 'break up' an enemy attack are not easy to pin down, although doubtless the experience of the Nazi invasion in 1941 and the traditional Bolshevik emphasis on the importance of nipping undesirable trains of events in the bud before they get out of hand are prominent among them. In all events, Soviet military doctrine is heavily laced with endorsement of preemption as a preferred strategy at the edge of war, on the premise that whatever uncertainties there might be at the moment of decision, inaction would probably carry greater risks than proceeding with an attack if the survival of the Soviet state were in jeopardy.

This Soviet conception of the utility of preemption is in no way comparable to the Western notion of a 'splendid first strike' aimed at so thoroughly degrading an enemy's capacity to wage nuclear war that he would be physically deprived of any remaining options to inflict significant retaliatory harm. It is highly unlikely that the Soviet military leadership harbours any delusions that it either currently possesses such a capability or stands within grasp of it anywhere within the forseeable future. The standard distinctions in Western strategic discourse between 'first strikes' and 'second strikes' (as well as between 'tactical' and 'strategic' nuclear operations) are entirely alien to the idiom of Soviet military philosophy. The Soviet belief in the merits of going first rests less on any assumption that doing so will substantially disarm the opponent than on a conviction that tremendous psychological and military advantages can be gained by getting the initial jump on the adversary and forcing him constantly thereafter to operate in a reactive mode.

This intellectual orientation of Soviet doctrine may partially explain the evident Soviet determination to acquire a credible hard-target kill capability against US silo-based ICBMs, even though the US alert bomber force and deployed SSBN fleet would remain survivable. One can readily imagine a favoured crisis scenario in the minds of Soviet planners in which a portion of the Soviet ICBM force is launched in a preemptive counterforce attack against the US ICBM inventory, home-ported SSBN fleet, and command and control infrastructure. Following such an attack, the United States would find itself in a state of utter societal disorganisation and chaos; left with a sharply diminished retaliatory arsenal and a highly degraded or nonexistent battle management capability, and facing a Soviet adversary who not only remained militarily untouched but also stood poised with a large residual nuclear force and a fully alerted air defence capability. In such a situation, Soviet planners might believe, the rational response for the US leadership would be to retain its surviving forces as instruments for negotiating a settlement from a position of weakness rather than to execute a SIOP-scale retaliation against Soviet cities, which would only trigger a devastating Soviet counter-response in kind. Even if the United States were to opt for some sort of sub-SIOP nuclear reprisal rather than merely throwing in the towel forthwith, the Soviet Union would — by the logic of this thinking — still retain the

the upper hand in the engagement. Whatever losses it might sustain, it would none the less remain in the favoured position of pursuing objectives it had established in advance in a conflict whose rules were overwhelmingly of Soviet making.

There is no evidence in Soviet doctrinal writings that Soviet military leaders believe they could preempt against the United States with impunity, and the rationale behind their emphasis on preemption is certainly not to pursue the key to a quick and easy victory (or the illusion that such a victory might even be possible). Rather, it seems to reflect a conviction that the least miserable option at the brink of a hopelessly unavoidable nuclear catastrophe would be to strike first and decisively so as to secure a measure of initiative and control, without which even a pyrrhic victory would remain beyond reach.

Restraint is Foolhardy

Part and parcel of the Soviet doctrinal emphasis on timely preemption is a thoroughgoing rejection of Western crisis-management concepts such as demonstration strikes, escalation control, limited nuclear operations, and other signalling ploys for intrawar bargaining and communication of resolve. Soviet writings typically dismiss such concepts with open scorn as clever but naive and misguided American notions that fail to appreciate the harsh realities of modern warfare. Partly this attitude reflects a deep-seated Soviet military scepticism about the likelihood that large-scale nuclear force application can be subjected to finely-tuned control under the stresses and confusion of battle. Primarily, however, it reflects an abiding doctrinal axiom that any half-measures once the threshold of armed conflict has been crossed would risk sacrificing the initiative and compromising the prospects for a decisive and prompt victory. As one Soviet military writer has put it, 'any delay in the destruction of [the enemy's] means of nuclear attack will permit the enemy to launch nuclear strikes first and may lead to heavy losses and even to the defeat of the offensive'. Implicit in this doctrinal orientation is the notion that deterrence is solely a passive peacetime function of deployed forces in being, and that once deterrence fails, the task of strategy is not to continue the process of diplomatic dialogue through the measured use of violence, but to employ nuclear force with whatever intensity necessary to defeat the enemy militarily in the shortest possible time.

Numbers Matter

As noted earlier, Soviet doctrine does not categorically insist that absolute superiority over the enemy is a precondition of acceptable strategic preparedness, nor does it maintain that there is some magic level of deployed forces whose achievement will assure strategic sufficiency. Hardware is only one ingredient in the composition of Soviet strategic power. An equally important ingredient in Soviet eyes is strategy, and an effective strategy adroitly pursued can significantly compensate for material shortcomings in the Soviet military arsenal: At the same time, Soviet doctrine seems to indicate — and the pattern of Soviet arms acquisition over the past decade seems to confirm — a Soviet belief that strategic adequacy requires the deployment of as much weaponry in all categories as Soviet fiscal and technological assets and such external constraints as arms control agreements and the tolerance of the United States will allow. Although some Soviet declaratory statements since the beginnings of SALT have professed a willingness to settle for some roughly-defined strategic 'equivalence' to the United States (seemingly ruling out any determination to seek manifest superiority), these statements have been occasioned primarily by the political requirement for Soviet compliance with the spirit of *détente* and do not reflect an underlying belief that once having achieved such 'equivalence', the Soviets can complacently rest on their laurels. The concept of 'parity' is purely a Western legal construct artificially transposed to the realm of strategic affairs and has no discernible counterpart in known Soviet military thought. In practice, the Soviet insistence on 'equivalence' has tended to mean that the Soviets will not countenance accepting anything less than that and will seek to acquire as much beyond it — through self-serving negotiatory tactics at SALT and careful probing of US resolve — as they can reasonably get away with.

This belief in the value of abundant forces is apparent across the entire spectrum of Soviet military activity. For theatre war contingencies the Soviets have produced over 40,000 tanks, a truly dramatic achievement that exceeds that of the United States many times over. Their army is twice the size of ours. Their navy is also substantially larger. They are currently producing fighter aircraft at more than double the rate of the United States. At the strategic level, there is similar evidence of this doctrinal penchant for quantity in the large inventory of heavy Soviet silo-based ICBMs (numerically constrained only by SALT), the Soviet refusal to incorporate land-mobile ICBM limits into the SALT I Interim Agreement, the incipient proliferation of SS-20 MRBMs with their attendant ambiguity regarding rapid convertability to long-range SS-16s, and the Soviet indisposition to accept the reduced ICBM numerical ceiling embodied in the original Carter SALT proposal of March 1977. These activities may or may not represent visible signs of an underlying Soviet effort to achieve significant strategic advantage 'on the cheap' within the framework of SALT and *détente,* but they certainly attest to a closely-held Soviet military conviction that when it comes to strategic preparedness, there is safety in numbers and one can never have more than enough.

The sources of this Soviet belief in the value of an amply endowed military posture run far back into Soviet history and doubtless include traditional Soviet self-perceptions of inferiority, as well as the bitter memories of the costs of inferiority left by the near-disastrous Nazi onslaught of 1941. More recently, they have almost surely been added to by the embarrassing debacle the Soviets suffered in the Cuban missile episode of 1962. There has been much debate among Western analysts over whether or not it was the incontrovertible US strategic superiority that principally enabled the United States to emerge from that crisis so successfully. Whether or not the United States in fact exploited its superior nuclear posture with as much clever finesse as some observers claimed it did shortly after the event, there is every reason to believe that the Soviets, for their part, learned a lasting lesson about what it means to be on the *inferior* side in a nuclear showdown. In considerable part because of the Cuban crisis, Krushchev lost his job and became supplanted by a new regime with quite different strategic values, a massive programme of Soviet force expansion and modernisation was set into motion which has continued unabated to this day, and the Soviet leadership, by every indication, bound itself to an all but enshrined commitment never again to allow itself to slip into a state of such perceived weakness that it could be so easily humiliated by its principal adversary.

To say that Soviet military doctrine places an important premium on numerical abundance of forces (indeed, on as large a margin of military advantages as may be feasible) is not to argue that Soviet military planners harbour any belief that strategic superiority can either supply 'instant courage' in crises or that it necessarily constitutes a tool that can be employed in specific and preplanned ways to exact concessions from the adversary in coercive diplomacy and war. There is nothing in the Soviet military literature even remotely comparable to the kinds of sophisticated — if frequently unpersuasive — arguments one characteristically finds employed by proponents of strategic superiority in the West. The Soviet case for strategic advantage is more diffuse and tends to regard numerical force preponderance principally as a comfort-inducing investment against possible future contingencies whose precise character cannot be anticipated. In peacetime, such preponderance affords Soviet political leaders the freedom to act in crises with a favourable edge of self-assurance by shifting the burden of anxiety onto the opponent. In wartime, it would presumably provide Soviet commanders a cushion of reserve forces against the uncertainties of combat and thus help underwrite a more audacious strategy than might otherwise be possible.

Soviet Doctrine in Perspective

So much for the essentials of Soviet military doctrine as they appear in the books. It remains now to consider what they mean in practical terms as determinants of Soviet force structuring and as guides to Soviet behaviour in future crises that could erupt into war.

To begin with, it bears repeating a familiar refrain among students of Soviet military affairs that doctrine serves many purposes besides simply prescribing criteria for weapons development and use. It provides, for example, a systematic body of official 'truths' for reinforcing Soviet military morale and reaffirming the conviction of Soviet soldiers that they retain an important purpose even in an age of deterrence, in which the principal rationale of strategic weapons is to prevent wars rather than fight them. The repeated stress in Soviet writings that nuclear weaponry has not invalidated the possibility of achieving meaningful victory is perhaps the most eminent example of a doctrinal tenet that exists in considerable (though by no means exclusive) measure for this purpose.

Doctrine also provides a convenient set of bureaucratic rationales for the armed forces to employ in advancing and defending their institutional interests in the competitive arena of Soviet budgetary politics. The ambiguity in Soviet doctrine regarding whether a future world war would be short or protracted, for example, offers a ready justification for large strategic reserve forces, and the doctrinal insistence that no such war could be won without combined-arms operations serves, among other things, to help assure that all of the armed services receive a respectable piece of the action in the allocation of military roles and resources.

Finally, doctrine plays an important part in the Soviet strategic dialogue with the United States and aims in part to manipulate the perceptions and expectations of the US strategic leadership by casting Soviet military strength and prowess in the best possible light. The emphatic Soviet disavowal of such US strategic concepts as limited nuclear targeting and intrawar deterrence, and the equally adamant

Soviet insistence that any war would be intense and uncompromising from the outset, for example, have the partial aim of forewarning the United States that the Soviet Union will not abide by US rules in the event of war and neatly typify how doctrinal principles collaterally serve Soviet propaganda ends.

With these allowances accounted for, however, there remains much in Soviet military doctrine of operational significance for Soviet defence planners. Where the imprint of doctrine has been most vividly apparent has been in the physical complexion of Soviet strategic force developments during the past decade. It goes without saying, of course, that Soviet military doctrine is primarily the product of military men, whereas the ultimate responsibility for Soviet resource allocation and force structuring inheres in the civilian Party apparatus. It is also clear that the civilian leadership is under no compulsion to rubberstamp the institutional preferences of the armed forces. None the less, the entire range of Soviet military activity since the mid-1960s has accorded surprisingly — and disturbingly — with the central themes of Soviet military doctrine highlighted in the preceeding discussion.

This is not meant to imply that the Soviet force posture since Khrushchev's ouster has been a product of unrestrained doctrinal determinism or that doctrine has, in any sense, blindly 'driven' Soviet military procurement choices. There are, for example, observable inconsistencies between certain edicts of Soviet military doctrine and the realities of contemporary Soviet military preparedness, perhaps most notably apparent in the relatively low readiness of Soviet strategic forces for prompt combat employment. Soviet doctrinal writings harp constantly about the critical importance of maintaining the Soviet military machine peaked for launch on a moment's notice. Yet in contrast to the United States, which continuously maintains approximately half of its SSBN boats on operational patrol, the Soviet Navy deploys only a handful of its ballistic missile submarines on station at any given time and leaves the rest concentrated in their highly vulnerable home ports. Similarly, unlike the US Strategic Air Command, which constantly maintains a third of its bomber force on five-minute strip alert, Soviet Long-Range Aviation is not known to observe any comparable practice. One could fairly argue, perhaps, that these are not significant anomalies since Soviet doctrine posits preempting at some point during a gradually intensifying political crisis, in which the Soviet military would presumably have more than ample opportunity to generate its forces to full alert status. The fact remains, however, that they explicitly belie a recurrent refrain in Soviet declaratory commentary.

Furthermore, Soviet military doctrine, with few exceptions (most notably on the question of whether a conventional war in Europe would 'inevitably' escalate to the nuclear level), has remained more or less internally consistent and conceptually stable since around 1960, well before the post-Khrushchev weapons build-up began to lend real teeth to Soviet military pronouncements. The sharp discontinuity between the extravagant war-fighting rhetoric of Soviet military writings and the miniscule capability of actual Soviet strategic forces during the early 1960s clearly accentuates the fact that it has always been hard-nosed internal politics, leadership preferences and institutional interest adjudication rather than automatic obeisance to the doctrinal catechism of the Soviet military that determine the character of Soviet strategic programmes and policies.

On the other hand, it goes without saying that if there is a convergence of leadership predispositions with doctrine, then the latter becomes critically important as an explanatory factor. Although the evidence is far more presumptive than empirical, there is good reason to surmise that something much like this occurred shortly after the Brezhnev-Kosygin regime assumed power. The latter part of the Khrushchev era, one may recall, was a period of considerably turbulent Party-military relations, fed by Khrushchev's refusal to satisfy the demands of his marshals and exacerbated by the abortive Cuban missile venture, whose outcome most of the military and many in the Party felt was precisely a consequence of Khrushchev's inadequate defence preparations. With the advent of the new leadership in 1964, a fundamental change seems to have occurred. This is not the place for a detailed reconstruction of that period, but it is a reasonable inference from known events that following an intense Party-military debate in 1966 and 1967 over the nature of the Soviet security problem and the requirements for dealing with it, a mutual accommodation was struck between the Party and the military, in which the military was granted most of its strategic programme requests that Khrushchev had left unrequited in return for a renewed spirit of institutional cooperativeness in the defence policy process. Moreover, Khrushchev's political successors appear to have become increasingly persuaded by much of the logic of Soviet military doctrine and assimilated it into their own belief system (if they were not indeed already substantially persuaded even while Khrushchev remained in power).

Tacit proof of this hypothesis may be inferred from a number of subsequent developments. For one thing, there has been a remarkable degree of quiescense, if not outright amity, in Soviet Party-military relations since 1967, which seems to entail far more than mere surface calm. Senior Soviet military figures have been heard to intimate openly to Westerners that 'things have been a lot easier' since Khrushchev's departure and the patching up of Party-military conflicts over institutional roles and resource allocations that ensued in its wake. Secondly, there has increasingly appeared to be a blurring of the former institutional separation of Party and military in Soviet defence decision making since the late 1960s. The current Minister of Defence, Dmitri Ustinov, is a civilian with long-standing ties to the Soviet defence industrial community, and his appointment to that position broke a long tradition of assigning it to professional military men. The chairman of the important Military-Industrial Commission, L. V. Smirnov, is also a civilian. Ustinov is additionally a voting member of the Politburo, as was his immediate predecessor, Marshal Grechko, prior to his death in 1973. Brezhnev, for his part, has become a self-appointed Marshal of the Soviet Union. And all of these figures interact closely and regularly on defence policy matters in a number of high-level joint political-military planning committees with an apparent degree of harmonious collegiality that would have been almost unthinkable during Khrushchev's incumbency.

There is also the inescapable fact that recent developments in Soviet weapons acquisition and military construction bear unmistakeable earmarks of being significantly informed by the criteria of Soviet military doctrine. To list only the most obvious of these, there is the vigorous Soviet pursuit of a credible hard-target kill capability through the proliferation of increasingly accurate MIRVed ICBMs. There is evidence of growing Soviet interest in preserving a capability for wartime force reconstitution both at the theatre and strategic levels. There have been repeated demonstrations of Soviet interest in acquiring the requisite antisatellite capabilities to deny the United States the wartime use of its space-based command, control, communications and surveillance capabilities upon which its own strategic force effectiveness critically depends. Notwithstanding the ABM Treaty of 1972, there continues to be a highly robust Soviet research and development effort in advanced antiballistic missile technology and no evidence whatever that the Soviet military has relinquished its traditional emphasis on the importance of strategic defence in modern warfare. The Soviet air defence network, for which we have no comparable counterpart either present or planned, is widely known to be the most extensive in the world and continues to grow in effectiveness and sophistication. Finally, there is the whole spectrum of war-survival measures which the Soviets have been implementing in recent years, ranging from their hardened grain-storage facilities and their controversial population-defence programme to their less noted but far more significant steps to acquire a hardened and redundant command and control capability and to maintain central direction and control throughout any military emergency. None of these activities would be necessitated by a deterrent policy based on 'assured destruction' assumptions, yet each constitutes an indispensable component of any strategy seriously aimed at preparing for the possible eventuality of a major nuclear conflict.

Certainly this complex of programmes requires more in the way of explanation than simply the reductionist assertion that it was hatched from Soviet military doctrine. It exists partly because of normal programme momentum, partly because it is economically and technologically feasible, partly because Russians simply do things that way, and partly for a whole gamut of additional institutional, political and cultural reasons. At the same time, there is little about it that is palpably incompatible with Soviet doctrine, and enough about it that accords with the war-preparation and war-survival injunctions of that doctrine to strike any reasonable observer as being far too consistent to be coincidental. Soviet strategic doctrine is manifestly a combat-orientated operational philosophy that treats the possibility of nuclear war as a threat that cannot be simply wished away, and that orientation is precisely the dominant hallmark of the comprehensive Soviet military build-up that has been underway, SALT and *détente* notwithstanding, throughout the past decade. If for no other reason than this extraordinarily close correlation between theory and reality, it seems appropriate to conclude that at least as far as peacetime force development and deployment are concerned, Soviet military doctrine is very much a vital factor bearing on the shaping of Soviet strategic policy.

As for the extent to which Soviet doctrine provides reliable insights into the way the Soviets would comport themselves at the actual brink of a nuclear war, there is obviously far less that can be said with any confidence. For one thing, however explicit Soviet doctrinal writing may be in its depiction of the Soviet security problem, it is hopelessly elusive regarding what specific operational measures might be taken to cope with it were deterrence to fail. From everything available to us in the published Soviet military literature, we still lack any clear sense of what actual Soviet nuclear war plans involve, and we could possibly be gravely misled if we tried to infer them solely from the known doctrinal indicators. To use a crude analogy, enunciated Soviet military doctrine is somewhat comparable to the US Joint Strategic Objectives Plan (JSOP), a highly formal and widely coordinated national document which posits broad definitions of the strategic situation, general peacetime and wartime goals of US military forces, and rough criteria for achieving those goals that most members of the US political-military community can comfortably live with. Soviet doctrine is not in any sense, however, a source of specific 'how to' guidance for the Soviet political leadership or for commanders in the field, and it tells us nothing whatever about the sorts of detailed target lists, laydown strategies and preplanned rates of fire that doubtless figure in the Soviet counterpart to our SIOP.

Secondly and more importantly, Soviet doctrine may provide a valuable intellectual ordering device for Soviet political and military planners, but it certainly is not in any way binding on the Soviet leadership. Blessed as they are with both natural conservatism and a total lack of prior experience at nuclear war, the Soviet leaders would doubtless feel powerful compulsions toward caution, circumspection and restraint in any crisis that appeared in serious danger of escalating to the nuclear level. At such a moment of truth, they might well conclude that what appeared reasonable enough when it was being briefed in calmer times by the General Staff had suddenly become the consummate height of strategic insanity. Moreover, the Soviet force posture is now in the process of acquiring a rich breadth of potential that will soon permit far more sophisticated options than anything currently addressed in the Soviet doctrinal literature. Whatever that literature may say about the importance of massive preemption at the outset, the riskiness of incremental force application, and so on, the Soviet leadership still retains the intellectual and organisational capacity for improvisation under stress. It is altogether plausible that they would feel no compunctions about throwing the whole book of doctrinal edicts out the window in a crisis if they felt they had a better way to address the problem. What such a better way might look like is, of course, impossible to guess at in advance. The Soviet leaders themselves are probably as unsure as anyone else. The best that can be said now is that Soviet military doctrine tells us something, though far from all, about the way the Soviet leadership thinks about strategic problems and provides some general hints about the sort of intellectual mind-set they would probably take with them into a major nuclear crisis. Like all doctrines, however, it is merely a conceptual roadmap, not a rigidly binding route plan, and offers little of predictive value about future Soviet leadership behaviour other than to indicate that up to now Soviet leaders have tended to concentrate more attention than their American counterparts toward what to do should deterrence break down. Because of that, they would probably arrive at the threshold of any actual nuclear calamity at least having given somewhat more systematic thought to the choices and dilemmas they faced.

Note

* This paper war prepared for presentation at a seminar on Soviet military doctrine jointly sponsored by the Program for Science and International Affairs, the Center for International Affairs, and the Russian Research Center, Harvard University, Cambridge, Massachusetts, 13 February 1978.

5 RETHINKING SOVIET STRATEGIC POLICY: INPUTS AND IMPLICATIONS

Dennis Ross*

Over the last few years the American public has been warned with increasing urgency about the emerging Soviet strategic threat. Concern about the danger and purpose of developing Soviet military might and capabilities may have reached its zenith with the leading of 'Team B's' National Intelligence Estimate.[1] Among other things, Team B concluded that the Soviets rejected our stated objective of strategic parity, and on the contrary were engaged in a relentless drive toward comprehensive military superiority — a superiority which at the very least was designed to yield political pay-offs and at the very most would allow the Soviets to survive a nuclear war.

Given the composition of Team B — Paul Nitze, William Van Cleave, Richard Pipes *et al.* — it is hardly surprising that they would draw these kinds of conclusions. Indeed, Nitze and Van Cleave have for some time argued that the Soviets have not shared our strategic attitudes or concepts. Specifically they have argued that the Russians reject the principle of MAD, and either reject or more benignly ignore the concept of deterrence.[2]

Citing Soviet strategic doctrinal calls for superiority, weaponry which can be linked to or explained by this doctrine, and Soviet political objectives which are perceived as unchanging, Nitze and Van Cleave posit that the Soviets continue to 'cling to their goal of worldwide domination',[3] and therefore simply do not approach strategic matters the way we do.

What is clear from this line of argument is that it hinges not on a different set of Soviet attitudes or perceptions but rather on different Soviet goals — that is, the Soviets reject our strategic concepts because these concepts do not suit their goals and not because they think or approach these problems differently.

But is this really true? Indeed, is it not possible that for historical, ideological or systemic reasons the Soviets approach these questions, and conceive of appropriate answers, differently from American strategists? And is it not possible that by interpreting Soviet strategic behaviour according to our logic or preconceptions, and not theirs, we necessarily draw overly negative conclusions — for example, according to how we would logically or theoretically use them, the Soviet development of big missiles can only be interpreted in an offensive, threatening manner.

Aside from almost mindlessly linking intentions with capabilities, the problem with such an interpretation is that it blithely ignores the possibility that the Soviets may believe big missiles make deterrence more, not less, secure. That the Soviets could have such a different view of successful deterrence highlights our need to come to grips with the attitudes that underpin Soviet strategic policy. In an effort to do so, this paper will characterise the values of those primarily responsible for formulating Soviet strategic thinking, and will also show how these values relate to and are reinforced by ideological and historical factors.

In the course of this discussion the central argument of this essay will become clear: that although different subjective inputs yield a Soviet strategic mind-set whose emphases are different from ours, these disparities (1) need not be de-stabilising if understood, (2) allow Soviet strategic behaviour to be explained in terms of deterrence, and (3) indicate that even in the abstract, Soviet capabilities should not be interpreted in a totally offensive, threatening light. By way of additionally proving the latter point, and at the same time subjecting the all-too-prevalent notion that Soviet intentions can be derived from their capabilities to a critique,[4] we will point out that even where similar types of inputs shape American and Soviet strategic policies, they tend to produce different outputs. That is, although bureaucratic routine, institutional interests and military balance considerations influence both American and Russian strategic arms behaviour, these factors nevertheless render different strategic preferences and policy choices because they conform to separate experiences and traditions and are perceived through distinct conceptual prisms.

In order to outline these distinct prisms we will turn presently to an examination of the 'subjective' inputs into Soviet strategic policy. By subjective inputs we refer to such factors as the general belief system, military doctrinal perspectives, and systemically-determined needs. These subjective elements constitute what might be called the Soviet strategic conceptual framework or style.

The Soviet Strategic Style

In very general terms, one might say that a unique Soviet strategic style grows out of a peculiarly Russian-Soviet psychology. For example, a traditional emphasis on 'bigness' as a symbol of 'goodness' or greater effectiveness has seemingly maintained a persistent influence over

Soviet approaches to weaponry. Thus a former SALT negotiator Alexis Johnson has observed, even with regard to the most advanced ICBM the Soviet approach remains the same as it has historically been toward artillery-like weapons: 'The bigger, the better.'[5] (In this connection, a suggestive relationship exists between the psychological inclination to favour super-sized missilry and the deployment of the SS-9 and SS-18 missiles.)

Similarly, the firmly rooted Russian-Soviet sense of insecurity (the product of such factors as invasions, ubiquitously perceived threats and enemies, and the traditional economic, industrial and general developmental inferiority when compared to the West) has very likely bred a natural inclination to overcompensate and over-insure on security matters. The possession of far more numerous and, particularly in the case of missiles, vastly larger weaponry than their chief adversary may reflect concrete examples of overcompensation. (Ideological symbolism also may bear on Soviet attitudes toward the number and size of weaponry; that is to say, the belief that the Soviet Union, as the leading socialist state, should have a superior military capability of some kind may find expression in the possession of superior size as well as numbers of arms.[6])

At any rate, psychological and indeed socio-cultural elements may yield Soviet predispositions when it comes to dealing with matters concerning the most efficacious kinds of weapons, their necessary amounts, how much is enough for defence, and the overall relationship of strategic nuclear forces. While psychological factors may thus inspire wide-ranging inclinations,[7] the Soviet strategic conceptual framework or style has been more directly shaped by Soviet military and strategic doctrine[8] — which, of course, also bears the imprint of historical experiences and ideological beliefs and expectations.

With regard to Soviet strategic theory, it is important to emphasise that Soviet strategic thinking about the nuclear missile age, unlike our own, generally reflects the basic biases and interests of its military establishment. That this is so is largely explained by the immobilised nature of Soviet strategic thought until Stalin's death, the deeper roots of pre-nuclear Soviet strategy, institutional resistance to any fundamental change in thinking, and, perhaps most significantly, the absence of authoritative specialists capable of redefining basic military roles and purposes. With respect to the latter factor, it is worth noting that as opposed to the US experience, where high-powered Rand-type civilians proceeded to educate our military in matters of war and peace in the nuclear age, in the Soviet Union there was no body of experts outside the defence establishment who could provide a fresh approach to the problem.⁹ Consequently, the moulding of Soviet nuclear strategy has been heavily influenced by the attitudes, actual experiences, basic traditions and institutional preferences of the Soviet armed forces.

As a result, Soviet strategic doctrine tends to be conceptually grounded in more traditional military concerns and considerations; that is, it focuses on the more classical and standard roles assumed by the military in warfare — for example, emphasising the ability to ensure success in warfare and, as an underpinning factor, highlighting the importance of having Soviet military capabilities direct their primary thrust against targets of military value (weapon systems, troop formations, etc.) In this sense, deeply engrained Soviet military traditions such as 'combined arms' (success in warfare is contingent on the use of all arms and services) and the 'primacy of the offensive' (emphasis on pre-emption) continue to have as much meaning in current Soviet strategic doctrine as they had in the pre-nuclear era.

While more traditional American military principles might also still dominate our strategic theory had civilians not shaped our strategic-nuclear attitudes, the fact that they have has produced a gulf between American and Soviet strategic prescriptions. Thus, whereas it is quite natural for Soviet strategic doctrine to emphasise a war-fighting thrust, it is not surprising, given essentially civilian definitions of nuclear deterrence, that American strategy does not.

The fact that there is a general distinctiveness between Soviet strategic-nuclear doctrine and American deterrence perspectives, however, should not be taken to mean that deterrence is not the Soviet military's primary mission. It is. The overwhelming destructiveness of nuclear weaponry leaves little doubt but that the military's most important function is deterring a nuclear strike against the Soviet heartland. What this general distinctiveness should be taken to mean is that the Soviets have a different operating definition for *strategic* deterrence; that is, while believing no less in its importance, most Soviet leaders, for military doctrinal and related historical and ideological reasons, conceive of strategic deterrence achievement in different terms than do their American counterparts.

To be specific, the general Soviet attitude toward successful deterrence is rooted in essentially traditional military maxims which emphasise the war-fighting capacity of weaponry. Consequently, as several observers have noted, 'Soviet doctrine and military posture do not distinguish between deterrent and war-fighting nuclear capabilities, but appear to view them as 'fused together' in dialectical unity'.¹⁰ In this connection, the Soviet view appears to be that the better their armed forces are prepared to fight and win a nuclear war, and the more any adversary knows this to be the case, the more successful is Soviet deterrence.

The underlying premise of this perception apparently is that the best way to guarantee that your enemy will never attack you is to convince him that no military advantage or meaningful success can ever be accrued by launching a first strike. The Soviets apparently strive to operationalise this premise in both verbal and practical-strategic ways: thus on the one hand, their claims of socialist victory-imperialist defeat in all-out nuclear war[11] (aside from having internal political-military payoffs[12]) might well be designed to convince the West that attacks on the USSR are at best futile and more likely are militarily disadvantageous, while on the other hand the Soviet development of a strategic posture capable of fighting wars and limiting damage to themselves might also be designed to dissuade an adversary from thinking it can gain any objective by striking first. Actually to achieve such a strategic posture, a counterforce-damage limiting strategic doctrinal orientation is apparently required.

Significantly enough, such an orientation conforms to the traditional military focus so dominant in Soviet strategic thinking, and, of equal importance, also corresponds closely to the Soviet's declaratory policy; for example, in an authoritative statement the late Marshal Grechko characterised the mission of the backbone of the Soviet strategic forces in a predominately counterforce manner:

> The Strategic Missile Forces, which form the basis of the combat might of our Armed Forces, are intended for the destruction of the enemy's means of nuclear attack, his large troop formations and military bases, the destruction of the aggressor's defence industry, the disorganization of his state and military command and control and of the operations of his rear and transportation.[13]

Similarly, from a specific damage limitation perspective, although the ABM agreement would seemingly suggest diminished Soviet interest in active missile defence, the military's continuing public obeisance to the concept of defence,[14] together with intensive research and development on a hyper-sonic 'Sprint-like' interceptor missile and transportable phased-array ABM radars (e.g. the X-3 radars),[15] leave room for doubt about whether the Soviets have closed the book on the achievement of an active ABM-damage limitation policy. That damage limitation remains a Soviet objective is at least implied by the Soviet passive or civil defence measures. In this regard, while the increasingly extensive Soviet civil defence measures to harden and disperse industrial complexes and populations, in conjunction with intensive civil defence public education, are ideologically useful as socialising and mobilising devices — as well as active reminders of the need for vigilance — they apparently have a damage limitation purpose as well. For example, Soviet officials have observed that civil defence measures are designed to enhance the country's 'ability to rapidly liquidate the consequences of enemy nuclear strikes, promptly render extensive and diverse aid to casualties, and secure the conditions for the more normal functioning of the facilities of the national economy'.[16]

Here again we are reminded of the Soviet vision of deterrence, that is that the Soviets, in the main, perceive the achievement of deterrence as being predicated on convincing one's adversary that he will be denied victory even should he strike first. In this context, active civil defence measures represent a crucial factor in limiting, and, at the same time, coping with damage that might be inflicted by an adversary; the better the civil defensive measures, the better the limiting and coping mechanisms, the less chance any adversary has (and must know he has) of ever being able to defeat or gain advantage over your country by striking first, or so the Soviet logic goes. That Soviet perceptions of the utility of civil defence correspond to this logic — reflecting its integral role in Soviet deterrence — is suggested by the following Soviet spokesman's statement: 'Improvement of Soviet Civil Defence and an increase in its effectiveness constitute one more *major obstacle* in the way of the unleashing of a new world war by the imperialists.'[17]

That the Soviets may thus believe that civil defence contributes to their deterrent[18] lends credence to the claim that the Soviet calculus of deterrence primarily derives from the premise that 'if your enemy knows he can't be victorious or gain advantage by attacking you, he won't'.

Before applying a particular phraseology to this Soviet conception of deterrence, it is important to point out that the Soviets do understand the logic underpinning retaliatory second-strike capabilities. At a minimum, the Soviets, wanting to be certain that the US is denied any possible incentive for striking first, appreciate the importance of having essentially invulnerable-survivable weaponry. Hardening of missile sites and the deployment of SLBMs ameliorate the problem of vulnerability and related incentives for attack, and thus were enacted by the Soviet Union.

Moreover, the Soviets have implicitly evidenced an appreciation of the deterring value of a retaliatory capacity; for example, as Brezhnev observed at the 24th Party Congress, 'any possible aggressor knows well that should he attempt a missile attack on our country, he will receive an annihilating retaliatory blow'.[19] Further, Admiral Gorshkov has even apparently assigned a second-strike role to the Soviet SLBMs by having noted that missile-carrying submarines represent a threat of inevitable 'nuclear retaliation'.[20]

Since the foregoing suggests that the Soviets accept the importance and utility of possessing retaliatory second-strike capabilities, we might reasonably conclude that the Soviet conception of deterrence is composed of two tiers of thinking. Firstly, for reasons partly flowing from the Soviets' more traditional military approach to strategic-nuclear questions, their primary tier or level of deterrence thinking focuses on conveying to an adversary that he cannot gain anything (and presumably stands to lose) should he contemplate attacking the USSR. A counter-force-damage limiting posture logically follows from this premise for deterrence. The second or sub-level, which may well be a product of American example or education,[21] supports and reinforces the primary level by further minimising incentives for attack by guaranteeing retaliation. It might be posited, therefore, that in Soviet eyes the most fully reliable deterrent is provided by having a mix of primarily pre-emptive and secondarily retaliatory capabilities.

In deterrence terminology, the Soviet philosophical or conceptual position might be classified as representing a deterrence strategy primarily based on denial. While American denial strategies traditionally have been placed in only conventional or tactical military contexts,[22] we are suggesting that the Soviets conceive of strategic deterrence on an essentially denial basis.

By 'deterrence through denial',[23] we mean actor A deters actor B by convincing B that he cannot carry out a successful attack; in other words, actor B is deterred by the knowledge that no military gain can be derived by striking first. B can be so convinced by A's visible capacity to disarm B (at least partially) and limit damage to himself. A deterrence-through-denial strategic posture, therefore, clearly requires some combination of the ability to destroy the other side's military force and at the same time provide additional measures for one's own defence.

As opposed to a Soviet deterrence-through-denial cognitive approach, one can characterise the traditional nuclear era calculus of Western-US deterrence as being largely based on a 'deterrence-through-punishment' logic; that is to say, actor A deters actor B from launching a first strike by being able to guarantee a severely punishing retaliatory attack. Stated simply, actor B is deterred from launching a first strike because he knows that any military advantage or gain that might accrue from such an attack would not be worth the cost or the pain that would result from A's retaliatory blow. Herein lies an important difference between the Soviet and the American[24] conceptions of deterrence — whereas the American deterrence-through-punishment approach accepts the fact that whoever strikes first will be militarily better off yet is deterred from doing so by the knowledge that unacceptable and horrendous damage will be wrought on his population and industrial base in retaliation, the Soviet deterrence-through-denial approach seeks to deny or minimise any advantage in striking first in the belief that reducing the prospect of military gain is a more certain guarantor of deterrence than is the ability to inflict wide-scale damage on an attacker's society.

What would seem necessary to produce a strategic deterrence-through-denial mind-set? In addition to having one's strategic-nuclear thought dominated by standard military biases and predilections, it is also logical to expect the existence of (1) a belief that your adversary is unremittingly hostile and out to destroy or defeat you,[25] and (2) a deep-seated sense of vulnerability to attack. In the Soviet case, the ideological belief system, together with general historical experiences, have almost certainly engendered the existence of both of these outlooks among the Soviet leadership.

After all, from the perspective of ideology, Soviet leaders have been inculcated with the belief that the Western 'imperialists' are inherently hostile to socialism, that they must continually seek to 'reverse the course of history', and that, therefore, the danger of war must persist as long as differing social systems exist. Indeed, in this context, Brezhnev has more than once stated, 'History teaches that while imperialism exists, the danger of new aggressive war remains.'[26] Not surprisingly, military spokesmen also acknowledge a direct relationship between the existence of imperialism and the continuing threat of war, only they tend to treat the subject with an air of greater certainty about its likelihood; thus the well-known military commentator Lt General Zhilin has stated, 'So long as imperialism and armed adventurism exist, *they will inevitably,* if only by virtue of their own momentum, unleash armed actions . . . .'[27]

In addition to the threat of aggressive war that imperialism inherently projects, Soviet leaders are also socialised to believe that the capitalist world understands the USSR to be its 'deadly enemy', must at some time destroy it, and seeks the opportunity to do so.[28] When this general belief is combined with the conviction that the imperialists will not be constrained from resorting to war by moral or value considerations (and relatedly will become more desperate as socialist successes multiply and the crisis of capitalism deepens), it is not surprising that Soviet leaders might conclude that the threat of wide-scale societal destruction will be insufficient to deter an imperialist attack. That is, Soviet leaders may believe that merely being able to inflict widespread destruction on capitalist population and industry is simply not enough to deter the West if its leaders see an opportunity to destroy-defeat socialism and thereby reverse the tide of history. Indeed, in order successfully to deter the West, so the Soviet thinking may go, the imperialists must be convinced that there is no hope of achieving their goal through military means.[29]

As for their sense of vulnerability, the rather sobering Russian-Soviet historical experience of isolation, encirclement and repeated invasion must certainly have contributed to a feeling of vulnerability to attack. In addition, the basic conspiratorial framework of the Bolshevik *weltanshauung* which has engendered a very deep sense of suspicion and mistrust toward the Russian people and the outside world also figures to have heightened Soviet feelings of insecurity and vulnerability. Put briefly, the Soviets have a more expectant view of invasion, a sense of vulnerability to such military onslaughts, and consequently have a natural predisposition to think in terms of 'frustrating', 'negating', or 'pre-empting' adversary attacks.[30] In sum, Soviet fears of vulnerability, together with their perception of Western hostility and persistent threat, have produced a natural tendency to conceive of deterrence in denial terms.

Beyond merely fostering a natural denial inclination, their comparatively greater expectation of war must also make the Soviets believe in the higher reliability of a deterrence posture based on denial. That is, because a strategic posture of denial, unlike one of punishment, is predicated on counterforce or war-fighting capabilities, it promises a 'rational' means of defence should deterrence fail. On the one hand, according to Soviet predispositions and perceptions of its adversary, this factor should dissuade an aggressor from attacking – thus producing the most reliable and credible form of deterrence. On the other hand, this consideration and its war-survival implications must also be more reassuring to a leadership that is charged with the responsibility of securing the survival and victory of socialism and yet continues to believe that nuclear war remains highly possible.

In this sense, it is not difficult to see why the Soviets might have little faith in the security provided by a posture of assured destruction.

Besides simply not believing that an assured destruction posture yields reliable and effective deterrence of their adversary, the Soviets must also view assured destruction — or deterrence-through-punishment — as unacceptable because it fails to provide any recourse or option should deterrence fail.

More than having little faith in assured destruction itself, there is also no small measure of distrust toward this posture when it is applied to a mutual or Soviet-American framework; after all, a Mutual Assured Destruction posture means the acceptance of mutual and assured vulnerability to retaliation. While in any event the Soviets may have intellectual difficulties in directly linking their security to that of their adversary's,[31] it is also quite probable that elements of the Soviet leadership fear that a situation of what Americans refer to as mutual vulnerability will leave the Soviet Union in an inferior-exposed position. In an environment of assured destruction, the Soviets do not see themselves having the same kinds of hedges against American breakthroughs in science and technology. Because they have always been concerned about superior American scientific prowess, the Soviets tend to be fearful that technological breakthroughs will yield US strategic advantages and make any military balance based on the premise of mutual vulnerability inherently unstable and threatening. Indeed, a Soviet spokesman rather explicitly argued against the Mutual Assured Destruction concept on the grounds that 'new scientific discoveries could lead to the creation of essentially new types of weapons, which could sharply upset the "balance of fear" [mutual vulnerability] and create a state of general instability'.[32]

In addition to believing that MAD might actually diminish or endanger Soviet security, there are those within the Soviet leadership who have solid institutional interest reasons for being opposed to a strategic posture based on assured destruction. Here we are principally referring to the Soviet defence establishment — the military, the defence planners, defence-heavy industries, etc. These groups are not likely to favour a posture of assured destruction (or deterrence-through-punishment) because it is inherently limiting; once the ability to inflict assured destruction or punishment is guaranteed, further increments of arms become largely unnecessary.

Indeed, here we are reminded that a deterrence-through-denial or counterforce posture is institutionally self-serving for the defence establishment.[33] Unlike a deterrence-through-punishment approach — with its intrinsic limits — a deterrence-through-denial posture is totally open-ended and without limits. To achieve even partially effective counterforce-damage limitation capabilities, one always needs more — thus as one's adversary upgrades his forces, he mitigates the ability of yours to carry out their counterforce mission, and further build-ups and/or qualitative improvements inexorably become necessary. Placing this factor in the super-power context, it is apparent that the warning systems and vast and redundant nuclear capabilities on both sides make a significant damage limitation capacity unachievable. To base one's force sizing and planning on an objective that even in minimal terms may not be attainable is in reality to provide a built-in dynamic for ever more weapons procurement and to eschew concepts of defence limits or controls.

Quite naturally, then, the Soviet military establishment has very strong institutional reasons to favour a strategic philosophy which provides a continuing rationale for ever-increasing defence expenditures and developments. Similarly, as mentioned earlier, the Soviet military also psychologically finds a posture of denial rather than of punishment or assured destruction consonant with its traditional missions, that is, directing Soviet military capabilities against the other side's military forces (not his cities), concentrating on the defence of the country, and not allowing Soviet cities to be held hostage, etc.

In sum, the military, for both broad security and institutional budgetary and psychological reasons, is likely to be opposed to MAD; additionally, the political leadership, out of security and ideological-philosophical considerations, is also likely to be chary of the stability and deterring value of a mutual vulnerability relationship.

At this point, having outlined the underpinning factors behind general Soviet adherence to a deterrence-through-denial perceptual framework, and, in addition, having noted why a denial or damage limitation strategic posture is generally preferable to a strategy of punishment or assured destruction, it is important to point out that there is a minority within the Soviet civilian-political elite which, while not actually advocating mutual vulnerability, seemingly does adhere to a logic of 'strategic sufficiency'; there are some in the non-military elite who *indirectly* argue that strategic superiority is unattainable, that counterforce strikes are at best futile and at worst destabilising, and that nuclear wars are not 'win-able'.[34] For example, in general terms, while A. Karenin has referred to the 'dreams [illusions] of nuclear superiority',[35] G. A. Trofimenko has questioned the ability to attain meaningful counterforce capabilities in an era where the invulnerability of the ballistic missile submarine 'makes the task of disarming the forces of retaliation insoluble in the observable stages of military technological development'.[36] Rather than questioning the feasibility of counterforce capabilities, V. M. Kulish has preferred to highlight the destabilising logic of a counterforce approach: 'Far-reaching international consequences would arise in the event that one side possessed qualitatively new strategic weapons which would serve to neutralize the ability of the opposing side to carry out effective retaliatory action.'[37]

The most significant challenge to the predominant deterrence-through-denial logic has come from Georgi Arbatov. Arbatov has suggested that 'prevention of nuclear war equally serves the interests of the US and USSR since nuclear war would be suicide for both'.[38] Similarly, in explaining why the achievement of political ends by military force has lost all meaning in the nuclear age, Arbatov has asserted that 'no policy can have the objective of destroying the enemy at the cost of complete self-annihilation . . . .'[39]

This latter statement by Arbatov directly counters the central premise of what we have identified as the general Soviet strategic perceptual attitude toward deterrence, viz. that whereas the Soviet 'denial' posture is predicated on the belief that the threat of great destruction may not be sufficient to deter the West should they see the chance to defeat socialism, the Arbatov position quite clearly maintains that the spectre of their own destruction will always be enough to deter an aggressor. The Arbatov position, therefore, seems to reflect a deterrence-through-punishment logic and at least implies that a minority within the Soviet elite does accept such an approach.

Because a discussion of who constitutes this minority and why their perspective is different is beyond the scope of this essay,[40] we will restrict ourselves to a cursory explanation of why their views are not likely to predominate in the area of strategic doctrine and attitudes.[41]

Two general reasons account for this. The first might simply be that the formulation of strategic theory-doctrine remains largely within the province of the military. In the area of devising strategic needs, force sizing, force employment, or overall strategic theory-doctrine, there is no effective counter to the Soviet military. Indeed, in this regard, there may be only a smattering of civilians that even have knowledge of the character and composition of Soviet military capabilities – for example, at the outset of SALT, such a senior non-military official as the Chief of the Soviet delegation, Deputy Foreign Minister V. S. Semonov, apparently knew very little about the basic data concerning Soviet strategic forces and weapon systems.[42]

That, outside of some small pools of expertise, there may be no independent civilian source of substantive analytical advice on strategic matters, suggests that even while leading political members of the

Politburo ostensibly make broad strategic decisions and shape doctrinal approaches in the Defence Council, they do so on the basis of almost exclusive military input and recommendations. As a consequence, given the military's tradition, historical attitudes, institutional preferences, ideological outlook (and seeming exclusivity of input), one cannot expect there to be any real change in a strategic theoretical approach that emphasises deterrence based on denial.

While strategic-military thinking or doctrine puts the military on record and certainly influences political leadership attitudes, the fact that it conforms to the leadership's predisposition or inclinations also determines whether there is any impulse to question it. In this context, the second reason why the minority's strategic attitudes will not predominate, at least in the near future, can be highlighted. To begin with, it is important to note that the cardinal difference between the bulk of the Soviet elite and the remainder, who are inclined to favour the 'Arbatov position', relates to their differing estimates over whether the West still believes that it can *militarily* defeat socialism. Thus while all within the Soviet elite — given the ideological-historical prism through which they see the world — share the same long-range goals for the USSR and perceive the West as hostile and threatening, there is a difference over the perception of Western rationality. On the one hand, the minority (the Arbatov position) accepts the premise that Soviet nuclear and overall military power has already and demonstrably (for example *détente,* Helsinki, SALT, acceptance of failure in Asia, etc.) (1) sobered the American imperialists, (2) impelled them to give up their penchant for dealing with the Soviet Union from a 'position of strength', and (3) forced them to recognise the futility of contemplating attack on the USSR and militarily trying to 'export counterrevolution' to defeat 'anti-imperialist' national liberation movements.[43] Thus massive growth in Soviet military capabilities is perceived as unnecessary, of little utility, and, by possibly catalysing American action, even counterproductive.

On the other hand, the dominant view seems to be that the current realism of Western policies, while being good for world peace and the future, may nevertheless be transitory because in the face of inevitable Soviet successes, Western-imperialist leaders will be driven to count on, in Brezhnev's words, 'achieving military supremacy, undermining the foundations of peace and, at a favourable moment, resolving the international dispute between capitalism and socialism by military means'.[44] In this sense, Western 'irrationality' may occur at any time. Thus to minimise the extent to which the West may waver in its realism, continually to reduce the prospect that it will think about attempting to resolve its struggle with socialism through military means, and, in the final analysis, to be prepared for sudden Western reversals or threats, policies based not on military sufficiency but rather on upward openended military development will continue to be perceived as necessary. To the majority of the Soviet political elite, then, continual military growth and indeed a deterrence-through-denial orientation will, for the forseeable future, be more reassuring than any alternate approach.

Before concluding this section, it should be added that even were the Arbatov-type views to become more accepted among the political leadership, one would not necessarily see any significant change in Soviet strategic behaviour or deployment policy. The clearest explanation for this relates to the operational character and constraints of the Soviet decision-making system. Without detailing the precise reasons, suffice it to say that the Soviet system has become increasingly oligarchical. As a result of its growing oligarchic character, and largely because of ideological-legitimating factors of Party infallibility, the myth of leadership homogeneity and, relatedly, the absence of institutional means for authoritatively resolving disputes, a premium is put on minimising elite conflict and maintaining the leadership coalition.

In the abstract, coalition maintenance is engendered by the operation of a unanimity principle;[45] in the actual Soviet environment, a consensual decision-making style in the Politburo evidently occurs,[46] approximates a coalition maintenance unanimity characteristic, and carries with it logical policy implications — that is, the operation of a unanimity principle dictates policies that must win the minimal acceptance of every leading institutional actor. In practical terms, this means the pursuit of lowest common denominator policies, or, in effect, the whole Politburo literally 'signs-off' or actively consents before highlevel political action or policies can be undertaken.

With regard to major allocative decisions — for example, agreeing to a basic strategic arms thrust or orientation — one can expect essentially consistent policies that change only at the margins. After all, those actors that most support and identify with the current thrust of strategic policy are not likely to acquiesce easily in any major change. Indeed, while the military's ability to say 'x is necessary for our security' makes it difficult to imagine any such changes, the exigencies of internal elite politics seem to guarantee that for any modification at all the military and like-minded institutional actors will be able to exact some mollifying price.[47]

In the end, even should a change in strategic attitudes occur in the

Soviet political leadership, the political realities of the Soviet system suggest that the military establishment, together with its supporters in the political elite, are sufficiently well ensconced in the leading political bodies to prevent any rapid or radical change in Soviet strategic behaviour. Thus, we are once again reminded that Soviet strategic policy responds to Soviet, and not American needs or logic. It therefore should be interpreted according to Soviet, and not American, reality.

In this section, we have dealt at some length with what we have called the subjective input into Soviet arms policies. By subjective factor, we have most particularly referred to the Soviet strategic style or conceptual framework. In this regard, we have pointed out that the combination of a largely military formulation and peculiarly Russian-Soviet ideological and historical outlook has forged a strategic doctrinal framework somewhat different from that held in the US.

As a result, Soviet attitudes toward strategic deterrence are not symmetrical with American views; however, while not being consonant with the American conception, the Soviets nevertheless do accept and adhere to a principle of deterrence. In this sense, Soviet strategic-nuclear doctrine should be placed in a deterrence-achieving light and not in an exclusively offensive-aggressive context. Indeed, what may appear to us as threatening strategic declaratory statements and weapons deployment may reflect a Soviet doctrinal input that conceives of deterrence on a denial basis. Relating this factor to apparent 'counterforce' weaponry and damage limiting software — e.g. SS-9s, SS-18s and ABM radars — it might be said that such capabilities represent the seeming marriage between capabilities and doctrine. However, it must remain the 'seeming' marriage because the doctrinal-conceptual factor represents but one, albeit important, input into Soviet strategic weapons policies.

In saying this we refer to the fact that a variety of other, what might be termed objective, inputs help to shape the contours of Soviet strategic policy. For example, bureaucratic routine, institutional interest and strategic balance considerations — factors which are likely to influence the arms decisions of any modern industrialised great power — affect the type and number of weapon systems the Soviets deploy. To indicate how these factors affect Soviet strategic deployment and, therein, to show why Soviet strategic intentions should not be directly inferred from their military capabilities, we shall turn to a more detailed discussion of their operation in the Soviet political setting. (Since bureaucratic tradition and institutional interests

Rethinking Soviet Strategic Policy

are closely related, we shall discuss them in tandem.)

Bureaucratic Tradition and Institutional Interest

In the Soviet Union, bureaucratic tradition and routine make the prevailing patterns of weapons acquisition and deployment difficult to alter. In addition to general military style and preferences, these patterns essentially emerge from (1) long-term strategic plans and (2) the technology available during the preliminary stages of weapons development.

With regard to the first, the technological requirements of modern weaponry have necessitated long lead times between the initiation of a preliminary design and the operational deployment of a weapon system. As a result, long-range development plans of the order of 10 to 15 years have apparently been formulated to guide Soviet procurement policies. While long-range strategic planning is certainly also found in the US, Soviet 'plans' in general impose more rigid constraints on development. Whereas American planning constitutes more of a fiscal guide with allowance for discretionary authority, Soviet plans, as Matthew Gallagher points out, tend to impose a 'specific set of instructions for detailed production targets and precise schedules for fulfilment'.[48] When one relates this general factor to the number of competing groups that have a stake in (and must agree to) the composition of the more specific weapons 'blueprint',[49] it is not hard to see why Soviet long-term strategic plans give rise to basic patterns of weapons development. As for the second, the limits of technology during the initial phase of development provide the impetus for clear-cut weapons design patterns; that is, technological constraints may permit only a certain kind of design during one period and yet because these designs become firmly entrenched they set the direction for future periods.

These designs become so entrenched because of the rigid nature of the Soviet weapons development and design establishment. This establishment is characterised by a dominant set of routines and by clearly established processes of work, and is known for its conservatism with respect to new approaches. Consequently, as one observer has noted, there is a built-in tendency to favour the improvement of old designs to the creation of completely new ones.[50] (The Mig-series fighters, (T)-series tanks, Frog-series battlefield support missiles, etc. seem to bear out this contention.)

The supportive relationship between a design necessitated by the technology of the time and the design sector's conservative style and routine is evidenced by the Soviet development of their ICBMs. For example, the first Soviet ICBM, the SS-6, had a decidedly large booster which was required by the only technologically available atomic warheads — bulky and low-yield plutonium fission warheads. Even though subsequent breakthroughs in thermo-nuclear weapons technology allowed the reduction of size and weight of warheads, the SS-6 programme, followed-on by similar 'heavy' missile SS-7s and SS-8s, fostered a Soviet tradition of powerful boosters.[51]

What understandably makes this and other Soviet weapons traditions difficult to reverse is the fact that the interests of the responsible designers, among others, are enhanced by the continuing operation of these weapons patterns. That is to say, the *institutional interests* of those segments most closely identified with various kinds of armament are served by the maintenance of the prevailing weapons approaches. In this connection, the institutional interests of designers, producers, and their attendant services and branches in the armed forces, require that relevant weapons production continue, that follow-on systems be developed and deployed, and that future generational systems have incorporated into them characteristics commonly associated with the work or function of a specific set of designers, producers and services.

It is important to add that since the institutional and personal prosperity of these groups is often contingent on the level of activity in their respective spheres, there is, as the memoirs of the famous Soviet weapons designer Alexander Yakovlev indicate, rather fierce competition over the allocation of resources for the various systems.[52] Indeed, Yakovlev, in writing about the possibly damaging consequences of the Mig-15 being chosen over his own Yak-25, indirectly highlighted how the selection of another design group's weapon system could adversely affect the health and morale within one's institutional base: 'I was worried about the situation developing in our design bureau. You see behind me stood 100 people who might lose faith in me as the leader of the design collective.'[53]

In addition to fierce designer and producer competition, it should be emphasised that all of the various branches of the military obviously wish to sustain deployment of those arms which are defined as either crucial to their respective missions or necessary for their continuing institutional well-being. Thus the leading elements of the Strategic Rocket Forces will seek persistent upgrading and successor generation ICBMs, those in the Navy will press for and justify the utility of capital ships, and the PVOs will push for better air defence capabilities.

Rethinking Soviet Strategic Policy

In short, because the persistence of weapons programmes and styles secures the institutional, and, in a sense, also reflects the political primacy of the relevant design, producer and military segments, armaments traditions do not die easily in the Soviet political-military universe. Hence, in subjecting the widespread notion that Soviet capabilities directly inform us about their intentions to a critique, it is important to point out that in many circumstances Soviet military capabilities may be far more reflective of dominant bureaucratic traditions and institutional interests than the mere product of any purported intent. For example, with reference to the Soviet rejection of American SALT proposals to equalise throw-weight asymmetries (perhaps the factor most alarming to those concerned about Soviet weapons capabilities), the Soviet unwillingness to retreat on this issue may well be 'less the result of a calculated intent to maximise future counterforce' potentials and far more a function of the need to avoid upsetting standard institutional practices, styles and interests in the Soviet missile design and manufacturing establishment.[54] Indeed, Soviet commentator G. A. Trofimenko has suggested as much by complaining that the US makes proposals that are 'radically at variance with the tradition and principles of the other side's [i.e. Soviet] military-technical policy'.[55]

While a strong case for the impact of bureaucratic tradition and institutional interest on the type of Soviet weapons deployments can thus be made, it must nevertheless be remembered that general Soviet deployment decisions do not occur in an external vacuum and hence do not respond only to an internal dynamic. The Soviets must, after all, be aware of threats and opportunities that present themselves within the context of their strategic relationship with their major adversary. Thus, we shall presently turn to the probable role that strategic balance considerations have on broad Soviet weapons policies.

Strategic Military Factors and Balance Considerations

In the abstract, it would appear to be a truism that the Soviet military and political leadership, at the very least, must take into account American military capabilities, and the climate of relations between the two, when weighing the choices for or the pace of weapons deployment. In this regard, Soviet leaders cannot afford to ignore, in the most general sense, how their strategic weaponry stacks up against the overall American capacity and threat. Thus questions must be addressed concerning the nature of projected American military threats, related areas of US superiority, appropriate Soviet responses to perceived disadvantages or threats, and the relative ability of the Soviet defence posture to fulfil its political-military missions. The answers to such questions no doubt affect Soviet perceptions of strategic needs.

It should be noted that while these kinds of questions and their answers are of concern to the military, they may have even greater utility when used to justify politically the acquisition of institutionally desirable weaponry. In any event, whether out of believed necessity, political utility, or as a useful rationalising vehicle to serve the military's interest, one can expect that perceptions of the general balance will have a significant effect upon, and thus rate as a major input into, Soviet strategic weapons deployment.

By way of example, it is useful to take a specific weapon system and portray the way in which strategic-military needs may have underpinned its deployment. In viewing the case of SS-9 deployment (a particularly significant case because it was cited by our then Secretary of Defence as clear evidence of Soviet first strike intentions[56]), it can be seen that a number of potent strategic needs and concerns were answered by its acquisition. Firstly, in a broad strategic sense, the SS-9s were needed to provide the Soviets with a more certain capability to penetrate any prospective (and in reality soon to be deployed) American ABM system. Because the SS-9 carried vastly improved chaff-decoy penetration aids and the first Soviet-developed multiple re-entry vehicles (MRVs), it, unlike other Soviet missiles, seemed to guarantee penetration of an American ABM.

Secondly, in the context of strategic arms balance considerations, the SS-9 helped to overcome certain Soviet deficiencies and thus ensured a rough equality with the United States. Simply stated, deployment of a super-sized missile with a tremendously large warhead yield (the SS-9 carried either a 25 MT warhead or three 5 MT re-entry vehicles) largely offset the American technological superiority in guidance and accuracy. Consequently, the Soviets gained a comparable position to the US in their ability to destroy hard-targets. To place this factor in the strategic context of the mid-to-late 1960s, it might be said that whereas the deployment of large numbers of cheaper and smaller SS-11s allowed the Soviets to catch up and overcome the American quantitative lead in land-based ICBMs, the SS-9 acquisition enabled the Soviets to equalise in part American qualitative-technical advantages.

In the end, strategic-military considerations alone probably were an influence on the decision to deploy the SS-9. However, they did not represent the only input, and this fact again permits us to highlight a central premise of this paper, namely that Soviet weapon systems are the product of a number of variable inputs. To the degree to which this premise is true, it casts doubt on a cardinal assumption built into the hypothesis that intentions can be specifically linked to or derived from strategic capabilities — that is, that because a weapon system can do something, it must perforce have been designed for that purpose.

In the case of the SS-9, the supportive confluence of bureaucratic tradition-routine (e.g. the powerful booster tradition), institutional interests (e.g. the 'big-missile' design team[57] and the Strategic Rocket Forces) and a set of strategic-military needs and values (e.g. more secure ABM penetration, offsetting US qualitative advantages in guidance and targetting), probably directed and determined SS-9 deployment far more than any long-range and inchoate 'first-strike' design or intent.

It should be added that because these various inputs naturally complemented the doctrinal (i.e. denial) reasons which favoured the deployment of the SS-9, their impact was enhanced. In this sense doctrinal or subjective factors, by indirectly consecrating certain bureaucratic traditions or institutional interests, may make them especially hard to challenge. For example, challenging a big missile tradition which serves the interests and prerogatives of designers, producers and elements of the Strategic Rocket Forces, is made far more difficult by the existence of a strategic doctrine which emphasises the importance of denial capabilities.

However, lest one conclude that subjective or conceptual factors totally determine which institutional traditions or interests will be favoured, the character of the Soviet political system must be kept in mind. That is, given a coalition maintenance decision-making process, the existence of powerful leadership segments with institutional and vested interests in the prevailing strategic arms policies presumably allows for only small margins of change in policy. Thus even should strategic conceptual attitudes be transformed, significant changes in strategic policy cannot be expected. This leads one to conclude that objective factors — bureaucratic tradition, institutional interest, strategic balance considerations — have an impact on strategic weapons deployment independent of subjective or conceptual inputs.[58]

In the final analysis, a number of inputs ranging from bureaucratic tradition and interest to peculiar Soviet strategic doctrine ultimately direct Soviet strategic arming policy. Two implications are suggested: firstly, discerning intentions (usually sinister) from Soviet weapons capabilities is at best problematical — after all the existence of multiple inputs suggests that there is not a direct relationship between the function and purpose of Soviet weapon systems[59] — and secondly, the existence of multiple inputs suggests that little change can be expected in the character and pace of Soviet strategic weapons programmes. In this regard, the built-in logic and momentum of a number of the inputs, coupled with the lowest common denominator nature of the Soviet decision-making process, will likely preclude any substantial transformation of Soviet strategic policies. Consequently, American decision-makers, while not reading into Soviet weapons capabilities negative or overly theatening intentions, should nevertheless be prepared for continual growth in Soviet strategic programmes; necessarily, therefore, Soviet superiority in the static indicators of nuclear power (missile launchers, warheads, throw-weight, etc.) and more pronounced asymmetries in Soviet and American force structures will ensue unless the United States undertakes a range of new strategic programmes. How the United States should best respond to the challenge of Soviet strategic arms development and to the related advent of Soviet numerical superiority is an extremely important question and one to which we shall now turn.

The Appropriate American Strategic Response

In determining the most appropriate response to the apparent direction of ongoing Soviet strategic programmes, the logical question to ask is whether Soviet superiority in static measures of nuclear power would have any real meaning? Given the length of this essay, rather than try to answer this question by fully analysing the issues it raises, I prefer to deal with it by briefly discussing the arguments of those who believe that the Soviet possession of such superiority would undermine strategic stability.

Perhaps the most thoughtful representative of this point of view is Paul Nitze. Nitze argues that Soviet superiority in indicators such as throw-weight and equivalent megatonnage (EMT) will produce a Soviet counterforce advantage. Because Nitze believes the Soviets will see that this counterforce advantage is capable of producing even greater throw-weight, and resulting military superiority after a Soviet initiated exchange of counterforce strikes, Nitze posits that the Soviets will be more inclined to use their nuclear weapons and engage in coercive policies.[60] To meet the challenge of this Soviet strategic threat, Nitze proposes that the United States 'batten down the hatches' and deploy a vast array of new weapons that enhance US throw-weight and counterforce capabilities.[61]

In addition to the fact that Nitze's characterisation of Soviet military advantage after an exchange of counterforce strikes is open to question,[62] his argument also falters on several other grounds. To begin with, Nitze, contrary to his own declamation, is fitting the Soviets into a US mould; he must necessarily assume that the Soviets finely calibrate strategic nuclear conflict, that they see psycho-political advantages in less than total nuclear strikes, and that they accept the feasibility of limited strategic war. Yet the Soviets give no evidence of believing any of these things.

On the contrary, Soviet military doctrine and declaratory policy explicitly reject such notions. To the Soviets, once strategic deterrence fails, there will be no middle or limited level of conflict and there will be no rules governing the war. Thus, according to G. A. Trofimenko, US attempts to bound and legalise nuclear missile war by 'ascribing to the Soviet Union intentions and readiness to wage a "limited strategic war" ' are doomed to fail because in any 'test of strength, the Soviet Union will not act in accordance with American "rules" . . . but in accordance with its own military doctrine — "with the aim of fully smashing any aggressor" '.[63]

Even if the concept of limited nuclear war were more compatible with Soviet strategic predilections or doctrine, there is good reason to believe that the Soviets would be extremely dubious about the practicality or utility of a US-Soviet counterforce exchange. On the one hand, given Soviet perceptions of the US leaderships's values and intent, the Soviets would be most unlikely to believe that their own limited or counterforce strike would be met only 'in kind' or in a limited way by the United States. On the other hand, Soviet perceptions of the US ability to launch on warning or under attack would also make the Soviets doubt whether any military advantage could, in fact, be gained by launching a limited counterforce strike.

While the Nitzian argument that the Soviets will be tempted to use their nuclear weapons is, thus, not persuasive, there none the less remains the question of whether the Soviets would be emboldened to try to coerce us. In this regard, because perceptions of US weakness and lack of resolve are probably crucial to any Soviet attempts to coerce us, what we choose to say about our capabilities and our intent will determine, to a great extent, whether the Soviets believe we are coercible. Consequently, a US declaratory policy that emphasises US strength and the ability of our forces to ensure our security and fulfil our political-military commitments is more likely to impress the Soviets than any asymmetries that may exist between our two strategic arsenals. Indeed, in light of Soviet perceptions of our 'irrationality', a strong US declaratory policy is likely to convince the Soviets that it will be difficult and, in fact, probably dangerous to try to coerce us.

This is not to say, however, that a forceful declaratory policy is sufficient to offset any or all measures of Soviet strategic superiority. Indeed, it is not. In the event that the Soviets achieved a disarming first-strike capability, or believed that they had achieved a position closely approximating such a capability, our public statements could do little to dissuade the Soviets from pursuing coercive policies.

However, because, for the forseeable future, a true Soviet first-strike capability will remain impossible, what the United States says and does publicly will have a major impact on Soviet behaviour. To ensure that our declaratory policy remains credible, and, therein, to guarantee that the Soviets neither achieve nor think they can achieve a disarming capacity, it will be important for the United States to re-inforce continually its second-strike capabilities.[64]

Beyond enhancing the credibility of our declaratory posture, such a policy will be necessary to ensure that neither the Soviets nor ourselves have any reason to doubt our ability or will to retaliate. An unquestioned retaliatory capacity is essential not only to convince our own leadership that Soviet advantages in certain measures of strategic power have little meaning, but also to guarantee that the differing US and Soviet strategic force structures and attitudes do not create an unstable strategic environment. In this latter sense, since an unquestioned US second-strike capability logically precludes any meaningful Soviet damage limitation abilities or incentives for striking first, an American deterrence-through-punishment approach can and should stably coexist with the Soviet deterrence-through-denial strategy.[65]

What one might conclude from this is that upgrading our second-strike capability would be an appropriate response to an ongoing Soviet build-up. It would maintain both mutual deterrence and strategic stability. At the same time, it would ensure our own security without needlessly making the Soviets doubt theirs.

The same cannot be said for the response that Paul Nitze recommends. After all, because approximately 75 per cent of Soviet strategic firepower exists in fixed, identifiable locations, substantially increasing our counterforce potential, as Nitze suggests, would have to make the Soviets feel more vulnerable and threatened.[66] Aside from actually reducing strategic stability,[67] such a response would also serve to reaffirm in Soviet minds the correctness of their strategic approach for, since the Soviet deterrence-through-denial mind-set is grounded on a very high threat perception of their adversary, American actions that pose a heightened military danger or threat must re-inforce Soviet strategic attitudes.

In short, Nitze's advocated response appears not only unnecessary but also counterproductive. While an alternative response — that is, one that upgrades systems of primarily second-strike role or utility — would probably not produce any immediate changes in Soviet strategic policies, it would at least serve to erode the credibility of dominant Soviet strategic attitudes. In this regard, the arguments of those in the Soviet elite who adhere to a more deterrence-through-punishment logic would have a greater chance of emerging and eventually having an impact.

In any event, since our security can be guaranteed by re-inforcing our second-strike capability, we need not depend on the Soviets accepting our strategic logic. By the same token, just because the Soviets do not accept our logic, there is no reason to accept or emulate theirs — particularly when theirs has no logical end point and appears irrational to us.[68]

What, in specific terms, does this suggest for our defence policy? It suggests that in designing our defence posture we ought to rule out the deployment of bigger throw-weight and highly accurate missiles such as the MX. On the other hand, we ought at least theoretically to 'rule-in' deployments of SLBMs, cruise missiles, and pentrating bombers. Depending on the political, military and psychological circumstances, upgrading or increasing any or all of these systems may prove necessary.

In addition, in order to provide hedges against possible future threats to our retaliatory capacity, we ought to emphasise broad-based R & D programmes in our defence posture. As John Steinbruner has pointed out, an R & D effort that emphasised (1) long-term developments independent of anticipated procurement, (2) competing technologies at the prototype stage, and (3) defensive protection of strategic forces, would not be destabilising and would allow for wide choice and rapid response if a serious threat to our strategic deterrent developed.[69]

Finally, to ensure overall deterrence, we should continue to emphasise the importance of conventional capabilities in our defence posture. This is so because in an era where assured nuclear deterrence makes the use of nuclear weapons nearly impossible — regardless of asymmetries in force structures — conventional arms are likely to become increasingly significant. As a result, in order to leave no doubt in allied or Soviet minds America's willingness to pursue its foreign policy goals and resist all threats to its interests, it will be important for the United States to complement its assured retaliatory strategic posture with a wide range of conventional capabilities.

In conclusion, we have suggested that as a result of various subjective and objective inputs, Soviet strategic deployment policies cannot be expected to change in the near future. Although Soviet superiority in certain static and dynamic measures of nuclear power will eventually ensue, we have argued that the United States need not 'batten down the hatches' and can afford to practice a kind of restraint. We have done so on the grounds that 'superiority' or asymmetries in the nuclear balance are neither militarily destablising nor politically detrimental.

On the contrary, we have posited that American security, and overall nuclear stability, can be guaranteed by US actions that relate primarily to consolidating 'defensive' second-strike capabilities. In the final analysis, it is possible that such an American response to the continuing and massive Soviet arms efforts can, in time, alter Soviet perceptions and convince a larger portion of their leadership that security, among other objectives, can be bought for a lot less. If it fails in this, only the Soviets will be the losers.

Notes

* Member of the Defense Department's Office of Program Analysis and Evaluation. This paper was written while he was a Fellow at the UCLA Center for Arms Control and International Security.

The author would like to thank Richard Betts, Bernard Brodie, Robert Jervis, Klaus Knorr, Roman Kolkowicz, and Jeffrey Porro for their very helpful comments on earlier drafts of this article. While not incorporating all of their good advice, the paper has improved as a result of their inputs. The views expressed in this article are those of the author alone, and are not necessarily representative of the views of the Defense Department's Office of Program Analysis and Evaluation.

1. For a good discussion of why 'Team B' war formed, who was on it, and what their conclusions were, see David Binder, 'New CIA Estimate Finds the Soviets Seek Superiority in Arms', *New York Times*, 26 Dec. 1976, pp. I, 14.

2. See for example Paul Nitze, 'Assuring Strategic Stability', *Foreign Affairs*, vol. 5. no. 2 (January 1976), and William Van Cleave, 'Soviet Doctrine and Strategy: A Developing American View', in L. Whetter (ed.), *The Future of Soviet Military Power*, ed. (Crane Russak, Inc., New York, 1976).

3. This is a quote taken from Nitze's statement in announcing the formation of the *Committee on the Present Danger;* while Nitze is a director, and one of those responsible for the formation of the committee, Van Cleave, at the very least, shares the values which underpin the committee.

4. Nitze, for one, appears to operate on the assumption that intentions can be inferred from capabilities. On at least one occasion he implied that attention to Soviet capabilities or publicly stated objectives really does inform us about Soviet intent. See Paul Nitze's letter to Adlai Stevenson, reprinted in the Congressional hearings on Civil Preparedness and Limited Nuclear Warfare, The Joint Committee on Defence Production, issued 28 April 1976, p. 111.

5. Alexis Johnson said this in a lecture at the Stanford Arms Control Center in August 1976.

6. David Holloway, 'Strategic Concepts and Soviet Policy', *Survival*, (November 1971), p. 366.

7. Shawn Johnston and I have been working on a more socio-psychological approach to this whole problem. Johnston, as a social psychologist, is introducing a number of interesting theoretical and methodological innovations into this field of study – e.g. 'attribution theory', 'information processing', etc.

8. Here we are using the term doctrine in its generic, not Soviet, sense – a body of principles that underpin a theoretical approach (to the strategic nuclear age). Matthew Gallagher and Karl Spielmann, *Soviet Decision-Making for Defense: A Critique of U.S. Perspectives on the Arms Race* (Praeger Press, New York, 1975), p. 36.

9. In Soviet terms, military doctrine is viewed as a 'higher formalized set of theses about the nature of a future war that reflects the broad guidelines adopted by the Soviet political and military leaderships for the development of the armed forces'. See Matthew Gallagher, 'The Military Role in Soviet Decision-Making', in M. MccGwire, K. Booth and J. McDonnell (eds.), *Soviet Naval Policy: Objectives and Constraints,* (Praeger Press, New York, 1975), pp. 55–6.

10. Leon Goure, Foy Kohler, and Mose Harvey, *The Role of Nuclear Forces in Current Soviet Strategy* (University of Miami Press, 1974), p. 8.

11. With regard to the outcome of all-out nuclear war the late Defence Minister Grechko said, 'we are firmly convinced that victory in this war would go to us – to the socialist system' *(Krasnaia Zvezda,* 28 March 1973). On another occasion, Grechko focused more directly on the theme that an imperialist attack would end only in an imperialist defeat – e.g. 'if the imperialist aggressor risks encroaching on our country, he will be beaten everywhere – on the ground, in the air, on the water, and underwater' (*Krasnaia Zvezda,* 4 March 1974).

12. Such statements have political-military payoffs – e.g. they help to preserve (1) a sense of innate socialist superiority and (2) high morale in the armed forces.

13. A. A. Grechko, *Na Strazhe Mira i Stroitel'stva Kommunizma* (On Guard Over Peace and the Building of Communism) (Voeizdat, Moscow, 1971), p. 41.

14. Goure, Kohler, and Harvey, *The Role of Nuclear Forces in Current Soviet Strategy,* pp. 116–17.

15. See Clarence Robinson, 'Soviet Grasping Strategic Lead', *Aviation Week and Space Technology* (30 August 1976).

16. Quoted in Goure, Kohler, and Harvey, *The Role of Nuclear Forces in Current Soviet Strategy,* p. 120 – from N. V. Karabanov *et al., Filosofskoye Naslediye V. I. Lenina i Problemy Sovremennia Voiny* (The Philosophical Legacy of V. I. Lenin and Problems of Contemporary War), Translations on U.S.S.R. Military Affairs, no. 930, (29 July 1973), p. 96.

17. Ibid.

18. Another statement by the above Soviet commentator specifically underscores this contention: 'Soviet civil defence does not incite, does not promote and does not provide impetus to war.' It is clear that this view is in direct contrast to the American premise for stable deterrence, namely, that stable deterrence is based on having cities held hostage.

19. *Pravda,* 31 March 1971.

20. Quoted in Goure, Kohler, and Harvey, *The Role of Nuclear Forces in Current Soviet Strategy,* p. 115.

21. Soviet appreciation of invulnerable-retaliatory capabilities followed American deployment of such forces and open discussion of the importance of such capacities. See Benjamin Lambeth, 'The Sources of Soviet Military Doctrine', in F. B. Horton, A. C. Rogerson, E. L. Warner (eds.), *Comparative Defense Policy* John Hopkins, Baltimore, 1975), p. 207.

22. The distinction between deterrence through denial and deterrence through punishment comes from Glann Snyder, *Deterrence and Defense* (Princeton University Press, 1961), pp. 14–16. Snyder and also Steven Canby (*The Alliance*

and Europe Part IV: Military Technology and Doctrine, Adelphi Paper no. 109, pp. 2—3) apply denial strategies to essentially conventional or tactical military contexts. (Snyder, however, implies that they can have a more strategic utility.)

23. Yair Evron, who spent the summer of 1976 at the UCLA Arms Control Center, used this phraseology to describe Israeli deterrence attitudes — he at least partially inspired my own research.

24. It should be noted that the Schlesinger Doctrine represents a step away from a strategic-nuclear posture based purely on deterrence through punishment.

25. This is to say that if your adversary perceives an opportunity to attack you, he will.

26. See *Pravda*, 28 June 1972; 28 March 1973; 21 Jan. 1974, etc.

27. Lt General P. Zhilin, 'Military Aspects of Detente', *International Affairs* (Moscow December 1973), p. 25.

28. See Goure, Kohler, and Harvey, *The Role of Nuclear Forces in Current Soviet Strategy*, p. 48 — taken from Professor F. Ryzhenko, 'Peaceful Coexistence and the Class Struggle', *Pravda*, 22 Aug. 1973.

29. To any observer of the Soviet media, it is clear that the Soviet literature is replete with references to the absolute importance Soviet military power plays in making imperialists understand that military means cannot solve the historical struggle between the differing social systems.

30. See Goure, Kohler, and Harvey, *The Role of Nuclear Forces in Current Soviet Strategy*, pp. 1—8.

31. The point here is that the Soviets have a long-standing habit of relying only upon themselves for their security. To be seemingly dependent on an adversary runs very much against the grain.

32. Iu. Kostko, 'Military Configuration and the Problem of Security in Europe', *Mirovaia Ekonomika i Mezhunarodnyye Otnosheniia*, no. 9 (September 1972), pp. 19—20.

33. We will be discussing the role of institutional interests as an input into Soviet strategic deployment in the next section.

34. Because explicit Soviet political-military doctrine (such as the legitimacy and need of socialist superiority, definition of military missions in terms of defeating the enemy, etc.) cannot be directly challenged, political-military writers must criticise these precepts implicitly — e.g. by subjecting American efforts in these areas to critiques, the futility of striving for superiority or meaningful counterforce can be highlighted. The arguments used against the prominent US efforts can be applied to comparable Soviet attempts as well. Indeed, the Karenin, Trofimenko and Kulish quotes which were essentially referring to American capabilities are being treated here as having general, Soviet and American, applicability.

35. Thomas Wolfe, *The SALT Experience: Its Impact on US and Soviet Strategic Policy*, Rand report R-1686-PR (September 1975), p. 190.

36. G. A. Trofimenko, 'Some Aspects of American Political-Military Strategy', *SShA* (October 1971), p. 26.

37. V. M. Kulish, *Military Power and International Relations* (translated by JPRS), 8 May 1973, p. 174.

38. Quoted in Goure, Kohler, and Harvey, *The Role of Nuclear Forces in Current Soviet Strategy*, p. 59.

39. Ibid. — see *World Marxist Review*, no. 2 (February 1974), p. 56.

40. Put very briefly, adherents of the 'Arbatov deterrence logic' are to be found in what might be termed the foreign affairs apparatus (the Foreign Ministry, relevant institutes in the Academy of Sciences, the International Department of the Central Committee, etc.) and among the economic managers in the state bureaucracy. Institutional functions and resultant interests largely explain the differing perceptions of some in these groups; i.e. on the one hand, the first group's responsibilities range from assessing American and Western

statements and behaviour to concretely furthering Soviet political objectives through a negotiatory, non-military process. Beyond possibly being influenced by that which they analyse, the members of the foreign affairs apparatus certainly find their general prerogatives and importance enhanced by the pursuit of military-political policies which make negotiations more likely and feasible. Similarly the state economic planners, who are responsible for the growth, development, and modernisation of the Soviet economy, are institutionally desirous of policies that hold the promise of providing them with larger budgets and resulting greater influence. In this connection, only under conditions of a relaxation of tensions and a heightened sense of Soviet security can the desired policies of greater Western trade and diversion of defence monies to internal construction be pursued.

41. Marshall Shulman argues that, in fact, this different attitude has already been accepted by the current political leadership; as proof he cites the Soviet acceptance of the ABM treaty and their public calls for equal security. However two factors argue against this interpretation. Firstly, the Soviets may have adhered to the ABM treaty not because they have accepted the principles behind it, but rather because they sought to prevent the US from deploying a technologically superior system. In this regard, while people like myself may not have believed that the Safeguard was technologically viable, it is quite possible that the Soviets believed that our superior system put them at a disadvantage — therefore it was important to pre-empt its deployment. Secondly, Soviet calls for equal security have been punctuated by declarations calling for Soviet advantages in the nuclear balance to offset asymmetries (e.g. geographic, technological, etc) favouring the US. Hence Soviet definitions of equal security may not be consonant with outs. See Marshall Shulman, 'SALT And the Soviet Union', in M. Willrich and J. Rhinelander (eds.), *SALT: The Moscow Agreements and Beyond*, (Free Press, New York, 1974).

42. .bid., p. 115.

43. Quoted in Goure, Kohler, and Harvey, *The Role of Nuclear Forces in Current Soviet Strategy*, p. 69.

44. *Krasnaia Zvezda*, 28 March 1973.

45. See John Schwarz, 'Maintaining Coalitions: An Analysis of the EEC with Supporting Evidence from the Austrian Grand Coalition', in Sven Groennings, E. W. Kelley, and M. Leiserson (eds.), *The Study of Coalition Behaviour* (Holt, Rhinehart and Winston, San Francisco, 1970), pp. 235–49.

46. See Brezhnev's comments on the Politburo operation made to Western correspondents in June 1973. Theodore Shabad, 'Brezhnev Who Ought to Know, Explains the Politburo', *New York Times*, 15 June 1973. Thomas Wolfe cites this and provides a good discussion of the consensual nature of Soviet decision-making. As Wolfe notes, Vladmir Petrov, 'Formation of Soviet Policy', *Orbis* (Fall 1973) and Gallagher and Spielmann, *Soviet Decision-Making for Defence*, pp. 28–33, are also quite useful.

47. An underlying and implicit theme of this section has been that the Soviet military has a very significant impact on decisions affecting Soviet strategic policy. Beyond the set of values and outlooks the political leadership shares with the military, the military's influence tends to be a function of their monopoly of information and the factional character of Soviet leadership politics. With reference to the latter, the support of the military is important at any time, but is especially important during times of leadership debate or instability.

An example of a mollifying price may be seen in the context of SALT; i.e. in return for acquiescing in SALT, one can argue that the Soviet military have had their weapons desires met — e.g. the weapon systems that are emerging now had lead times that coincided with the timing of Soviet decisions to enter into SALT I agreements. If there is, in fact, a correlation here, it may be that the seeds of

SALT's ultimate destruction are planted by the internal trade-offs necessitated to arrive at the preliminary SALT agreements.

48. Gallagher, *The Military Role in Soviet Decision-Making*, p. 52.

49. Here we refer to the rival services in the military, the General Staff, the defence industries – Military-Industrial Commission, Defence Council, etc.

50. Such attitudes and style interact with and reinforce the generally lower rate of Soviet technological progress – i.e. the slower rate of Soviet technological change makes it natural to think in terms of refining old systems rather than creating new ones, Arthur Alexander, 'Weapon Acquisition in the Soviet Union, United States, and France', Horton, Rogerson, and Warner, *op. cit.*, p. 429.

51. Edward Warner, 'Soviet Strategic Force Posture: Some Alternative Explanations', in Horton, Rogerson, and Warner (eds.), *Comparative Defense Policy*, p. 313.

52. Alexander Yakovlev, *Tsel'znizni: zapikski aviakonstrukotura* (The goal of life: notes of an aviation designer), 2nd ed. (Izadatel'stvo Politicheskoi Literatury, Moscow, 1968).

53. Ibid., p. 491. Also quoted in Warner, 'The Bureaucratic Politics of Weapons Procurement', in MccGwire, Booth, and McDonnell (eds.), *Soviet Naval Policy*, p. 76.

54. Thomas Wolfe, *The SALT Experience*, p. 190.

55. Quoted in ibid., p. 152. See also G. A. Trofimenko, *SShA*, p. 190. (September 1974), p. 18.

56. Then Secretary Laird said that the SS-9 proved 'they are going for our missiles and they are going for a 1st strike capability. There is *no question* about that.'

57. Warner, 'Soviet Strategic Force Posture', p. 313.

58. Here one sees the nexus between objective and subjective factors. On the one hand, systemic operation emphasises the importance of institutional weight and interest. On the other, conceptual attitudes can be affected by strategic balance considerations and US strategic actions.

59. Our characterisation of Soviet strategic doctrine in deterrence framework suggest that even were doctrine to be the only input, we would not be justified in interpreting Soviet intentions in exclusively aggressive terms.

60. See Nitze, 'Deterring Our Deterrent', *Foreign Policy*, no. 25 (Winter 1976-7), pp. 198–9.

61. See Nitze, 'Assuring Strategic Stability'.

62. Similar studies by other analysts come to very different conclusions about who would have a military advantage after a Soviet counterforce strike. For example, see John Steinbruner and Thomas Garwin, 'Strategic Vulnerability and the Balance Between Prudence and Paranoia', *International Security*, vol. 1, no. 1 (Summer 1976), p. 171.

63. G. A. Trofimenko, *SSHA: Politika, Voyna, Ideologiya* (Izdatel'stve Mysl', Moscow, 1976), p. 323.

64. For our declaratory policy to remain credible, it will also be important to enhance the quality of our conventional forces. In this regard, because nuclear deterrence is not particularly sensitive to disparities or asymmetries in force structures, conventional arms are likely to become more not less important; i.e. since the nuclear forces on one side deter those on the other, strategic nuclear arms may become little more than shields behind which the sword of conventional power may be used. For our public statements to be credible, therefore, we will require the weapons that remain usable.

65. It should be pointed out that the Soviet denial strategy is geared toward what it takes to deter the United States and not to what it takes to deter the Soviet Union. In this regard, the Soviets, not unlike ourselves, believe that it takes much more to deter their adversary than to deter themselves.

66. That the Soviets would, in fact, feel more theatened and vulnerable is suggested by the Soviet reaction to the Schlesinger Doctrine and its call for increased counterforce or 'hardpoint kill' weaponry. For example, not only has Brezhnev himself been reported to have attributed the US retargetting plan to an American design to achieve a first-strike capability, but Soviet commentators have consistently declared that the changing US targetting emphasis makes wars more likely and reflects a US attempt to fight a nuclear war under favourable circumstances. (For a Soviet argument in terms similar to these, see an article by Major General Simonyan in *Krasnaia Zvezda* entitled 'The Concept of "Selective Options" ', 28 September 1976).

67. Contrary to what he argues, Nitze's proposed response is likely to reduce strategic stability in a crisis; after all, increasing our counterforce capability will make the bulk of Soviet strategic firepower vulnerable — this vulnerability will combine with the Soviet pre-emption doctrine to increase the Soviet impulses to strike first in a crisis.

68. It should be pointed out that the non-compatibility of Soviet and American strategic attitudes or doctrine need not rule out SALT agreements. SALT agreements will remain possible, but they will have to be of an incremental kind; attempts to achieve comprehensive agreements, which are based on common formulae for stability, are unlikely to be successful.

69. John Steinbruner, 'Beyond Rational Deterrence', *World Politics,* vol. 29, no. 2 (January 1976), pp. 242–3.

6 THE SOVIET MILITARY AND SALT
Raymond L. Garthoff*

The Strategic Arms Limitation Talks (SALT), begun more than a decade ago, have now become a familiar feature in the international political landscape and an important element in US—USSR relations. Much more than any other arms control and disarmament measure negotiated to date, SALT deals with the most vitally important elements of national power of the two countries. More than any other, it has engaged the alert and active attention and participation of the senior military authorities of both countries. The present discussion deals with attitudes of the Soviet military toward SALT, Soviet military objectives in SALT, the role of the Soviet military in SALT, the interaction of SALT with the Soviet military posture and military thinking, and some effects of SALT on evolving Soviet political-military relationships.

Soviet Attitudes toward SALT

In December 1966 and January 1967 the United States advanced, in private, a proposal for bilateral talks on limiting strategic arms — specifically anti-ballistic missile (ABM) systems. The Soviet response was cautious, noting that the question deserved attention, and not rejecting the idea, but couched in terms which left open options either for serious negotiation or for retreat to propagandistic embrace of drastic reductions by both sides down to a minimum deterrent 'nuclear umbrella' (an idea earlier championed by the Soviets in Geneva). For the next eighteen months, the Soviet side declined to agree on a time and place for beginning substantive discussions, despite repeated American importuning, including a personal argument for SALT by Secretary of Defence McNamara to Soviet Prime Minister Kosygin at Glassboro in June 1967.[1]

The precise role of the Soviet military leaders in this initial pre-SALT phase is not known, but it is highly likely (and in accordance with published Soviet military statements) that their predominant reaction was a compound of suspicions — suspicion both of disarmament and of arms control; suspicion of the United States in general, and in particular what it was up to in proposing SALT; suspicion that arms budgets would be reduced; and suspicion of likely further involvement of Soviet political leaders and political considerations in decisions on military programmes. These military attitudes reinforced the wariness of the Soviet political leaders, but did not override the readiness of the latter to keep the possibility of SALT open and under continuing consideration.

The first substantive position taken by the Soviet side was a firm statement at the very outset of the exchanges that strategic offensive arms, as well as anti-ballistic missile systems, must be included in any talks. This position, made known in January 1967, was promptly accepted by the US — perhaps to the surprise of the Soviet side. We do not know whether this position was advanced by the Soviet military or (as the author believes more likely) by the political leaders to provide a basis for 'out-bidding' the US in moving to the propaganda high ground of proposing drastic nuclear disarmament in case the course of the talks threatened to reveal Soviet unreadiness to agree on apparently reasonable limitations, owing to the relative weakness of Soviet strategic forces at that time.

A second Soviet position which became clear in the 1967 diplomatic exchange was a strong stand eschewing an approach based on freezing the existing strategic balance. The Soviet leaders, political and military, were wary that the US might call for a rigid 'freeze' of force levels, at a time when the US had a heavy strategic preponderance in all categories of intercontinental forces — ICBMs, SLBMs and heavy bombers. In January 1967, when SALT was proposed, the US had operational 1,054 ICBMs, 576 SLBMs and 650 B-52 heavy bombers while the USSR had only 500 ICBMs (many in 'soft' deployment), 100 old short-range SLBMs and 155 inferior heavy bombers.[2] The US total of 2,280 was thus three times the Soviet total of 750 operational units (and still nearly twice the Soviet total of 1,200 if the additional ICBM and SLBM launchers then under construction in the USSR were counted).

Concerning strategic defensive systems, the problem from the standpoint of the Soviet military and political leaders was different: they were reluctant to accept limitations on their own freedom of action. ABM deployment at Moscow, publicly disclosed by Secretary of Defence McNamara immediately preceding the American overtures on SALT (and the concomitant step toward ABM deployment in the US marked by the January Administration request for 'contingent' funding for such deployment) was not yet operational, although it had been under construction for over two years. The Soviet ABM system was cumbersone and costly; hence it was being deployed only around Moscow (as had been the case with the billion dollar deployment of the pioneer Soviet air defence missile system, the SA-1, around Moscow – and only around Moscow – a decade earlier). But Soviet military doctrine and related political-military commentary in the press (such as the late Major General Nikolai A. Talensky's articles after 1964)[3] were based on the assumption that deployment of all means of strategic defence was morally and politically justified, and strategically sound and stabilising. This was challenged implicitly by the US proposal (which had initially focused exclusively on ABM systems). Moreover, a ban or sharp limitation on ABM deployment, coupled with growing American strategic offensive superiority (or an arms control freeze of the existing US superiority), would have consigned the Soviet Union to permanent inferiority and one-sided vulnerability. In an unconstrained arms race, at least the Soviet Union had a good chance of achieving *mutual* vulnerability, and of mitigating the near-complete nakedness of the Soviet Union to American missile attack. Hence the Soviet military insistence on coupling possible strategic offensive limitations with ABM limitations, and hence, too, the Soviet reluctance to become committed to SALT until their own strategic offensive force build-up had at least brought the Soviet Union within sight of parity with the United States in intercontinental capabilities.

The US decision in September 1967 to deploy a nationwide ABM defence, despite Secretary of Defence McNamara's obvious reluctance and his efforts to rationalise it as directed against a potential Chinese threat, and despite renewed public and private reaffirmation of American desire to proceed with SALT, did compel the Soviet leaders to calculate seriously the impact on the strategic balance of a major US ABM deployment. The prior Soviet testing and developing of an ICBM had not prevented the US from leaping far ahead of the USSR in deploying a much larger and much more capable strategic offensive force, and if the same thing were to be repeated with ABM systems as well it would seriously prejudice and could confound Soviet aspirations to achieve strategic parity with the United States.

By mid-1968 the Soviet leaders decided to enter SALT and see what it could offer as against the alternative of an unrestricted strategic arms competition with the United States. By the time SALT was originally scheduled to convene, on 30 September 1968, the American strategic offensive force levels had long ago levelled off, while the Soviet build-up of modern silo-protected ICBMs was proceeding apace, and a modern SLBM production programme was underway. Accordingly, in some contrast to the situation at the time SALT had first been proposed, by September 1968 the US had 1,054 ICBMs, 656 SLBMs and 565 B-52s, while the USSR had operational about 875 ICBMs, 110 SLBMs and heavy bombers. Counting additional Soviet ICBM and SLBM launchesr under construction, the totals over-all were 2,275 for the US and 1,650 for the USSR.

SALT was postponed for slightly over a year as a consequence of the Soviet invasion of Czechoslovakia (on 20 August 1968, literally on the eve of the planned announcement of a forthcoming US-USSR Summit meeting in Leningrad and the commencement of SALT), then the advent of a new American Administration, the decision of that Administration to review its military policy and SALT position, and other delaying factors. But throughout that year the Soviet side reaffirmed its readiness to begin SALT. From the standpoint of development affecting the strategic balance, the difference of that year was of some significance in two respects: firstly, the US moved from initial testing (beginning in August 1968) to development of deployable multiple independently-targetable reentry vehicles (MIRVs); and secondly, the Soviet ICBM and SLBM build-up had proceeded to an extent that now virtually assured parity in the bilateral strategic balance in numbers of missile launchers. As of November 1969, when SALT actually got underway, the US force levels remained unchanged from September 1968 except for a slight decline in the number of B-52 bombers, while the USSR then had 1,140 ICBMs operational and some 380 more under construction, about 185 SLBMs operationsl and 175 more under construction, and 150 heavy bombers. Thus the totals, including Soviet ICBMs and SLBMs under construction, stood at 2,235 for the US and 2,030 for the USSR. Meanwhile, the Soviet Union had virtually completed its ABM deployment underway with 64 ABM launchers at Moscow, while the US was launched on a major ABM programme now called 'Safeguard', somewhat reoriented from the 'Sentinel' programme of 1967 to stress defence of ICBMs, but still nationwide and with well over ten times the number of ABM launchers and interceptors comprising the Soviet deployment.

The Soviet military leaders do not limit their view of 'the strategic balance' to a comparison of US and USSR intercontinental strategic forces. As we have learned in SALT, they insist on considering in conjunction with these elements other US and Allied nuclear forces capable of striking the Soviet Union. In this respect, it may be somewhat misleading to list only these intercontinental forces in comparing force levels. None the less, the Soviets have recognised in the SALT I and II agreements the key role these elements bear in the strategic equation, and it is important to bear in mind these developments in the changing intercontinental strategic balance, even though this summary does not cover many other important aspects of, and factors affecting, the overall strategic balance. Both the reality and perceptions of the strategic balance are, and have been recognised to be, important both in military and in political terms.

During the critical gestation period of SALT, from 1967 to 1969, the Soviet military leaders (as well as political leaders) came to realise several important things affecting their approach to SALT:

(1) The United States remained interested in SALT under conditions of near-parity, and not only when it had a three-to-one superiority in strategic offensive forces;
(2) The United States had demonstrated its capability and will to build up qualitatively and quantitatively superior forces rapidly in strategic bombers in the 1950s, and in ICBMs and SLBMs in the 1960s, and it could do so again with ABMs and MIRVs in the 1970s if strategic arms competition remained unrestrained;
(3) The United States had indicated it was prepared to place maximum reliance on unilateral means of verification, in contrast to its earlier demands for on-site inspections to verify strategic arms limitation agreements;
(4) Bilateral strategic arms limitations, if mutually acceptable terms could be negotiated, would contribute to a general lessening of tensions between the Soviet Union and the United States, particularly important given increased Sino-Soviet tensions, and consonant with Soviet political strategy in Europe as well;
(5) There were measures which the Soviet Union and the United States could take that would reduce the possibility of the outbreak of nuclear war, and SALT could serve as a useful and appropriate forum to raise and consider such matters.

Of these, the second point was undoubtedly of highest importance to the Soviet military leaders. They remained suspicious of US intentions in SALT, but saw possible advantage if strategic parity would be accepted by the United States and if limitations could be agreed which would prevent a new US surge in strategic deployments threatening this newly-won and still precarious Soviet prospect of achieving strategic parity.

Throughout the SALT negotiations (including the period since the 1972 SALT I agreements were reached) foreign analysts have cited Soviet military statements warning of the possibility of nuclear war, of American aggressive intentions, and of the need for vigilance and for continued efforts to maintain Soviet military might.[4] (Soviet authors have done the same in reverse, the most extensive being a 1971 book called *First Strike*,[5] reviewing American military statements and weapons programmes and alleging a US proclivity to seek a first strike capability.) These Soviet statements in support of the Soviet military effort no doubt in part reflect real continuing Soviet military concerns; in part they probably are rationalisations for desired programmes; and in part they may represent instruments in bureaucratic manoeuvre by those opposed to SALT or at least to far-reaching Soviet moves in SALT.

It is evident from the virtual absence of references to SALT in Soviet military publications and in most statements by military leaders in the early 1970s that there has been a strong current of reserve and reluctance toward SALT among the military. There has been more, and more favourable, reference since the mid-1970s. Much of the explanation may lie simply in concern at undercutting the case for maintaining a strong military posture — a concern which continues since the SALT agreements have been reached. When Army General Viktor G. Kulikov, Chief of the General Staff and First Deputy Minister of Defence, endorsed the SALT I agreements before the Supreme Soviet in August 1972, he coupled with this support reference to the fact that the Party and Government at the same time 'display constant concern for raising the defence capability of the Soviet Union', affirming that 'the Soviet Armed Forces possess everything necessary to reliably defend the state interests of our Motherland'. He also noted (as did other speakers) that 'the ABM Treaty halts the further build-up of ABM systems in the USSR and the USA, preventing the emergence of a chain reaction of competition between offensive and defensive arms'.[6] Marshal Grechko stressed this same point on the occasion of the ratification of the ABM Treaty by the Presidium of the Supreme Soviet a month later,[7] underlining the arms control aspect of greatest significance to the Soviet military (as well as political) leaders.

Soviet Objectives in SALT

A number of foreign policy, economic, strategic — and bureaucratic — considerations have been noted by various observers as contributing to the formulation of Soviet positions and objectives in entering SALT.[8]

The Soviet political leaders have been particularly concerned with political, economic and diplomatic objectives, but they have also shared the interest of the military leaders in military considerations and objectives. The most fundamental political objective has been American recognition of parity of the USSR with the US — parity in the broadest political and political-military as well as strategic sense, spelling an end to Soviet inferiority in its relations with the United States. The SALT agreements reached in May 1972 reinforced in Soviet eyes the 'Basic Principles on Relations between the USA and the USSR' signed by the President in Moscow at that same time.[9] In a political-military context these agreements reflected and bore witness to American recognition of the fact that there exists a military parity in the broad sense of inability of either side to prevail militarily over the other and hence an inability to coerce the other side; in terms more familiar in the West, it reflects an equal vulnerability of both sides and therefore a state of mutual deterrence of nuclear war. Soviet commentaries since May 1972 have consistently stressed this parity, and have refrained from any discussion (even from publication) of asymmetrical specifics in the numbers of strategic missile launchers allowed under the SALT I Interim Agreement, even though these numbers favoured the Soviet side; they know that other asymmetries have favoured the United States, and they do not wish to engage in debate over pluses and minuses on matters of relative detail which do not affect basic parity.

As early as 1968, the Soviet side had agreed that the main objective of SALT would be to achieve and to maintain stable US-USSR strategic deterrence through agreed limitations on the deployment of strategic offensive and defensive arms. Soviet representatives stressed then, and throughout SALT, that limitations must be so balanced that neither side could obtain military advantage and that equal security should be assured for both sides.

The military leaders in Moscow, while sharing or at least accepting these political and political-military strategic objectives, also continue to hold to a military doctrine which calls for preparing to wage war if deterrence should fail. Also, they are naturally more concerned with the specifics of the strategic military balance notwithstanding overall parity in a broad military-political sense.

Among the considerations leading to serious Soviet interest in SALT has been the pressure of an economic pinch.[10] The Soviet leaders have not been compelled by economic pressures to become interested in SALT or to reach any particular arms limitations. But they have found an important economic incentive for dampening down unlimited military competition with the US. And the Soviet military leaders realistically recognise the constraints which competing economic needs have always placed on military programmes in the Soviet Union. The economic situation of the USSR contributed to the initial Soviet

The Soviet Military and SALT

decision to enter SALT, and growing economic pressures probably played an important role in leading to Soviet agreement to the SALT accords.

It is important to bear in mind that there are varied and sometimes competing interests among the military leaders (and among civilian military-industrial chiefs), since they have differing stakes in particular weapons programmes and military forces. 'The military' by no means always speaks with one voice.[11] But over-all, the principal basic objectives of the Soviet military in SALT have been:

> (1) to assure that the terms of any negotiated strategic arms limitation would result in no military disadvantage and, if possible, some advantage to the USSR;
> (2) to preserve maximum leeway for Soviet military research and development and deployment programmes, except when specific limitations are justified by limitations of comparable value placed on US military programmes;
> (3) to forestall an extensive US development of ABM systems, even at the cost of foregoing comparable Soviet ABM defence; and
> (4) to preserve the right to maintain Soviet offensive and defensive forces required to counter third-country forces, excepting only special cases where a US-USSR limitation was deemed paramount (e.g. ABM limitation).

In engaging in SALT, the Soviet military have also had certain specific second-order objectives:

> (1) to avoid any on-site inspection in the USSR and to obtain agreement instead to rely on national technical means of verification;
> (2) to obtain, if possible, inclusion of the full range of American nuclear delivery forces deployed within striking range of the Soviet Union in the forces subject to limitation; and
> (3) to ensure that the SALT negotiations not become an opening which would compromise Soviet military secrets, in the first instance to the US, and for an even wider-range of matters on which the US was informed to third countries and the world at large (and, for that matter, to the Soviet public).

The Soviet side, probably at the insistence of the political leadership, also decided some time prior to the beginning of SALT to pursue in that forum the tangential but significant objective of seeking agreement with the US on measures to reduce the possibility of the outbreak of nuclear war between the two countries as a result of accident, unauthorised use of nuclear weapons, misconstruction of some technical development or weapons test, or provocative action by a third nuclear country. The attitude of the Soviet military leadership toward this objective is not known, but there are no indications of military opposition to it, and it is more likely that the military agreed on this objective so long as it did not involve intrusion into the secrecy surrounding Soviet military command and control arrangements.

The strong preference of the Soviet military for caution in disclosure of Soviet military interests and concerns clearly contributed to the generally passive and reactive Soviet stance with respect to proposals for arms limitation. As a consequence, the United States took most initiatives in raising propositions and advancing proposals. The Soviet military seemed to be on guard against revealing their own concerns and weaknesses. Particularly with respect to possible MIRV limitation in SALT I this was unfortunate. More generally, while American views on this question were divided, the advantages of staking out the ground in proposals probably favoured the American side.

Role of the Soviet Military in SALT Negotiations and Decisions

SALT represented the first arms limitation negotiation in which the Soviet military played a direct and major role. Soviet military representatives and experts have attended other disarmament and arms control negotiations as advisors (particularly the conference on measures to avert surprise attack in 1958), but never with the seniority of direct participation represented in SALT.

The Soviet leaders initially contemplated having a senior military man, possibly Marshal Matvei V. Zakharov, then Chief of the General Staff, head their delegation, but they decided instead to follow the pattern they understood the US had in mind of having a senior civilian official as chief negotiator, and to make a senior military representative the deputy chief of their delegation.

During the first three 'rounds' of SALT I, from late 1969 to the end of 1970, the second-ranking member of the Soviet SALT Delegation was Colonel General Nikolai V. Ogarkov, then First Deputy Chief of the General Staff of the USSR Armed Forces. For a man with this senior position and broad responsibilities to devote eight months in a fourteen-month period to service on a delegation abroad — in addition to time spent in Moscow in preparation for each round of negotiation —

demonstrates the seriousness which the Soviet Government and the Soviet military ascribed to SALT. General Ogarkov continued in 1971 and 1972, and to a lesser but significant extent since then, to devote considerable attention to SALT matters in Moscow, and he attended the Summit Conferences in 1972 and 1974, where SALT was a major issue. In the fall of 1973 he was promoted to Army General (four-star rank) and made a Deputy Minister of Defence, and in January 1977 he became Chief of the General Staff and First Deputy Minister of Defence, and a Marshal of the Soviet Union. He continued to participate directly in high-level SALT negotiations in Moscow in the spring of 1977 and the fall of 1978, and together with Minister Ustinov met with German Chancellor Helmut Schmidt in Moscow in June 1980 on the European theatre nuclear arms problem.

In addition to General Ogarkov, Colonel General of the Engineering Technical Service Nikolai N. Alekseyev was a member of the Soviet SALT Delegation in the first two rounds of negotiation in 1969 and 1970. General Alekseyev was then serving as deputy to Colonel General of Artillery A. V. Gerasimov, a Deputy Chief of the General Staff and Chairman of the Scientific and Technical Committee of the General Staff. Shortly after his return to Moscow in the early fall of 1970, General Alekseyev replaced General Gerasimov. At that time, in a reorganisation this position was moved from the General Staff to the Ministry of Defence, and General Alekseyev became a Deputy Minister — thus at the time outranking General Ogarkov, and leading to General Alekseyev's departure from direct participation in the Delegation in 1971. But he continued to be actively involved in SALT matters in Moscow, in view of the responsibilities of his position. In 1979 he was promoted to Marshal of the Signal Troops.

Succeeding Generals Ogarkov and Alekseyev as the senior Soviet military representatives on the SALT Delegation were Lieutenant General Konstantin A. Trusov, a senior General Staff officer with a background of work overseeing advanced weapons development, and Lieutenant General Ivan I. Beletsky. General Trusov remained a member of the SALT Delegation from early 1971 (except for brief absences in 1974 and in 1977 for reasons of health) until 1978. He was promoted to Colonel General in 1976.

Colonel General Anatoly A. Gryzlov, a seasoned General Staff officer since World War II, was assigned to disarmament and arms control matters in the late 1950s, and attended all significant disarmament conferences from the Surprise Attack Conference in 1958 through SALT (as well as participating in unofficial exchanges in the so-called 'Pugwash Conferences'). General Gryzlov was identified as 'advisor on military matters' in the SALT sessions in 1969 through September 1971, when poor health required his retirement (he died in 1974). General Gryzlov had also headed an Arms Control Section of the Main Operations Directorate of the General Staff, which coordinated working level preparations for SALT in the Soviet military establishment.

General Gryzlov's successor, Lieutenant General Ivan I. Beletsky, appeared as an 'advisor' on the Soviet Delegation at the beginning of SALT II in November 1972. In all subsequent SALT sessions, he served as a full 'member' of the Delegation. In 1973, General Beletsky was promoted to Colonel General, and he probably heads the Arms Control Section of the General Staff. Both he and General Trusov seem to have had virtually full-time SALT responsibilities throughout SALT II. After General Trusov left in 1978, he was succeeded by Major General Viktor P. Starodubov, a Strategic Missile Forces officer who earlier served as an advisor on the SALT Delegation, as a colonel, from 1972 into 1974.

Among the key military men also deeply involved in SALT in Moscow have been Generals Kozlov and Akhromeyev. Colonel General Mikhail M. Kozlov was involved in SALT from its inception by virtue of his position as Chief of the Main Operations Directorate and Deputy Chief of the General Staff. When General Ogarkov became a Deputy Minister of Defence in December 1973, Kozlov succeeded him as First Deputy Chief of the General Staff. In that capacity, he played a prominent part in the two SALT-involved Summit meetings of 1974, especially at Vladivostok. In the spring of 1979, General Kozlov was succeeded as First Deputy Chief of Staff by Colonel General (soon Army General) Sergei F. Akhromeyev (who had probably earlier succeeded to Kozlov's former position as Chief of the Main Operations Directorate). Generals Kozlov and (later) Akhromeyev also met with at least three delegations of American senators visiting Moscow in November 1978 and January and August 1979 which had expressed the wish to discuss the SALT II Treaty with authoritative military as well as political officials.

A number of other Soviet officers, some of general officer or flag rank, have participated directly in the SALT talks as 'advisors' or (a less prestigious category) as 'experts'. Advisors during SALT I were: Vice Admiral Petr V. Sinetsky, a submariner serving on the General Staff, probably as the senior naval officer in the Arms Control Section, who served through all of the SALT I sessions (excepting one absence for health); Rear Admiral Mikhail A. Kovalevsky, who served in 1970; Major General Igor A. Afonsky, once the youngest general officer in the Soviet armed forces, representing the Strategic Missile Forces command, who attended all SALT I sessions (and appeared again at meetings on SALT at the third Summit in Moscow in June 1974); Major General of Aviation Aleksei M. Gorbunov, an Air Defence specialist, who attended all the sessions of 1969 and 1970; Colonel Aleksandr A. Fedenko, a World War II heavy bomber officer, presumably representing the interests of the Soviet Long-Range Air Force, who served first as an 'expert' and then as an 'advisor' from 1969 until the end of 1971, when discussion of bombers was suspended; Engineer Colonel Boris T. Surikov, an Air Defence Forces specialist and author of articles on air defence and ballistic missile defence, who served from late 1971 through early 1972; Engineer Colonel (later Major General) Vasily N. Anyutin, author of a book on ABM defence and serving in the Air Defence Forces, who was present as an 'expert' in 1971 and and 'advisor' in 1972; and as we have noted Colonel Viktor P. Starodubov of the Strategic Missile Forces served first as an advisor in the final SALT I session in 1972. During the seven years of SALT II an additional fourteen field-grade Soviet officers from all services were assigned as advisors to the Soviet Delegation (and yet others have served in SALT I and II as 'experts' or interpreters).

One officer who first appeared in SALT II in 1973 as an adviser then left the Delegation to become the Soviet Commissioner on the Standing Consultative Commission (SCC) established in 1973 in accordance with the SALT I accords – Major General Georgy I. Ustinov. (The United States named a civilian official as its Commissioner, with a brigadier general as his deputy; the Soviet deputy is a civilian from the Ministry of Foreign Affairs.) Several military officers have served on the SCC staff, some who had served as advisors in the SALT II Delegation and others who had not.

This resume of direct Soviet military participation in the SALT I and II negotiations shows the recognition by the Soviet military of the importance of SALT.

The US has throughout SALT been represented by capable senior military officers with excellent staffs, but the scale of military representation has been more limited. The US Delegation had an Air Force lieutenant general from 1969 through 1972, and an Army lieutenant general from 1973 through 1979, as a member of the Delegation representing the JCS, but there have been no other general officers and relatively fewer other military advisors on the American side. (In addition, the US Delegation has included a senior civilian representative of the Secretary of Defence, for whom there is no Soviet civilian equivalent.)

As one would expect for a serious negotiation, the Soviet side has sent highly qualified specialists in the key areas under discussion, as we have seen: strategic missile experts, ABM experts, submarine and ASW specialists, and strategic bomber officers, all working under senior officers of the General Staff concerned with advanced weapons development and procurement.

In addition to military representatives, the USSR has included in its Delegation two senior figures from the scientific-technological-military production field. Academician Aleksandr N. Shchukin, a highly respected 'elder statesman' in military applications of science and technology, was active throughout *all* SALT I and II sessions, from 1969 through 1979 – despite the fact that he was sixty-nine years old when SALT began! A reserve major general in the engineering-technical service, he is principally a civilian scientist, and played a key role as the representative on the Delegation of the Military-Industrial Commission, of which he is a deputy chairman. Petr S. Pleshakov also served throughout SALT I and into SALT II from 1969 to 1974, despite his other responsibilities initially as a deputy minister, later first deputy minister, and after 1973 Minister of Radio Industry (producing radars, computers, electronics, and communications equipment for military as well as civilian uses). He, too, is a reserve officer, as are many Soviet scientific and industrial production personnel; his reserve rank is lieutenant general of the engineering-technical service. (On the US Delegation, there has been one equivalent representative, Dr Harold Brown from 1969 through 1976, formerly director of a nuclear weapons laboratory, later head of the Directorate of Development, Research and Engineering of the Department of Defence, and then Secretary of the Air Force before his SALT duty, and Secretary of Defence after January 1977.)

SALT led to establishment of direct coordination between the Ministry of Defence and the Ministry of Foreign Affairs, reportedly early in 1969, also with participation of Academy of Sciences political and technical institutes, and of representatives of the industrial production ministries. Appropriate sections of the Central Committee apparatus, and of the personal staff of the General Secretary, also play an important coordinating and tasking role.

The participation of senior levels of elements in addition to the Ministries of Defence and Foreign Affairs was manifest in the SALT negotiations at the first Moscow Summit meeting in May 1972, when Deputy Prime Minister Leonid V. Smirnov played an important direct part in the final negotiation of the SALT I Interim Agreement limiting strategic offensive arms. (Smirnov also participated in the Moscow

The Soviet Military and SALT

negotiations with Secretary Vance in March 1977 and October 1978.) Smirnov has for years chaired the important Military-Industrial Commission (VPK), which handles coordination between the Defence Ministry, ministries concerned with military production, and Academy of Science institutes contributing to military research and development. The Minister of Defence, Marshal Dmitri F. Ustinov, oversaw this sector as Party Secretary and a Politburo Candidate Member, before becoming Minister and a full member of the Politburo in 1977.

The highest body dealing specifically with military and defence matters is the Defence Council. Although formally acknowledged only in the new Soviet Constitution in 1977, and nominally responsible to the Presidium of the Supreme Soviet, the Defence Council has existed at least since 1970 and in practice represents an elite national security committee of Politburo members. Chaired by Party Secretary General and Supreme Soviet Presidium Chairman Leonid I. Brezhnev, this body includes Prime Minister Aleksei N. Kosygin, Minister of Defence F. Ustinov, Foreign Minister Andrei A. Gromyko, KGB Chief Yury V. Andropov and full members of the Politburo. Its full membership is not known. If not a member formally, in any event an important participant in its deliberations is Chief of the General Staff and First Deputy Minister of Defence Ogarkov. Other advisers and consultants are called upon to attend on occasion, including senior Defence Ministry and General Staff officers, and Smirnov and other VPK members. It is known to have dealt with SALT issues on a number of occasions.

The highest authority is the Politburo of the Central Committee of the Communist Party of the Soviet Union. The key Soviet decisions on entering SALT and all major positions in SALT are determined by the Politburo. Also chaired by Brezhnev, this body includes the other political leaders who do not usually concern themselves with defence or foreign affairs. In an unusual circumstance, during the intensive five days of negotiations on SALT at the first Nixon-Brezhnev Summit Conference in Moscow in May 1972 the Politburo (which normally meets weekly) met at least four times.

In 1973, Marshal Grechko (along with Foreign Minister Gromyko and KGB Chief Andropov) was added to the Politburo. Previously, he had attended not as a member but rather by special invitation on occasions when policy questions under discussion directly concerned him — which occurred increasingly often. His successor in 1976, Dmitri Ustinov, was also promoted from candidate membership he already held as a Party Secretary to full membership in the Politburo. Also, soon after Marshal Grechko's death and replacement by Ustinov,

Brezhnev was promoted to Marshal of the Soviet Union (in May 1976), followed by Ustinov (in July 1976).

Military men did not directly participate in the Summit meetings of Soviet and American leaders dealing with SALT in 1972 and 1973, but senior Soviet military representatives (including Colonel General Kozlov) did participate in certain of the Summit SALT discussions at Yalta and Vladivostok in June and November of 1974. Others, including Marshal Ogarkov, participated in Moscow SALT negotiations by Secretary Vance in March 1977 and October 1978. At the Vienna Summit in June 1979 senior military men of the two sides met for the first time. (No American military representatives or Defence Department officials participated directly in any of the Summit meetings until 1979, except for a non-SALT role for Secretary of the Navy John Warner in 1972).

Soviet military participation in the SALT planning and decision-making, and in the actual negotiations, has been active and vigorous at all levels. The effect of this active role has probably been to exert a conservative and cautious influence on Soviet positions, but it has not precluded reaching a number of significant agreements.

SALT and Soviet Military Policy and Programmes

The first significant effects of SALT on Soviet military programmes were felt long before the representatives of the two sides appeared at the green negotiating table. The Soviet political and military leaders were led by the persistent high-level American request for SALT throughout 1967 and 1968 to give the idea careful consideration. And even the prospect of Soviet entry into SALT had an impact in certain instances — particularly with respect to the Soviet ICBM build-up.

As we have noted, US strategic offensive forces had levelled off by mid-1967, and each step toward deployment of an ABM system was accompanied by private as well as public urging of strategic arms limitation talks. At the same time, as the Soviet ICBM deployment programme moved toward numerical equality with the US, and the SLBM program got underway, Soviet ABM development continued to yield disappointing results.

In 1967, the Soviet leaders decided to curtail by one-third the originally planned deployment of 96 ABM launchers in 12 complexes around Moscow, even abandoning some construction already underway. It is unlikely that this move was intended to signal restraint to the US; rather, it appears to have represented a decision, based on the

The Soviet Military and SALT

relatively poor performance of the existing ABM system, to cut back on even the modest original deployment around Moscow. (Work on the other eight complexes with a total of 64 launchers and associated battle engagement radars continued, reaching completion shortly before SALT began in late 1969, and construction of three additional sophisticated large phased-array radars for long-range detection and tracking continued on through the mid-1970s.) This pattern of ABM development suggested, as early as 1968, that the Soviet side might be prepared to agree, in SALT, to an ABM limitation at 75-100 launchers for defence of Moscow.

Reflecting these developments, there was a sharp drop in 1968 in the frequency of claims to an effective ABM defense of the USSR — a claim for years routinely sounded by Soviet military spokesmen. This change clearly reflected Soviet reconsideration of their originally more or less automatic commitment to ABM deployment. Following the US 'Safeguard' deployment debate, reference to Soviet ABM defence capability resumed in 1970, but again, as agreement on an ABM treaty became more likely in 1971, virtually all references to a Soviet ABM capability ceased, not to be resumed again.

During the period from 1966 through 1969, as we have seen, the Soviet ICBM force was growing by about 300 new silo launchers per year. The Soviet military and political leaders were determined that the Soviet Union should equal the US at least in number of ICBM silos, and preferably in modern ICBMs and SLBMs combined. By the time the Soviets were prepared to begin SALT in 1968, the USSR had more ICBM launchers operational and under construction than did the US (although slightly fewer in protective silos). The USSR was, however, still lagging badly in SLBMs, just beginning deployment of a Polaris-class submarine (the nuclear-powered 'Y' class, with 16 launchers).

The delay of SALT from September 1968 to November 1969 gave the Soviet Union the advantage of having an additional 375 ICBM and SLBM launchers operational and under construction. At this point, having surpassed the US in numbers of ICBMs, the Soviet leaders decided to stop the build-up of ICBM launchers. After SALT began, no additional groups of ICBM silos were begun for a year (only a few individual silos needed for filling out standard groups — six silos per SS-9 group, ten silos each for SS-11 and SS-13 groups — were started in late 1969 or early 1970). Indeed, three groups of SS-9s in early construction were abandoned in 1970. Construction of the remaining groups continued, for a putative total of 1,527 ICBM launchers at operational complexes (including 134 of the older SS-7s and 8s on 'soft' launching pads). Construction of Y-class submarines with SLBM launchers continued apace, as the Soviet Navy still had very few.

The Soviet cessation of its ICBM build-up was, in my view, intended as a 'signal' in SALT, although it also reflected Soviet intention to shift to a new generation of improved ICBMs, if SALT did not preclude having more and the ICBM build-up resumed. One can only surmise, but it seems likely that the Soviet decision at that time was a contingent one, designed to seek the benefit for SALT purposes of a display of restraint, while keeping the door open for a renewed build-up if SALT did not result in a timely agreement limiting ICBMs. The 'signal' in SALT was gently prompted by some unofficial Soviet spokesmen, but did not really 'catch' until well into 1970, partly owing to seasonal construction patterns but mainly because of the usual caution in reporting favourable intelligence. The Soviet side did not receive a response to this signal.

About a year after the first signal, as the SALT talks began to stalemate, a new 'signal' of a different kind was made as a limited deployment of new missiles was undertaken − construction began on some 80 new ICBM launcher silos (and some new underground control chambers). This signal hit a little more rapidly, in the early spring of 1971, just before agreement was reached by the highest US and USSR Government leaders on a new approach in SALT. Probably as a consequence of the agreement of 20 May 1971 on new guidelines for the talks, no additional ICBM launchers were begun thereafter − again a positive signal by the Soviet leaders, unilaterally restricting their own deployment for the year until actual agreement on ICBM limitations was reached in SALT I.

Sceptics of the value of the SALT accords suggest that the Soviet Union probably had no intention to build more ICBMs in any case. While conceivably this was so, it may be observed that these sceptics were often the same people who had projected much higher levels of Soviet ICBM deployment, had doubted the 'signals' of 1969-70 and 1971-72, and had most ardently during those years argued the need for limiting Soviet ICBM (and particularly SS-9) deployment. In fact, as we have noted, during the two and a half years of SALT negotiations leading up to the Interim Agreement of 26 May 1972 on strategic offensive arms, the Soviet ICBM build-up was unilaterally limited to 80 additional ICBM launchers, in contrast to the 300 to 350 each year for the preceding three years, apart from the Soviet agreement to build no additional ICBM silos over the five years duration of the Interim Agreement.

The Soviet ICBM force build-up, restraints and limitation should be considered in light of the fact that this matter was viewed by the Soviet military also in terms of requirements vis-a-vis third countries. Both the USSR and the US would need to consider possible use of some portion of their ICBM forces against China. But for the Soviet military that possibility, as well as possible use against yet other countries, and against US bases in Eurasia, required balancing ICBMs for these roles against MRBMs and IRBMs. In 1969 it became publicly known that the USSR was deploying 120 SS-11 missiles capable of being fired at targets either in the United States or in the Eurasian periphery. Shortly thereafter, it became clear that a number of MRBMs and IRBMs were being phased out; in all, over 100 MRBM and IRBM launchers were deactivated by 1972. In all, probably more than 300 ICBMs were deployed primarily for possible use against peripheral continental, rather than intercontinental, targets. (Some 60 of the 80 new launchers begun in 1971, incidentally, were for SS-19 missiles in an expansion of two SS-11 deployment fields oriented towards peripheral targets in Eurasia rather than toward the United States.) In the SALT negotiations, the Soviet side none the less agreed to count launchers for all such missiles as ICBM launchers, recognising that the US could not agree to exempt weapons which could be fired at targets in the United States.

Thus we see that the very proposal for SALT, and then the two and a half years of negotiations leading to the May 1972 SALT I accords, almost certainly *did* have an effect — a restraining effect — on Soviet ICBM deployment, and may have reinforced other considerations leading to an early levelling off at a very low level of ABM deployment. On the other hand, a steady SLBM build-up continued.

The SALT II negotiations also were reflected in, and influenced in at least a modest way, actual Soviet missile deployments. Throughout the SALT II negotiations, the United States was well in advance of the Soviet Union in MIRV deployment. Indeed, Soviet MIRV development and deployment in the 1970s lagged behind US expectations. Contrary to the contention of some critics of SALT, the United States had in 1972 projected a Soviet initial MIRV deployment *earlier* than the actual 1975 start, and also a faster deployment rate. (American estimates on Soviet MIRV accuracy were, on the other hand, behind the actual pace of development.) As a consequence of the American lead in MIRV deployment, it was the United States which set the relatively high MIRVed missile sublimits (1,320 at Vladivostok, later modified to include strategic cruise missile (ALCM) and MIRVed airborne ballistic missile (ASBM) carrying heavy bombers in that total along with MIRVed ICBMs and SLBMs, with a new 1,200 ceiling for MIRVed ballistic missile launchers). The United States later pressed for a MIRVed ICBM sublimit as well, which would pinch the Soviets more than the US, and a MIRVed ICBM launcher limit of 820 was finally agreed. The Soviet Union had planned (in line with the Vladivostok agreement), and had begun construction, of about 100 launchers of MIRVed ICBMs *above* the 820 limit, and they accordingly abandoned that construction. So SALT II did impose direct limits of at least 100 on the Soviet MIRVed ICBM (SS-17 and SS-19) silo deployment programme. This example again clearly disproves the contention that SALT has never required the Soviet Union to modify and restrain its existing build-up, although it remains true that both the United States and the Soviet Union have preferred as a general rule to set limits at or above existing and even currently programmed force levels.

We do not know in detail what the views of the Soviet military were on the pace and levels of strategic force build-up at various stages of the SALT process. It is likely that particular services had their own advocacies.

The Air Defence Forces probably lobbied for higher levels of ABM deployment in SALT I, but even the military leadership probably was prepared to agree to forego Soviet ABM deployments if the US also would do so. It seems clear that the Soviet military leaders (and probably the political leaders too) preferred to keep the Moscow ABM deployment, particularly to provide defence against small third-country strikes and accidental launchings (remote though the latter possibility would be), and perhaps also to have the benefit of some operational experience with an ABM system. But it is not clear that a complete ABM ban could not have been negotiated; the possibility was not fully explored. In 1980, the Soviets began to reduce the number of active ABM launch sites they had maintained since 1969.

The Soviet military, not unlike the American, was evidently inclined to prefer specific deployment limitations, but no more than minimal restraints on research and development and on system modifications and improvements. None the less, initial opposition was overcome to such limitations as a ban on deployment of future 'exotic' types of anti-ballistic missile systems, as well as to development and testing of various ABM systems, such as space, air, sea and land-mobile based, and rapid refire, systems.

The strongest military consideration pressed by the Soviet side, and one representing a major difference with the US, was the insistence that strategic offensive arms for purposes of SALT include all nuclear delivery means capable by virtue of their deployment location of striking the USSR or the United States. This position underlay their opposition to early US proposals in 1970 to limit Soviet MRBMs and

IRBMs deployed against targets in Europe, the Middle East, and Asia, but the US did not press this proposal. Much more difficult has been the persistent Soviet attempt to include in some manner US forward-based systems (FBS) deployed within nuclear strike range of the USSR. These are mostly aircraft dual-capable (for nuclear or non-nuclear attack) based on US air bases in Allied territory or on US attack aircraft carriers. It is not necessary to discuss this issue — which bedevilled SALT I until May 1971, and SALT II until Vladivostok in 1974, and remains active for SALT III — save to note that the issue was probably posed by real concerns, exaggerated in their own minds, on the part of the Soviet military. The political leaders probably found these arguments convincing but not overriding in the context of the SALT I accord or in the Vladivostok formula for a ten-year SALT II agreement on strategic offensive arms. If the matter had been raised primarily to cause the US difficulties with its Allies, or for tactical negotiating reasons, it would have been much more readily disposed of. The Soviet side has already indicated it will be an issue in future SALT III negotiations on long-range theatre nuclear forces (LRTNF) limitations or in general strategic offensive force reductions.

The FBS issue represents, but does not exhaust, the category of 'worst case' calculations which each side can conjure up to justify hedges in limitations favourable to itself as counterweights to these conceivable advantages to the other. The US has had its share, including the exaggerated concerns of some American officials during the SALT I negotiations over so-called 'SAM upgrade', the possible upgrading of components of surface-to-air missile (SAM) anti-aircraft systems converting them into low-grade ABM systems. Despite strong Soviet military (and political) suspicions that this concern was both fraudulent and involved unwarranted attempts to impinge on air defence systems, the strength of the American concern did lead the Soviet side to accept obligations not to convert or upgrade SAM missiles, launchers and radars to ABM missiles, launchers and radars, and to agree not to test such SAM components against strategic ballistic missiles, and not to deploy SAM or other phased-array radars of a certain power (except agreed special and limited purposes). Real concerns were met without undue impingement on Soviet air defences once exaggerations of concern were set aside.

Perhaps the chief instance of Soviet refusal to accept an American proposed limitation in the SALT I Interim Agreement was the definition of 'heavy' ICBMs. In retrospect, it is clear that the Soviet SS-19 (and possibly the SS-17) would not have been allowable within the US proposed limit, and the Soviet military could never have accepted a limitation which precluded their deployment of the long-awaited MIRVed ICBM counterpart to the US Minuteman III. The no 'significant increase' in silo size is less constraining and thus permitted a compromise wherein the Soviets agreed not to retrofit SS-9 class missiles in the SS-11 silos (the main American concern at the time), but kept the opportunity to deploy the SS-17 and the SS-19 in modified SS-11 silos, and the SS-18 in SS-9 silos.

In the SALT negotiations, each side has of course presented national positions, so that it would usually only be possible to infer which positions were adopted because of 'military' concerns and preferences, as distinguished from those non-military leaders and negotiators. But the examples above illustrate some of the particular interests of the Soviet military as reflected in the SALT negotiations.

It is reasonable to assume that Soviet military men may have sought to couple with their approval of the SALT limitations commitments by the political leaders to continuation or intensification of some other non-limited military programmes, although we can only infer from what has been happening in the Soviet military forces since the SALT accords of 1972. It is, for example, quite possible that the powerful PVO (Air Defence Command) 'lobby' sought and secured an assurance that foregoing ABM defences would not be followed by unilateral or negotiated cutbacks in air defences — notwithstanding the gap in logic of maintaining costly (and relatively ineffective) strategic air defences when the massive missile forces of the potential opponent would be unopposed. (Of course, the Soviet Air Defence and other military leaders do make a case for maintaining extensive air defences to defend against possible air attack by other powers on the Eurasian periphery.) Similarly, the military leaders doubtless secured agreement to proceed with MIRVing much of the ICBM force by modifying existing launchers for new MIRVed missiles, and with deploying the additional modern SLBMs allowed under the Interim Agreement.

There is strong basis to conclude that the Soviet military leadership sees the current programmes to improve the SLBM force and, above all, to replace about half of the SS-11 force with MIRVed SS-17s and SS-19s and all of the SS-9 force with SS-18s, as necessary and prudent actions in order to preserve parity by matching the build-up of US Minuteman III, Poseidon and Trident strategic forces. These Soviet efforts to catch up and then keep up with the US are, however, seen by many in the United States as threatening to move *ahead* of the US in strategic offensive strength. These conflicting perspectives of the two sides have posed a major problem for the SALT negotiations.

Turning now from discussions of some interacting influences of

The Soviet Military and SALT

Soviet deployment programmes on SALT and vice versa, it may be useful to consider some aspects of doctrine and military thinking particularly pertinent to SALT and also interacting with it.

Military Doctrine

By 1969, the Soviet military leadership had reached the conclusion that strategic superiority in the sense of a first-strike option permitting escape from a crushing retaliatory strike was not possible for either side in contemporary conditions. They recognised that, with the existing level of development of nuclear missile forces, it had become impossible in practice for an attacker to destroy such forces completely, and consequently that it had also become impossible to prevent an annihilating retaliatory strike. In other words, a kind of 'nuclear balance' in terms of capabilities for mutual destruction had come into being. At the same time the military were concerned that this balance could be threatened if one side — the US — achieved a highly effective anti-ballistic missile defence while the other side — the USSR — did not have such a defence. Hence their willingness to support the political leadership in its desire to avoid heavy expenditures on an unpromising and even dangerous further round of the strategic arms race caused by extensive ABM deployments — if a mutually equitable limitation could be reached with the United States.[12]

These views came slowly, in part because they were not self-evidently consistent with the standard military statements implying Soviet victory in a nuclear world war if one should come. Such public statements in the military press and on national military commemoration days have a number of purposes, prominently including indoctrination and morale-boosting of the armed forces and the public. Also, specifically with respect to ABM defences, since the early 1960s it had been standard military litany to claim in a general implied way the *existence* of reliable anti-missile defences (although beginning in 1967 a muted countercurrent to this view began to be expressed). Moreover, as noted earlier, it had been the established Soviet view that ABM defences were naturally 'good' — a position still publicly echoed by Prime Minister Kosygin in London in February 1967, and privately during his visit to the United States in June of the same year.[13] By 1969, however, claims that ABM defence was 'good' while offensive weapons were 'bad' had ceased, and by early 1971 claims to an ABM defence of the Soviet Union had quietly been dropped.

Some controversy has arisen in Western commentaries over the significance of the Soviet agreement to the 1972 ABM Treaty with its clear acceptance for the indefinite future of assured vulnerability of the USSR (as well as the US) to missile attack. Some commentators who are opposed to the idea of 'Mutual Assured Destruction (calling it 'MAD') are also reluctant to conclude that the Soviet leaders subscribe to such a doctrine. They rightly note that Soviet military doctrine has long stressed 'damage limitation', and that the USSR continues to maintain extensive strategic anti-aircraft defences. Moreover, a comment by Marshal Grechko in 1972 that 'research and development directed toward resolving the problems of the defence of the country against nuclear missile attack' is not limited[14] suggests that the military did not originate, and may have been cool toward, the Soviet position in favour of an explicit ban on deployment of a ballistic missile defence of the territory of the country. However, these considerations do not negate the fact of the Soviet acceptance in the ABM Treaty of mutual assured vulnerability of the Soviet Union and the United States to missile attack. The Soviet leaders value doctrine, but they are not always doctrinaire.

The SALT negotiations thus far have not led to the kind of far-reaching dialogue on military concepts that some of us have hoped to see emerge from SALT. There was early significant agreement on certain basic concepts such as mutual deterrence, equal security and strategic stability. But views on specific prescriptions for 'strategic stability' in particular have differed significantly. Moreover, each side has stressed those aspects of stability of greatest concern to it and in terms of support for its current proposals. (This has led to some interesting reverse field running by both sides at different stages of the negotiation.) But the net result has been to negotiate in a classical bargaining fashion as much as to persuade by debates over doctrine and strategic concepts.

An example can illustrate the difficulty in engaging in discussion of doctrine. During an exchange on stragetic stability in the SALT plenary meetings in the spring of 1970, the Soviet side referred to the possibility that ICBM silos might be empty by the time of an enemy strike, since the ICBMs in them could already be in flight owing to information gained from technical early-warning systems. The US Delegation took the occasion of this remark to make clear that the US held any 'launch on warning' doctrine abhorrent, and a statement to that effect by the Secretary of Defence was subsequently placed on the SALT plenary record. The Soviet side declined, however, to pick up a suggestion that it too make an official statement of the Soviet position, because the Soviet military were consistently adamant against any discussion of such matters of operational doctrine. (In addition, there is now considerable evidence from Soviet internal military discussions that the Soviet Union had adopted some form of launch-under-attack contingency concept.)[15]

SALT and Soviet Political-Military Relations

SALT has affected political-military relations in the USSR in a number of ways.[16] Probably both the political and the military leaders have gained broadened perspectives, the former through acquainting themselves with military matters in ways other than those familiar from Politburo reviews of the military budget, and the latter through thinking more in terms of political uses — and limits on uses — of strategic forces rather than exclusively in terms of deterrence and contingent war-waging requirements. This development should probably be regarded as a significant dividend from SALT; so, too, should the introduction of Soviet military leaders into a bilateral US-USSR dialogue on strategic matters.

As noted earlier, SALT was reportedly responsible for the establishment in the late 1960s at the 'working level' of a Ministry of Foreign Affairs and Ministry of Defence joint working group to study the issues and to draft positions for higher level review. Politico-military matters have traditionally been handled only through occasional *ad hoc* meetings, so this has led to greater contact and probably better mutual understanding. Similarly, SALT has contributed to drawing members of the staffs of research institutes — especially the Institute on World Economics and International Relations, and the USA Institute — including a number of retired military officers, into writing and publishing commentaries on a wide variety of political-military and strategic themes. Many of these articles display high professional competence. The role of these institutes in influencing Soviet policy decisions on SALT has probably been limited, but their indirect influence may be appreciable.

In general, the Soviet military has had a very strong voice in SALT not only owing to its responsibilities for security, but also owing to a near monopoly of expertise and relevant information. Soviet military leaders, well aware of this advantage, will not easily share this source of power. None the less, there will probably continue to be some greater diffusion of information and opportunity to comment on political-military issues.

In the negotiations, the Soviet military were initially very conservative and restrictive, and displayed traditional suspicion of Western intelligence 'fishing'; they even objected to discussion of matters involving military secrecy in the presence of *Soviet* civilian officials engaged in SALT. Marshal Grechko at the beginning of SALT in 1969 ordered the Soviet Delegation to provide no quantitative or qualitative information on Soviet military and technical capabilities. General Ogarkov, on one occasion early in SALT, took aside his US military counterpart and suggested that it was not necessary to talk specifically about military concepts in the SALT discussions.[17]

It should be observed that for some time the Soviet commitment to SALT was highly tentative — not only prior to the actual beginning of the talks in November 1969, but until April 1971. By the end of the first round of talks, in December 1969, the Soviet military (as well as political) leaders had concluded that the US was indeed serious about SALT, and after high-level correspondence between President Nixon and Prime Minister Kosygin, and Kissinger-Dobrynin discussions, over the period of January to May of 1971, they concluded that a mutually acceptable limitation *could* be negotiated. The critical juncture was reached in deliberations in Moscow at the time of the 24th Communist Party Congress in April 1971. Marshal Grechko supported Brezhnev in these discussions. And from that time on, the highest-level role in SALT on the Soviet side was assumed directly by General Secretary Brezhnev, now the champion of detente.

There were signs during SALT I that the Foreign Ministry negotiators did not always appreciate fully the depth of certain military concerns, and this may also have been true among higher level political leaders. Certainly by the time of the April 1972 visit of Dr Kissinger to Moscow and the first Summit meeting a month later, Brezhnev and several other senior civilian leaders were deeply involved in detailed negotiation. (To a lesser extent, because the initial gap generally was less, SALT has probably also helped to bring some American civilian leaders more deeply into strategic matters.)

Soviet presentation of its own 'scare' picture of American strategic capabilities at the third Summit in June 1974 (at a meeting in Yalta) may represent a step forward in civilian engagement with military evaluations, and in frankness in the dialogue between the two sides. On that occasion. Colonel General Kozlov and other Soviet General Staff representatives (including General Afonsky, who had served as an advisor on the Soviet SALT delegation) assisted Brezhnev in presenting an impressive picture of American strategic forces and capabilities (including FBS, as well as intercontinental forces), operational and planned under current programmes, of overwhelming superiority. The Soviet military may have overstated their case in order to stress their point, but they — and the Soviet political leaders — evidently believed that there was a valid point to be made. Marshal Grechko personally stressed this case to Secretary Kissinger at that time. And some of the Americans were, indeed, impressed. It was significant that the Soviet military were allowed to have their say directly in negotiations at the Summit.

In general, frank exchanges could lead to a more healthy awareness by each side of the differences in perspective and inherent biases both sides display in their military evaluations. In evaluating the 'threat' from the other side, each side tends to hedge by conservative estimates of its own capabilities in a retaliatory situation, while judging the maximum capability of the other side in an initial surprise attack. Moreover, each side in its military evaluations looks ahead at what the other side *may* have the capability to do in the next several years, but again is conservative about its own prospects. Such biases in the military evaluation process make much more difficult the process of agreeing on equitable and mutually acceptable asymmetrical limitations on the strategic forces of the two sides. But recognition of the problem, and that it does not (at least not entirely) spring from international attempts of the other side to gain unilateral advantage, is at least a step toward facilitating solution. Other factors, such as public ventilation of 'worst case' 'threats', and also attempts to build 'bargaining chips' through additional military programmes (or worse, so labelling new programmes which it is *not* intended or desired to 'cash in' in negotiated trade-offs and limitations) further compound the problem. But the direct involvement of the military on both sides may help to gain mutual respect and confidence in negotiations seriously pursued.

Several important achievements in SALT were facilitated by recognition of common political-military interests of the two sides. One important example was the agreement to rely on national technical means of verification, and its highly significant corollary commitment not to interfere actively or passively with the other side's operation of its means of verification. Similarly, notwithstanding the reluctance of the military on both sides to be drawn into discussions of traditionally secret procedures concerning security of means of command and control, both also were prepared to seek agreement on the measures included in the 'Agreement on Measures to Reduce the Risk of the Outbreak of Nuclear War Between the USA and the USSR', and the Companion 'Agreement on Measures to Improve the USA-USSR Direct Communications Link', both negotiated at SALT and signed on 30 September 1971 (and in the 'US-USSR Agreement on the Prevention of Incidents On and Over the High Seas' negotiated in separate parallel talks and signed on 25 May 1972). Finally, there was no difficulty in agreeing on the establishment of a Standing Consultative Commission to deal with details of implementation of the SALT agreements. This body has a considerable potential, and has proved useful to date in working out detailed implementing procedures on dismantling systems being reduced, and in clarifying uncertainties over compliance with the SALT agreements. As we have noted, its composition is mixed civilian and military personnel on both sides.

Concluding Observations

The Soviet military approached SALT warily. Its active participation in the negotiation probably contributed to a constructive, if conservative, approach. Public statements of Soviet military leaders and other articles in the Soviet military press have practically ignored SALT; they have continued to stress the requirements for deterrence and for waging war if deterrence should fail; and they have criticised new American military programmes. None the less, they have refrained from taking positions that would preclude agreements.

In SALT, the Soviets have accepted mutual deterrence, both through advocacy of equal security for the US and the USSR and even more tellingly through sponsoring an ABM limitation specifically precluding a defence of the country against overwhelming strategic missile attack and thus ensuring mutual vulnerability. They have accepted strategic parity as reflected in the SALT agreements, and as a goal for further agreements. They have acknowledged the strategic offensive-defensive and action-reaction interrelationships. They have recognised the importance of crisis management, agreed on specific measures to deal with possible nuclear accidents or unauthorised nuclear or missile firings, advocated defence of the National Command Authorities of both sides, agreed on upgrading the 'Hot Line' Moscow-Washington Direct Communications Link through satellite communication, and agreed on consultations in crisis situations to avoid the outbreak of nuclear war.

SALT has led Soviet military and political leaders both to understand as never before the indivisibility of strategy and arms control, and therefore of certain political-military considerations which impact on internal Soviet decision-making on military affairs. SALT has also led to recognition of the importance of both strategic and 'political-military' interaction between the US and the USSR, and indeed has enhanced considerably the importance of that interrelationship.

Finally, in addition to the substantial first step in arms control marked by SALT I and the prospective further stabilisation of strategic arms competition under SALT II, SALT as a common endeavour of the two superpowers may, despite contrary indications in public polemics, also have led to the beginning of a more realistic common understanding of the strategic military balance and of a stabilising role for strategic military power, as well as of limitations on that power.

Notes

* An earlier version of this essay appeared as 'SALT and the Soviet Military', in *Problems of Communism* (January-February 1975); this chapter is a revised, updated and expanded discussion.

1. For accounts of the US proposal, its background and origin, and initial Soviet reactions, see John Newhouse, *Cold Dawn: The Story of SALT* (Holt, Rinehart and Winston, New York, 1973), pp. 86-95; and Raymond L. Garthoff, 'SALT I: An Evaluation', *World Politics*, vol. XXXI, no. 1 (October 1978), pp. 1-25.

2. These figures on US and USSR strategic force levels, and others cited later, are drawn from authoritative sources including not only the unclassified versions of the Annual Reports (or 'Posture Statements') of the US Secretary of Defence, but also later declassified 'sanitized' versions of the classified Reports, and the unofficial but well-informed annual *Strategic Balance* publication of the International Institute for Strategic Studies in London, including refinements and corrections presented in later years as well as those current for the dates indicated.

3. See, for example, Major General Nikolai A. Talensky, 'Anti-Missile Systems and Disarmament', *International Affairs*, no. 10 (Moscow, October 1964), pp. 15-19.

4. In particular, see Leon Goure, Foy D. Kohler and Mose L. Harvey, *The Role of Nuclear Forces in Current Soviet Strategy* (Center for Advanced International Studies, University of Miami, Coral Gables, 1974), *passim;* Lawrence T. Caldwell, *Soviet Attitudes to SALT,* Adelphi Paper, no. 75 (The Institute for Strategic Studies, London, 1971), esp. pp. 6-19; Thomas W. Wolfe, 'Soviet Interests in SALT', in William R. Kintner and Robert L. Pfaltzgraff, Jr (eds.), *SALT: Implications for Arms Control in the 1970s*, (University of Pittsburgh Press, Pittsburgh, 1973), pp. 21-54; Thomas W. Wolfe, 'Soviet Approaches to SALT', *Problems of Communism*, vol. XIX, no. 5 (September-October 1970), pp. 1-10; C. G. Jacobsen, *Soviet Strategy – Soviet Foreign Policy* (Robert Mac Lehose and Co. Ltd., Glasgow, 1972), pp. 71-121; Thomas W. Wolfe, 'Soviet Interests in SALT: Institutional and Bureaucratic Considerations', in Frank B. Horton III, Anthony C. Rogerson, and Edward L. Warner III (eds.), *Comparative Defence Policy* (The Johns Hopkins University Press, Baltimore, 1974), pp. 113-20; Thomas W. Wolfe, *Soviet Power and Europe, 1945-1970* (John Hopkins University Press, Baltimore, 1970), pp. 273-7, 437-41 and 499-510; and Samuel B. Payne Jr, 'The Soviet Debate on Strategic Arms Limitation: 1968-72', *Soviet Studies*, vol. XXVII, no. 1 (January 1975), pp. 27-45.

5. Yury N. Listvinov, *Pervyi Udar* (First Strike) (IMO, Moscow, 1971), 183 pp.

6. As quoted in 'Interest of Strengthening Peace: Joint Session of the Foreign Affairs Commissions of the Council of the Union and Council of Nationalities of the USSR Supreme Soviet', *Izvestiya*, 24 August 1972.

7. As quoted in 'Important Contribution to Strengthening Peace and Security: Session of the Presidium of the USSR Supreme Soviet', *Pravda*, 30 September 1972.

8. In addition to the writings cited in footnote 4 above, see in particular the excellent discussion by Marshall D. Shulman, 'SALT and the Soviet Union', in Mason Willrich and John B Rhinelander (eds.), *SALT: The Moscow Agreements and Beyond* (The Free Press-MacMillan, New York, 1974), pp. 101-21; and see David Holloway, 'Strategic Concepts and Soviet Policy', *Survival* (November 1971).

9. See *Documents on Disarmament 1972* (United States Arms Control and Disarmament Agency, Washington, 1974), pp. 207-325, for the texts and other official documents relating to the SALT I agreements. Of greatest significance was the ABM Treaty, limiting the US and the USSR each to no more than two anti-ballistic missile defence sites with no more than 100 ABM launchers and interceptors at each, and further limiting development and deployment of ABM systems. (A Protocol signed at the third Summit in June 1974 reduced the allowed ABM sites to one on each side.) The SALT I Interim limiting the numbers of ICBM and SLBM launchers each side could have for a five year period, during which negotiations would continue for a more comprehensive offensive strategic arms limitation, expired in October 1977, but both sides declared their intention to continue to abide by its terms while the SALT II negotiations continued.

10. See in particular Wolfe, *Problems of Communism* (September-October 1970), and Wolfe, in *SALT: Implications for Arms Control in the 1970s*, pp. 24-8.

11. In addition to the writings of Thomas Wolfe and Samuel Payne cited in footnote 4 above, see Matthew P. Gallagher and Karl F. Spielman Jr, *Soviet Decision-Making for Defense: A Critique of US Perspectives on the Arms Race* (Praeger, New York, 1972); and Douglas Garthoff, 'The Soviet Military and Arms Control', *Survival*, vol. XIX, no. 6 (November-December 1977), pp. 242-50.

12. The statements in this paragraph are a paraphrase of statements by Army General S. P. Ivanov, 'Soviet Military Doctrine and Strategy', and Major General V. I. Zemskov, 'Wars of the Contemporary Era', both in *Voyennaya mysl* (Military Thought), no. 5 (May 1969), pp. 47 and 57 respectively. This is an authoritative Ministry of Defence organ not intended for open circulation. See also the extensive direct citation and discussion in my article 'Mutual Deterrence and Strategic Arms Limitation in Soviet Policy', *International Security*, vol. 3, no. 1 (Summer 1978), pp. 112-47. See also Stanley Sienkiewicz, 'SALT and Soviet Doctrine', *International Security*, vol. 2, no. 4 (Spring 1978), pp. 84-100.

13. See 'Kosygin is Cool to Missile Curb', *The New York Times*, 10 February 1967, and 'Transcript of Kosygin News Conference at the UN', *The New York Times*, 26 June 1967.

14. In *Pravda*, 30 September 1972.

15. See Garthoff, *International Security*, vol. 3, no. 1, pp. 129-32.

16. Two useful studies which review the role of the Soviet military in SALT, expressions of military views on SALT related issues, and political-military relations in the SALT context, are [Lt Col., USAF] Edward L. Warner, *The Military in Contemporary Soviet Politics: An Institutional Analysis* (Praeger, New York, 1977), Chapter 6, pp. 220-67; and Thomas W. Wolfe, *The SALT Experience* (Ballinger, Cambridge, Mass., 1979), esp. pp. 49-77.

17. Newhouse, *Cold Dawn: The Story of SALT*, p. 192, refers to this comment, although his account of the incident is somewhat inaccurate in other specifics.

PART THREE:

THE USE OF THE MILITARY INSTRUMENT

7 SOVIET RISK TAKING AND CRISIS BEHAVIOUR
Hannes Adomeit

Soviet Military Power

One of the most widely accepted assumptions about Soviet foreign policy is the view that a growth in relative Soviet military power induces higher risk-taking propensities. It is a fact that there has been a spectacular growth in Soviet military-strategic power since the early 1960s and a somewhat less dramatic increase in conventional, including naval, capabilities. But the record of Soviet behaviour at present suggests, if anything, the absence of a positive correlation between growth in capabilities and an increase in potentially dangerous ventures in foreign policy. Is the view that 'capabilities have a way of begetting intentions' then nothing but one of the many projections of Western analysts, derived, perhaps, from the observation of United States foreign policy?[1] How important has Soviet military power been in the achievement of political objectives in general and, more specifically, in crisis situations?

Local Conventional Superiority

Stalin clearly recognised the political significance of military power — the political advantages to be derived from advancing the Red Army as far as possible into Eastern Europe, Germany and the Balkans in the west, into Iran in the south, and into north-east China, Manchuria, Korea and Sakhalin in the Far East. In the last case, powerful Soviet military offensives were not halted until *after* the announcement of Japanese capitulation. The overriding political steering of the military campaigns is also reflected in criticisms in the memoirs of many Soviet generals. In recurring conflicts over saving lives and resources versus making speedy military advances Soviet generals frequently urged the minimising of losses, but Stalin pushed them ahead to maximise territorial gains; as a result history received a tremendous propulsive kick from the Russian military boot. Almost everywhere, with the exception of Iran and the Soviet occupation zone in Austria, Soviet military presence was translated into Soviet political control. All this is well known.

It is less well known that official criticism of Stalin's policies as a rule has scarcely touched on his achievements in foreign policy. During his de-Stalinisation campaign, Khrushchev found only two specific foreign-policy measures worthy of criticism: Stalin's handling of war preparations and intelligence before June 1941, and his policy towards Yugoslavia. It is equally significant that a Soviet historian, Roy Medvedev, who has written a most scholarly, thorough and scathing analysis of the origins and consequences of Stalinism, does not conceal his disappointment with the still inadequate military push history received during the war. Medvedev reasons, more in sorrow than in anger, that:

> Very real chances for the victory of the socialist revolution arose throughout continental Europe during the Second World War. Much depended on the fortunes of the German-Soviet conflict. If it had been less successful for Hitler in 1941, he would not have declared war on the United States in December. The Red Army would have moved into Western Europe while Britain had not yet recovered from her defeats. Not only Eastern Europe but also Western Europe would have been liberated by the Red Army. The face of Europe today would be quite different.[2]

Khrushchev's very limited criticism of Stalinist foreign policy; Medvedev's arguments from 'correct', 'internationalist' positions, accusing Stalin of never being a 'Marxist in essence', but at the same time regretting the failure to 'liberate Western Europe' by military intervention; the emphasis of the present leadership under Brezhnev on not underestimating the 'objective achievements' of Soviet foreign policy under Stalin — all this leads to one major conclusion. In Soviet perceptions, the use of force and the acceptance of risk in this process are subject primarily to criteria of *expediency,* not legitimacy or morality. If Soviet military power can 'objectively' serve to further Soviet state interests, and thus, by definition, strengthen world socialism, the acceptance of risk is considered *a priori* as 'just'.

What remains to be said in the present context is that Stalin's military advances in the West and Far East during and immediately after the war were operations without risk as defined here. Only the break-up of the war-time alliance led to the emergency of crisis and war risks for Stalin.

The Period of American Nuclear Monopoly

The question arising in this period of Soviet strategic inferiority is not primarily whether revisionist historians in the West are right that 'the bomb served to toughen the United States approach to disputed Central and Eastern European issues even before it was actually used' at Hiroshima and Nagasaki, or that the American nuclear monopoly gave Truman sufficient confidence 'to attempt major reversals in negotiations over Poland, Germany, Hungary, Bulgaria and Rumania'.[3] This author is unconvinced by the 'evidence' put forward to support these theses. The important question is rather whether there is any indication that Stalin was sufficiently impressed by American nuclear power to restrain his risk-taking in foreign policy. This, in essence, is asking two questions: Did Stalin know and appreciate the significance of an entirely new weapon? How did he act in foreign policy?

Stalin was 'casually' informed of the existence of the atomic bomb by President Truman on 24 July during the Potsdam Conference (if he did not know earlier from Soviet intelligence), and the effectiveness and destructiveness of the new weapon was demonstrated on 6 and 9 August 1945. Yet Stalin's outward reaction at the Potsdam Conference was as casual as the way in which he was informed; Truman thought he showed no special interest. But there is no reason to dismiss what Zhukov said in his memoirs, that Stalin understood the significance of the atomic bomb and that, when informed by Truman about the 'new weapon of unusual destructive force', he remarked to Molotov the same evening that he was going to tell I. V. Kurchatov, the scientist responsible for the nuclear weapons programme, 'to step things up'.[4] This version is confirmed by a Soviet physicist, Igor N. Golovin, who said in 1966 that the decision to build the atomic bomb was taken as early as the summer of 1942 and that, after the first explosion of an atomic bomb took place at Alamogordo on 16 July 1945, Soviet scientists were ordered to speed up their efforts.[5] Considering the huge energy requirements necessary for gas diffusion to separate U-235 from U-238, the complex engineering problems and the limited technological potential in a war-ravaged country, it is justifiable to call the Soviet nuclear-weapons programme a top-priority project based on the political will to abolish the American nuclear monopoly.

However, the appreciation of the destructiveness and the political implications of nuclear weapons was not reflected in Soviet foreign policy before June 1948, for nuclear deterrence began in earnest only during the Berlin crisis. Soviet conventional superiority in Europe in the wake of substantial American demobilisation programmes, troop withdrawals, dissolution of overseas air bases and substantial cuts in defence budgets undoubtedly provided a temptation for Stalin to initiate risky probes of Western determination, while in Washington the recognition of significant conventional deficiencies had a paralysing effect. In the opinion of a contemporary observer, 'The most determined opposition to the use of force [to break the blockade of Berlin] came from the JCS [Joint Chiefs of Staff] who viewed the problem in purely military terms. Secretary of State Marshall, who had been a soldier most of his life, was equally opposed to breaking the blockade'.[6]

In the event of war, everything pointed to a protracted struggle in which the United States could only gradually bring to bear her strategic invulnerability, naval superiority, superior industrial resources and nuclear weapons, and had to hope this could be accomplished before the development of a Soviet strategic air force could jeopardise these advantages. When in February 1948, at a meeting with Bulgarian and Yugoslav Communist leaders, Stalin acknowledged that the United States was 'the most powerful state in the world', without giving his reasons for thinking so, it is safe to assume this assessment was based on a combination of these strategic factors favourable to America.[7]

In the light of these considerations it is hard to agree with the view that 'the era of the American monopoly of the atom bomb passed without any special advantage accruing to the United States on its account'.[8] While strategic air power did not deter the Soviet Union from taking risks, it almost certainly set a limit, and thus deterred further exploitation of conventional military advantages.

Soviet Strategic Inferiority

The successors of Stalin, with Khrushchev emerging by 1955 as the *primus inter pares,* initially continued the shift from confrontation to *détente* begun by their predecessor in Europe after the end of the Berlin blockade in the spring of 1949 and in Asia after the stalemate reached in the Korean war. The post-Stalin 'thaw' and the 'Spirit of Geneva' appeared at the time to be lasting and to exclude the outbreak of serious crises and military confrontations. Parallels to present East—West relations are evident.

In 1956 and 1957, however, developments in missile technology and the twin crises of Hungary and Suez converged to arrest and reverse the swing from confrontation to coexistence. Soviet intervention in Hungary was an important factor in this context, not because the United States considered it an opportunity to give military substance to the Dulles rhetoric of 'roll back' but because it shattered the hopes, even among many Western Communists, that a fundamental change in the Soviet system and Soviet foreign policy had taken place.

As regards the Suez crisis, the frequent invocation of the dangers of escalation, the declaration of a readiness to send Soviet 'volunteers' and, finally, Bulganin's letters of 5 November 1956 to Eden and Mollet (asking them how Britain and France would have felt if they had been attacked 'by more powerful states possessing every kind of destructive weapon' and reminding them that there were countries which 'could have used other means such as rocket techniques') — all these were innovations in the style of foreign policy which were to affect its substance.

In the Middle East crises of 1957 and 1958 and in the Taiwan Straits crisis of 1958, different elements of conventional and strategic threats were brought to bear on the course of events (or at least the attempt was made.) Whatever the specific elements of the crises in the Middle East and Far East, there are fundamental similarities in several respects. The Soviet leaders invoked Soviet advances in the military-technological field, notably in the missile race, *in general terms,* leaving ample room for ambiguity by not linking them to specific contingencies or automatic obligations; when they did so, there was only a *remote* risk of crisis between the super-powers; and when the danger of escalation and the preparedness by the USSR to use nuclear weapons was most emphasised, the *actual dangers* of military conflict involving the super-powers *were least.* This pattern was broken when Khrushchev, instead of reacting to events, took the initiative in Central Europe.

Khrushchev's resumption of coercive diplomacy against the Western position in Berlin on 10 November 1958 immediately raised the question of how he thought he could succeed where Stalin had failed ten years earlier. If anything, the Western hand had been strengthened in Western Europe and in Berlin since 1948, and the *status quo,* still fluid in 1948, had hardened by 1958. Khrushchev did not show any inclination to replay the counter-productive sequence of blockade and airlift, so, unless something entirely new could be pulled out of the hat, Soviet pressures against Berlin were doomed to failure from the very beginning.

Khrushchev's rabbit jumped out from the columns of *Pravda* only four days after the speech in which he had challenged the Western position in Berlin: 'The production of the intercontinental ballistic rocket has been successfully set up.' Two months later, at the XXIst Party Congress, Khrushchev went one step further and claimed that '*Serial* production of the intercontinental ballistic rocket has been successfully organised.'[9] By early 1960 he reported to the Supreme Soviet that the USSR had achieved superiority over the USA 'in the creation and mass production of intercontinental ballistic rockets of all types',[10] and in March 1960 he asserted bluntly, 'the Soviet Union is now the world's strongest military power', thus ostensibly reversing what Stalin had said privately to Djilas in 1948.[11]

That the production, capability and superiority claims were directly linked to Soviet political objectives in Berlin is undeniable. However, in the period from November 1958 to August 1961 Khrushchev failed to wring substantial concessions from the West in Berlin, despite military-strategic threats — those concessions which the West had made at Geneva having been withdrawn after Camp David. In addition, the highly successful U-2 reconnaissance overflights (which made headlines only after one of the planes had been shot down on 1 May 1960) threatened to reveal that the emperor did not have any clothes on after all. The whole edifice of missile deception began to crumble. American intelligence estimates of Soviet ICBM capabilities began to be scaled down (though they were not reported in the press until after August 1961), while the United States' own intercontinental ballistic missile (ICBM) programme jumped from 9 to 60 operational missiles between 1960 and autumn 1961, whereas the USSR had by that time deployed only a 'handful'. And only one month after the closure of the Sector border between East and West Berlin, American officials began to claim a wide and growing margin of strategic superiority.[12] If the Soviet leaders still hoped to exploit Western anxieties about the military-strategic balance, the time to act was getting short. Khrushchev did act in August 1961: the Berlin Wall was built.

The isolation of one particular variable in foreign policy decisions always contains the seeds of over-simplification and perhaps even serious distortion. Security considerations, domestic factors and the increasingly difficult predicament in which East Germany was to find itself in the spring and summer of 1961 are almost certainly equally as relevant to the basic principles of the Soviet decision to accept the risks inherent in the building of the Berlin Wall as the military aspect. But if it is correct that Khrushchev's strategy was based on the exploitation of exaggerated Western anxiety about Soviet strategic power and well-founded concern about Soviet conventional superiority in Central Europe, then military factors may have been instrumental at least in the timing of the Soviet decision.

This conjecture could be further supported by other considerations about the dynamics of deterrence in Berlin. In July 1962, when the USSR again resumed testing of atomic weapons (a significant fact in itself, considering the emerging Cuban venture), an editorial in *Pravda* asserted that a similar resumption of tests in the autumn of 1961 had inhibited the reactions of Soviet adversaries to the Berlin Wall.[13] Later sources were to elaborate on that issue and state that the testing of super-megaton weapons had a 'sobering effect' on Western leaders, who did not dare 'to risk unleashing a military conflict with the Soviet

Union in the autumn of 1961'.[14] Oleg Penkovsky confirms that the Soviet military was concerned about the risks of Western counteraction and the vulnerability of the USSR *vis-à-vis* United States' strategic power.[15]

On the basis of this evidence the author is not convinced that the outcome of the Berlin crisis was interpreted by Khrushchev as a 'setback' or 'failure', as many Western analysts believe. From the Soviet point of view the lesson of August 1961 could very well have been that *compellence* had failed, but that *deterrence* of Western counteraction had been quite successful. It could have demonstrated to Khrushchev the temptations inherent in the fact that military power can more often be profitably employed for denial and the safeguarding of the *status quo* than for compelling an adversary to do what he would otherwise refuse to do.

If this was the lesson Khrushchev had drawn from the Berlin crisis, it would go far to explain the preparation for the challenge to the United States in Cuba: the attempt to create a *fait accompli* (as in Berlin) and then try to 'get away with it' under cover of a strong deterrent posture. This interpretation would be corroborated further by indications that Khrushchev's position in the CPSU Praesidium was strengthened rather than weakened at the XXIInd Party Congress in October 1961 — a tribute, or grudging admission, by his colleagues and rivals that the strategy of *fait accompli* had been (or could be) quite successful.[16] Finally, it should be remembered that it is only in retrospect that the building of the Berlin Wall appears as the culminating point in the Soviet campaign against the Western position in Berlin.

Between the Berlin and Cuban crises, Khrushchev made it clear that his position was still that the 'long-since ripe question of signing a peace treaty with the two German states' had not escaped his hands. In the summer of 1962 the atmosphere began increasingly to resemble that of the previous summer. Backed by a resumption of nuclear tests on 21 July, Khrushchev proposed a menu of plans to remove the Western garrisons from West Berlin, while Marshal Konev administered sporadic harassment in the air corridors. On 5 September, Moscow declared in a diplomatic note: 'The question is not one of discussing incidents and consultations. It is necessary, at long last, to liquidate the occupation regime in West Berlin . . .'.[17]

It could be argued that linkage between Berlin and Cuba existed only in the sense that Khrushchev attempted to divert Western attention from the build-up of Soviet military power to an issue that was no longer an issue; to dismiss this argument lightly would indeed be foolish. However, the fact remains that a successful outcome of Soviet risk-taking in Cuba would have made things 'mature' in Berlin and would have justified the transformation of an allegedly diversionary issue to a real problem in a climate of American acquiesence to Soviet military-strategic advances.

In retrospect it is quite easy to accuse the victim of failure as a 'hare-brained schemer'. But if it is true, as argued above, that in Moscow the lesson of the Berlin crisis was that, while compellence had failed, deterrence of Western counteraction had worked, the same logic could have applied to Cuba. Moreover, the Soviet Union had made it clear on a number of occasions that it disliked the idea of missile sites in Italy and Turkey and Polaris bases in Britain, so why should the United States not apply the same reasoning and react to bases in Cuba in the Soviet manner — with verbal outrage but with military restraint? (Only after the crisis was over was it sound to argue that the Soviet leaders should have applied another analogy: American missiles in Yugoslavia or Rumania, or Chinese missiles in Albania.)

Little can be gained by asking whether American conventional superiority in the Caribbean or American strategic superiority was ultimately more important in Khrushchev's decision to break off the venture. By deciding on the 'quarantine', the Kennedy Administration had by no means excluded the ultimate means of redress by force— a massive air strike and intervention. Once the extent of American determination was made credible beyond reasonable doubt in Robert Kennedy's conversations with Ambassador Dobrynin on 27 October — the United States 'had to have a commitment by tomorrow that those bases would remove them' — one possible alternative was to raise the conflict to the nuclear level.[18] Considering American strategic superiority, this alternative could only have ended in vastly greater damage for the Soviet Union.

A second alternative, military action in Berlin, would not have remedied but compounded the basic dilemma for the Soviet leaders, because there was nor reason to believe that any outbreak of military conflict in Central Europe would have remained below the nuclear threshold. A counter-move in Berlin was, perhaps, being considered during the crisis. Foreign Minister Gromyko implied as much when he reported to the Supreme Soviet in December 1962 that already the Cuban missile crisis 'had brought the world one step, perhaps only half a step, from an abyss'; it also made 'many people think how the whole matter might have developed if yet another crisis in Central Europe had been added to the critical events around Cuba'.[19]

In sum, as regards the military factors of Soviet risk-taking, the

Khrushchev era shows a surprising correlation: the acceptance of risks despite the relative military-strategic inferiority. Perhaps, the most appropriate epitaph on the Berlin and Cuban crises could be that the former demonstrated to the Soviet Union the possibilities inherent in creating a *fait accompli* under the umbrella of mutual nuclear deterrence and the ineffectiveness of the adversary's strategic power to compel an actor to 'undo what has been done'. In contrast to that, the Cuban case showed that deficiencies in capabilities (and negative changes in the military and political *status quo*) have a way of begetting intentions to remedy them, but that the frustrated attempt to employ the same strategy as in Berlin had seriously put into question the general applicability of a strategy of *faits accomplis* in the nuclear age. The new leaders were not to forget these lessons.

Strategic Maturity and Approximate Parity

In the last phase of Khrushchev's rule, the discrepancy between claims and capabilities, between doctrine and power, and the neglect of conventional military forces had increasingly come under attack from the traditional and modernist schools of the Soviet military establishment. As soon as Khrushchev was deposed, a platform acceptable to both groups was put forward by Marshal M. V. Zakharov, who was reinstated as Chief of General Staff by the new leadership.

Zakharov expressed previous criticism of military leaders and the spirit of the new times by saying, in obvious reference to Khrushchev, that 'subjectivism is dangerous in any activity', but 'particularly dangerous in military affairs which deal with problems of the country's defence'; these observations applied especially to persons who claim 'strategic far-sightedness' but lack a 'rudimentary knowledge of military strategy'.[20] While Zakharov warned against over-emphasis on strategic weapons (endorsing the remark of the then Commander of the Tank Forces Academy, Marshal Rotmistrov, the year before, that it was dangerous to rely on 'one weapon, and that an untried one'),[21] he also ruled out a complete dismantling of the new look and warned against those 'leaders who are under the spell of the old experience, who turn this experience into a fetish and, by their authority and high position, obstruct the coming into being of everything that is new, progressive and outstanding'.

What came into being were not only substantial modernisation programmes for the ground and air forces, new types of naval vessels, the equipment of the armed forces with greater fire-power and mobility, new types of aircraft, a greater airlift capability and, more recently, some quantitative and qualitative improvements in the Soviet 'offensive-defensive mix' in East Central Europe. First and foremost, the new leaders decided to embark on a rapid and vast expansion of Soviet strategic capabilities.

The top priority attached to catching up with the United States in this field is demonstrated by the *quantitative* leaps from the deployment of 200 land-based ICBM in 1964 to 800 in 1968, and to numerical superiority over the United States during SALT I with 1,530 missiles). While the momentum of the deployment of land-based ICBM launchers has been arrested for the time being by the SALT Agreement of 1972, efforts by the USSR to catch up still continue in the field of submarine-launched ballistic missiles (SLBM) — the agreement permits expansion of the Soviet Navy up to 62 'modern submarines' and 950 SLBM launchers. In *qualitative* terms the same trend is indicated by the steady, year-by-year increase in the All-Union science budget, by the deployment of new types of missiles and by the recent successful testing of a multiple independently targetable re-entry vehicle (MIRV) system. Whatever the remaining quantitative and qualitative disparities in Soviet strategic capabilities *vis-á-vis* the United States, the USSR has deployed forces capable of deterrence, surviving a first strike and war-fighting.

In view of these facts it is at first sight all the more surprising that, as early as January 1970, a new theme was advanced in the Soviet scholarly literature. According to an editorial in the journal *USA: Economics, Politics, Ideology*, international politics in recent years had demonstrated the 'limited significance in itself of military power in achieving aims of foreign policy'.[22] If this is to be taken as a genuine conviction shared by the Soviet political leaders, it would be very difficult to explain the significant expansion and improvement of Soviet offensive and defensive capabilities. However, the general applicability of the doctrine of the limited utility of military power has been put into question by subsequent analyses emphasising that 'under the new correlation of forces in the world [in favour of socialism], military power has become less and less applicable for the attainment of the political aims pursued by US imperialism'.[23] This analysis is something entirely different, and implies a double standard: while military power has proved its utility for Soviet foreign policy, it has become a blunt instrument in the hands of imperialism.

Indeed, it is difficult to escape the conclusion that there exists an asymmetry in perceptions about the utility of military power. From the Soviet point of view, military power served not only to safeguard, but to expand the socialist system. It must appear to the Soviet leaders as an instrument of last resort to maintain Soviet control in East Central

Europe and one that has played a significant role in persuading West
Germany to recognise the 'realities' in post-war Europe; as a means
of achieving political equality with the United States by means of
military parity; and as a potential bargaining device in the
controversy with China. Domestically, the military as an institution
retains an important function in 'nation-building' or, more
appropriately, 'strengthening socialism' via 'military-patriotic
education' in the armed forces, paramilitary organisations and the
KOMSOMOL (League of Communist Youth).

Intervention Capabilities and Constraints

On the basis of interpretations that the political utility of military
power remains high in Soviet perceptions, it has been argued that the
real test for the proposition that 'capabilities induce higher risk-taking
propensities' is yet to come. The argument draws on the observation
that in Cuba in 1962, in the Middle East in 1967 and 1970, and in
North Vietnam in 1972, the degree of 'flexibility' available to engage in
local or limited war and to respond in kind to American naval
supremacy had been quite inadequate. Once genuine parity at all levels
— or perhaps a combination of overall parity with local superiority in
potential crisis areas — is achieved, and once substantial numbers of
Soviet attack aircraft carriers and naval task forces for intervention (or
the threat of intervention) have been deployed, the Soviet leaders will
consider the time ripe to teach the Americans a lesson. It reflects the
view that the Soviet Union has, at present, only put forward a *claim* to
super-power status, and that this will be translated into military and
political *substance* at a time of the Soviet leaders' choosing.

The horizon would be brighter if one could dismiss this hypothesis,
but, unfortunately, a lot can be adduced to uphold it. It is undeniable
that successive Soviet leaderships have shown a marked tendency to
manipulate the risks of crisis and to withdraw from a 'competition in
risk-taking' only when risks of war became evident. Recent Soviet
policies are ambiguous enough to justify apprehensions over the probes
in Cuba in September 1970, the unprecedented military involvement
of Soviet pilots in the civil war in the Yemen after June 1967 and in
Egypt in the summer of 1970, the expansion of naval activity in the
Red Sea and the Indian Ocean, and the unclear extent of Soviet
commitments in Somalia, a country considered important enough to
justify a four-day visit by the Defence Minister, Marshal Grechko,
in February 1972.[24]

There is also much ambiguity over the significance and scope of
Soviet naval expansion since 1964. In general terms, Commander

Herrick's observation, made in 1968, that 'the complete lack of strike carrier forces constitutes a fundamental, qualitative difference that necessitates resorting to the defensive in naval strategy', is still valid today.[25] It is also true that the size of Soviet naval infantry has remained relatively small, even after a tripling of its size from 5,000 to 15,000 over the past decade. The size and number of amphibious assault ships has also been expanded only very moderately, while the armament of the modern destroyers and cruisers consists predominantly of ship-to-ship missiles rather than heavy guns for amphibious assault preparation. Finally, the construction of the helicopter carriers, *Moskva* and *Leningrad* – and even of the *Kiev*, an aircraft carrier of 30,000 tons displacement, twice the size of the two previous helicopter carriers – does not appear to introduce a major qualitative change in the eyes of the editors of *Jane's Fighting Ships*, who would still consider it 'surprising' if the Soviet Union 'were to change the emphasis towards an offensive weapon concept'. They take into account that the new angled deck still does not permit fixed-wing aircraft operations, that there is a lack of suitable aircraft, expertise in arrester gear, mirror landing sights and catapults, and that the size of the carrier remains well below that of American counterparts.[26]

However, to draw the conclusion that we can rule out forever the possibility of a naval arms race would be premature. There is, for instance, a change in Soviet perceptions about the combat potential of aircraft carriers. In 1960 Admiral of the Fleet S. Gorshkov contended that 'the significance of aircraft carriers has fallen sharply. As battleships, they have already had their day and are inevitably moving into the past.'[27] By 1969 he had changed his opinion: 'Of course, one should not minimize the combat potential of aircraft carriers, especially, for instance, when they are brought to bear against poorly-armed countries'.[28] Also, the precise significance of the demands for an ambitious Soviet naval programme, forging the Soviet Navy into an instrument 'without equal', advanced by Admiral Gorshkov in a series of eleven articles in *Morskoj sbornik* in 1972 and 1973, remains controversial but does not appear to justify optimism.

Similarly, it would be premature to consider increased, and increasing, Soviet naval capabilities as a mere token, and not an instrument of Soviet super-power status. What some naval analysts seem to forget is that even a basically deterrent and defensive naval strategy does not at all exclude an offensive political concept. In contrast to some Western analysts, Admiral Gorshkov is convinced that 'Soviet sailors ... well understand the meaning of naval power in strengthening the international prestige of our country and its military capacity, in the defence of its enveloping sea borders and the safeguarding of the state interests of the USSR in the seas and oceans'.[29]

What *can* be said with some confidence is that the attempt to achieve parity with the adversary super-power on all levels would require a vast effort and even greater proportions of the Soviet economy for defence, and would probably take a long time. Moreover, the present Soviet leadership may be aware of the fact that in those instances where the Soviet Union hoped to take the lead in the arms race, or gave the impression that it was about to do so (e.g. in strategic aircraft in the 1950s and ballistic missiles and space programmes in the 1960s and early 1970s), the ultimate outcome was often a widening of disparities, and not a narrowing.

Similar considerations could apply to the manipulation of the risks of crisis and war in future military confrontations. There has been a tendency in the West to mobilise military power predominantly in response to clearly recognisable challenges, and to reduce forces once immediate dangers have, or seem to have, passed. In order to encourage these trends, dramatic confrontations could be counter-productive, and the Soviet leaders may well be aware of that.

The Soviet leaders can be seen as reacting to constraints and opportunities of the international system. Yet they are also part of the Soviet political system and have to consider domestic processes and pressures in their decisions to accept or reject risks.

Domestic Factors

In what has been ironically referred to as the 'end of rationality' (Horelick), recent scholarship in the West has stressed the importance of bureaucratic, governmental and organisational influences on decision-making, challenging the concept that international relations had to be understood primarily as a process of interaction among 'rational' state actors. Because of competing intra-governmental preferences, group and personality conflicts, inter-service rivalries and inaccurate or incomplete intelligence information and implementation, foreign policy had to be interpreted not (or at least not exclusively) as a series of calculated decisions but as an outcome of 'non-rational' processes.

There is some support for this interpretation among East European sociologists and international relations experts. To a Hungarian sociologist, 'it appears that we have got rid of the harmful illusion that the scientific nature of politics is identical with the situation in which decisions always conform to interest relationships, they are always choices among interests, and this always introduces an element of will into the struggle and realization of interests'.[30]

Concerning the analysis of Soviet foreign policy, it is often taken for granted that 'the dominant feature of bureaucratic politics in the Soviet Union is the continuous "struggle for power" '.[31] If this were the case, is it just the struggle among ambitious men for supremacy or a more fundamental reflection of institutional conflicts and 'interest relationships'? But how can either assumption or, more importantly, its relevance for foreign policy be proved, for there is a scarcity of information about Soviet decision-making processes, particularly in critical phases of crises. We are dealing here with a country that is characterised by a highly centralised structure of decision-making, by a monopoly of power concentrated in the Party and its core, by 'democratic centralism' and by a 'collective leadership' adhering to very similar beliefs on the basis of similar career patterns, rejecting any interference of autonomous, rival bodies in matters of foreign policy. These distinguishing factors of Soviet politics create conditions in which projections of Western theories about universal patterns of 'bureaucratic politics' may be quite misleading.

To question frequently assumed, but unproven, general concepts about linkages between domestic and foreign policy is not to reject from the outset their relevance for specific cases and phases of Soviet behaviour. Each Soviet post-war leadership has created different problems of control and different dynamics, thereby limiting the scope of sweeping generalisations.

Stalinist 'Accidents' and the 'Accident of Stalinism'

There is reason to believe that the 'continuous struggle for power' had only a marginal impact on Soviet foreign policy under Stalin. The enormous power Stalin had concentrated in his hands after Lenin's death ruled out any effective challenge of the leader, and right up to his death Stalin remained in a position to play off one faction against the other; rivalries between Molotov, Malenkov, Zhdanov and Beria could only hope to solve the problem of who would win Stalin's ear and who might succeed the autocrat in the event of his death. In these conditions, Stalin could more easily disengage himself from policies which proved ineffective. Since there was no question of anyone imposing on Stalin a particular line in foreign policy, it is necessary to analyse primarily the impact of Stalin's personality, and of Stalinism as a system, on Soviet foreign policy.

In the view of George F. Kennan, who met Stalin on several occasions during his long service in Moscow, 'Stalin was not really a normal man. Like Ivan the Terrible, he was the captive of a personal devil within his own soul.'[32] Not being a psychologist or psychiatrist, Kennan is cautious about linking Stalin's presumably abnormal personality to foreign policy, but many other Western analysts, although not knowing Stalin personally, have done so. Speaking about 'costly and risky ventures such as the aggression by proxy in Korea', Robert C. Tucker concludes that 'few situations could illustrate more convincingly the potential importance of personality, and specifically the pathological personality, in foreign policy.'[33]

Similar views have been expressed in the Soviet Union. The former Commissar of the Soviet Navy, Admiral N. G. Kuznetsov, for instance, speaks of Stalin's 'pathological mistrust',[34] and Khrushchev, in his 'Secret Speech' of 25 Feburary 1956, called Stalin a 'very distrustful man, sickly suspicious' and drew the lessons from the 'Yugoslav Affair' of 1948 and Stalin's 'mania for greatness' by saying that 'He [Stalin] had *completely lost consciousness of reality*; he demonstrated his suspicion and haughtiness not only in relation to individuals in the USSR, but in relation to whole parties and nations.' (Italics mine.)

From this point on it can be, and has been, argued that 'it was an historical accident that Stalin, the embodiment of all the worst elements in the Russian revolutionary movement, came to power after Lenin'.[35] If this Marxist version of history were true, it would be possible to concentrate exclusively on Stalin's personality, his 'excessive ambition', his 'mistakes' and 'violations of party rules' and conclude that his 'wilfulness' and 'arbitrary conduct' led to an aggravation of international tensions 'fraught with great danger'; this line of interpretation is, in fact, the essence of Khrushchev's remarks at the XXth Party Congress that 'during Stalin's leadership our peaceful relations with other states were often threatened because one-man decisions could, and often did, cause great complications'.[36] It would appear, however, that efforts to explain Soviet foreign policy under Stalin by reference to his personality are questionable intellectual devices, and that they are often used by analysts arguing from Marxist-Leninist perspectives to evade potentially sensitive political issues. As far as is known Stalin never lay on a psychiatrist's couch, so that it is difficult to decide the extent of irrational influences on Stalin's foreign policy, but, even assuming the presence of paranoid elements in Stalin's psyche, drawing inferences from them with which to speculate on foreign-policy behaviour must be considered fundamentally ambiguous. Fear of domestic and external conspiracies and exaggerated threat

perceptions can, of course, give rise to aggressive attitudes and
behaviour (which is not necessarily the same as actual risk-taking),
but it would seem just as logical for a constant pre-occupation with
real or imagined risks to result in *excessive caution*. This throws the
argument back into the political sphere.

A primarily political explanation of Stalin's 'paranoia' is inherent
in Djilas' perceptive analysis: 'Thanks to both ideology and methods,
personal experiences and historical heritage, he [Stalin] regarded as
sure only whatever he held in his fist, and everyone beyond the control
of his police was a potential enemy.'[37] This suggests something of
crucial importance, that there was an interrelationship between Stalin's
personality and historic, ideological and systemic factors, and that,
while Soviet leaders come and go and international conditions change,
basic constraints, commitments and requirements of the Soviet system
remain.

Extending this argument, it stands to reason that, in post-World War
II conditions, Trotsky, Khrushchev or Brezhnev might not have acted
very differently in foreign policy from Stalin. The Cold War served a
specific purpose, namely to tighten control at home and over a newly
created sphere of influence in East Central Europe, and no Soviet leader
has ever questioned the legitimacy of power changes in Europe
favourable to the USSR. Reliance on coercion and occasional 'armed
reconnaissance', if the risks could be expected to be controllable, is
certainly not specific to Stalin's foreign policy; Khrushchev may have
derided the 'shaking of the little finger' in the case of Yugoslavia, but
he did not criticise the successful shaking of the fist in Czechoslovakia
in 1948, nor did Khrushchev or Brezhnev find it ill-advised to go
beyond finger and fist shaking themselves. As for those situations
'fraught with great danger', wisdom is won only in retrospect. Had
Stalin succeeded in Yugoslavia, Berlin and Korea, had there not been
the significant costs of a formal draw, we may be sure that this
enhancement of Soviet power would have been ranked under the 'great
achievements' of Soviet foreign policy.

Khrushchev's 'Adventurism'

The sudden death of Stalin and the arrest and execution of Beria and
Abakumov in 1953 and 1954, which unfroze the monolithic power
structure at the top, created a situation in which no single leader
possessed the authority and power Stalin had monopolised. It is to this
period that Western images of Soviet 'power struggles' have the greatest
relevance. It was also a period of transition from 'totalitarianism' to
'authoritarianism', in which new demands had to be met so as to

proceed from extensive to intensive growth, from mobilisation to modernisation and from coercion to 'material incentives' and persuasion. Adaptation processes and de-Stalinisation notwithstanding, an oligarchic, conservative system emerged, relying on the retention of one-party rule, centralisation and basic principles of 'socialist legality' and *partiinost'*. As conflicts of personality and the policy preferences of individual leaders became inextricably linked with institutional conflicts in a genuine struggle for succession, the question is not so much *whether* Soviet risk-taking and crisis behaviour was influenced by these conditions as *how* and *when* they affected the development of events.

From a theoretical point of view there is no single answer to the question. One possible major consequence of personal and institutional conflict might be that the rivals are so pre-occupied with it that effective leadership becomes virtually impossible. In its extreme form, the resulting foreign policy would show paralysis, inaction and concentration on the absolutely necessary, day-to-day business. A second, less extreme, response could be a search for the relaxation of tensions at home and abroad, a policy of caution, restraint and risk-avoidance. A third possibility arises out of the temptation for individual leaders to take initiatives for bold action, radical change and new designs in order to out-manoeuvre more moderate, complacent and unimaginative rivals. It must be considered of major importance that Khrushchev adopted the last approach.

The 'Khrushchev era' — which was ushered in domestically by a new emphasis on heavy industry and defence (reversed after 1955), the gradual build-up of Khrushchev's power by strengthening the role of the party *vis-à-vis* the state bureaucracy headed by Malenkov, the extension of his influence to the secret police (MVD) and by an initially successful reliance on the support of the military — reached a crucial juncture at the plenum of the CPSU Central Committee on 25-31 January 1955 and the session of the Supreme Soviet on 8 February 1955. On the latter occasion, Premier Malenkov asked to be replaced 'by another Comrade with greater administrative experience'.[38] Given the circumstances, Molotov was the most likely candidate for the post of Chairman of the Council of Ministers. However, all available evidence suggests that he, too, was skilfully relegated to a secondary role by Khrushchev and isolated in a rapid succession of moves between the close of the Central Committee plenum and the session of the Supreme Soviet. Bulganin, although having much less administrative experience than Malenkov or Molotov, succeeded to the Premiership, and Marshal Zhukov took Bulganin's place as Minister of Defence.

These developments are significant in several respects. For one thing, Khrushchev's 'victory' was incomplete and rested on an unstable correlation of domestic forces; both Malenkov and Molotov remained in the Praesidium and thus could always join forces to put Khrushchev in his place when circumstances were ripe. Secondly, the military, which was to be brought into play again and again by Khrushchev as an ally, was headed by a leader whose prestige, self-confidence and political aspirations could at any moment turn into a liability and a major obstacle to Khrushchev's ascendancy. Thirdly, Khrushchev had begun to reject the limitations of 'collective leadership' and manoeuvred himself into the perennial dilemma of charimatic leaders, as described by Max Weber: the necessity to substantiate claims for supreme power by dramatic successes and breakthroughs.

In foreign policy, one of the major innovations was the initiation of an activist approach towards the countries of the Third World, notably the Arab East. There is no reason to doubt the word of Mohamed Heikal, Nasser's close associate, that Khrushchev had told him it had been 'Molotov [who had] wanted to keep Russia away' from the Near East; that Khrushchev knew 'that a defensive policy was wrong, that attack was the best means of defence, and that flexible diplomacy was needed'.[39] Some months before he was replaced by Shepilov as head of the Foreign Ministry, Molotov engaged in self-criticism saying 'We still suffer frequently from an underestimation of the new opportunities which have opened up before us in the post-war period. This shortcoming has also appeared in the work of the Ministry of Foreign Affairs. We must put an end to this.'[40]

Although Molotov was not allowed to implement the new line personally, the controversy over foreign policy in the Arab East is symptomatic of controversies in other areas. At the highest level of decision-making, the view persisted that Soviet foreign policy under Krushchev showed 'adventuristic' traits inherent in over-extensions of commitments and available resources. So long as Khrushchev could confront his colleagues with tangible successes at home and abroad, he could hope to maintain his position as the 'true and only heir of Lenin', but Khrushchev's position was still vulnerable. It remained so even after the important, but quite narrow, victory over the so-called 'anti-party group' (Malenkov, Molotov, Kaganovich, Bulganin, Shepilov *et al.*) and the reversal of a 'mathematical majority' against Khrushchev in the Praesidium in June 1957.

As a member of the Central Committee Secretariat was to say later, the members of the 'anti-party group' had 'at almost every meeting of the Praesidium of the Central Committee attacked everything new which followed from the teaching of Lenin and from life'; their criticism and obstructionism concerned 'questions of exercising leadership over the country, the building of the armed forces and foreign policy'.[41] While the composition of 'anti-party' (anti-Khrushchev) groups changed, the criticism continued and in fact strengthened as Khrushchev's inclination towards boldness and new initiatives in agriculture, industrial organisation and party matters ended in failure and significant segments of the military were alienated by his over-reliance on immature strategic power.

In foreign policy, the allegedly 'vast opportunities' arising from the disintegration of the Western colonial system had shown only ambiguous results, despite rocket rattling and economic and military aid. While Soviet influence was certainly extended, there was no extension of Soviet control. In Berlin, Khrushchev was able to score his last major foreign-policy success by engaging in a calculated risk-taking venture; however, indications that he was continuing to prepare a dramatic breakthrough beyond the mere strengthening of the *status quo* did, most likely, strengthen apprehensions in the Praesidium. The Cuban missile crisis finally put an end to the increasing degrees of risk Khrushchev could afford to take.

The critics of Khrushchev's domestic and foreign policy initiatives closed in on the new personality cult. Had he been willing to accept a genuinely collective leadership by 1963 or 1964, the shift to a relaxation of tension he embarked upon after Cuba might perhaps have saved him in the Praesidium.[42] But by not recognising and respecting the power of the hyra-headed opposition, he added another, this time final, miscalculation to the list of his underestimations of risks and costs.

A 'Businesslike' Approach to Risk

If the feature distinguishing Soviet domestic politics from those of other countries is indeed the perennial struggle for power, evidence of this has yet to appear as far as the present leadership is concerned. Predictions, made ever since October 1964, that the collective leadership would soon crumble and give way to major personnel changes at all levels were still unfulfilled by the time of the XXIIIrd Party Congress (March—April 1966). As the XXIVth Party Congress approached, similar predictions were made, but in April 1971, at the end of the Congress, all members of the Politburo had retained their seats while that body's voting membership was increased by the co-option of Grishin, Kulakov, Kunaev and Shcherbitskii, bringing its strength up to 15 full members.

There have been some other changes at the top in recent years. Mikoyan retired because of age; Shelepin lost his Chairmanship of the Committee for Party and State Control in 1965 but retained his Politburo seat; Shelest was demoted from his First Secretaryship of the Ukrainian Party in May 1972 and, together with Voronov, lost his membership of the Politburo in April 1973. Finally, in April 1973, three new members were added to the Politburo: Marshal Grechko, Yuri Andropov and Andrei Gromyko — all senior members of the Soviet establishment with broad experience in defence, internal security and foreign policy.

Despite all this, the leadership at the top, as well as membership of the Central Committee, have remained remarkably stable during the first decade after Khrushchev's fall. An oligarchy has arisen, with Brezhnev as *primus inter pares,* which appears to recruit new members according to group compromise and expectations that whoever is deemed fit for inclusion in the ruling group will conform to committee rules and not endanger his or any other member's position by a quest for supremacy.

The potential dangers of collective leadership of this type are illuminated in a Western study about group psychology and committee decision-making, The study concludes that members of a closely-knit group tend to become victims of 'groupthink', believing unquestioningly in the inherent morality of their procedures, and this belief inclines them to ignore the ethical and moral consequences of the their decisions; their illusion of invulnerability provides some degree of reassurance about obvious dangers, and they collectively construct rationalisations in order to discount warnings and other forms of negative feedback which, taken seriously, might lead them to reconsider their assumptions each time they recommit themselves to past decisions; it leads them to become over-optimistic and willing to take extraordinary risks.[43] Although these dangers may be real, they have so far failed to appear in the actions of the present Soviet leadership.

One of the major reasons may have been the new leadership's increasing reliance on research and advice, and the relegation of the analytical and cognitive function of ideology to a place of somewhat lesser prominence. At the XXIIIrd Party Congress, Brezhnev denied that the social sciences had 'merely propaganda significance' and existed solely to 'explain and comment upon practice',[44] and new research institutes at the USSR Academy of Sciences have been created: the Institute for the Far East, the Institute for US Studies, the Institute for Concrete Social Research and the All-Union Institute for Information on the Social Sciences. While extensive horizontal dissemination of information continues to be restricted, the vertical information flow must be expected to be intensive and of high quality. This, in turn, lessens the danger of wide discrepancies between subjective ('voluntaristic') hunches about risk and objective international conditions.

Another major reason why inherent dangers of collective leadership have failed to occur rests in the limitations imposed by the Soviet system, notably by problems of relative vitality and economic efficiency. The forecast codified in the CPSU Programme of 1961 that the Soviet Union would overtake the United States in industrial output by 1970 has failed to come true. The present leadership has refrained from making any more specific 'scientifically founded' predictions, but it has been estimated in the West that if the GNP of the United States grew at a meagre 3.5 per cent per annum, and if the Soviet GNP rose at the higher rate of 5 per cent, by 1985 the American GNP would still be over $1,500 billion, compared to the Soviet $800 billion.[45] Other Western forecasts which predicted approximate growth rates of 4.8 per cent (USSR) and 4.7 per cent (USA) for the 1970s were rejected as 'illusory' by a Soviet economist, writing in *World Economy and International Relations,* who pointed instead to the *projected* average growth rate of 6.8 per cent per annum in the current Five-Year Plan (1971-5).[46] At the time of writing, he did not know that the actual growth for 1972 would fall even below the 'illusory' 4.8 per cent to 4.0 per cent.[47]

In order merely to catch up with the adversary United States, Western Europe and Japan, let alone to overtake them, dramatic change is required. It just is not enough to achieve growth rates of the 1972 magnitude. As Kudrov writes in the article quoted above, 'an acceleration of economic growth rates can be regarded as adequate only if it is carried out as a comprehensive process of raising the technical and economic levels of production and its efficiency, if improvements in technology and processes are supported by the utilisation of the latest progressive achievements of science'.[48] But nothing has changed since Brezhnev's acknowledgement and warning at the XXIVth Party Congress that, regarding the efficiency of the Soviet system, 'the weakest links are those connected with the practical implementation of the achievements of science, with their assimilation in mass production'.[49] Brezhnev would like, in his own words, 'to create such conditions which would oblige enterprises to produce the newest types of products', he wants them 'literally to chase after scientific-technological novelties, and not to shy away from them, figuratively speaking, as the devil from incense'.[50]

These concerns reflect apprehensions, detectable also in the significant series of articles on 'Problems of the Contemporary Scientific-Technological Revolution', published in *Voprosy filosofii* between July 1968 and January 1969, that the USSR has had great dificulties in adapting successfully to the transition from extensive to intensive growth. They are evident also in the journal *USA: Economics, Politics, Ideology*, in which a thorough comparative economic analysis of the major capitalist countries was featured in 1972. Its author probably has the Soviet Union in mind when he cautioned that traditional economic indicators, and above all mere *quantitative* comparisons, were inadequate for assessing relative economic efficiency and power. While there had been tendencies for an approximation of economic power and economic development between the United States and her major rivals, it had to be underlined that 'in many fields of the scientific-technical revolution, the "technological gap" between the United States and her competitors is growing'. Because of high rates of innovation, investment in research and growth industries and the rapid introduction of computers, growth in the United States had become intensive, while it had remained extensive in Western Europe and Japan.[51] (And even more so in the Soviet Union, it should be added.)

It is therefore not at all evident, as other Soviet spokesmen have consistently argued, that the United States is 'no less' interested in economic contacts than the socialist states.[52] There is an asymmetry, and not 'equality', of interest. Firstly, 22 per cent of Soviet trade is already with capitalist countries, while the socialist countries' share of American trade is less than 1 per cent. Secondly, American shortage of energy supplies and the Soviet need for technology may establish a complementary and potentially fruitful economic relationship, though it is doubtful whether this kind of interaction — typical of the economic relations between developed and developing countries — is what the USSR wants in the long run.

While raw materials can be imported from a number of countries, or can to a certain extent be replaced by synthetic materials, advanced technology is concentrated in a few highly developed capitalist countries, and the only substitute is the extensive utilisation of capital and labour — a policy explicitly rejected by the Soviet leadership. Finally, higher productivity does depend on advanced technology, yet importing Western machinery tends to create undesirable dependence, is expensive and is impeded by bureaucratic red tape and inefficiencies in other areas of the economy. For instance, Soviet prospects for succes in the scientific-technological and economic competition are adversely affected by failures in agriculture and the squandering of precious foreign currency reserves for imports of butter and grain.

Similar considerations apply to defence expenditures. Of course, civilians in both countries and elsewhere would benefit if SALT and other arms-control agreements led to a significant reduction in defence spending. But it is a matter of common sense — unless one assumes miraculous cost efficiency in the Soviet Union — that the economic strain of achieving and maintaining strategic parity and a global military effort are substantially greater for a country with an estimated Net Material Product of $439 billion than for one with a GNP of $1,152 billion.[53]

If it is correct, as Soviet military spokesmen have frequently pointed out, that 'In our time science becomes one of the most important factors of the struggle for supremacy in the correlation of forces in the world arena';[54] if 'the military-technological policy of the CPSU is directed toward creating and maintaining military superiority of the socialist countries over the forces of war and aggression';[55] and, finally, if Soviet commitments and priorities are so established that a 'decisive speed-up in scientific-technical progress remains one of the chief tasks',[56] the codification of strategic parity, the 'special relationship' and the shift from 'confrontation to co-operation' do not appear exclusively as voluntary restraints on risk-taking propensities. They could also be the realisation of significant contraints forced upon the leadership by the deficiencies of the Soviet system.

Notes

1. Marshall D. Shulman, 'Relations with the Soviet Union', in Kermit Gordon (ed.), *Agenda for the Nation* (Brookings Institution, Washington, 1968), p. 388.
2. Roy A. Medvedev, *Let History Judge: The Origins and Consequences of Stalinism* (Knopf, New York, 1971), pp. 469-70.
3. Gar Alperovitz, *Cold War Essays* (Doubleday, Anchor Books, New York, 1970), p. 70.
4. G. K. Zhukov, *Vospominanie i razmyshlenie* (Novosti, Moscow, 1969), p. 713.
5. *The New York Times*, 19 August 1966.
6. Robert Murphy, *Diplomat Among Warriors*, (Doubleday, New York, 1964), p. 316.
7. Milovan Djilas, *Conversations with Stalin* (Harcourt Brace, New York, 1962), p. 182.
8. Adam B. Ulam, *Expansion and Coexistence: The History of Soviet Foreign Policy, 1917-1967* (Praeger, New York, 1968), p. 497.
9. *Pravda*, 28 January 1959, quoted by Arnold L. Horelick and Myron Rush, *Strategic Power and Soviet Foreign Policy* (University of Chicago Press, Chicago,

1965), p. 50 (italics added).
10. *Pravda*, 2 March 1960.
11. Ibid., 15 January 1960, as quoted by Horelick and Rush, *Strategic Power and Soviet Foreign Policy*, p. 50.
12. Horelick and Rush, *Strategic Power and Soviet Foreign Policy*, pp. 35-7.
13. *Pravda*, 23 July 1962.
14. P. A. Nikolaev, *Politika Sovetskogo Soiuza v germanskom voprose* (Izdatel'stvo 'Nauka', Moscow, 1966), pp. 290-4; N. N. Inozemtsev (ed.), *Mezhdunarodnye otnosheniia posle vtoroi mirovoi voiny*, vol. I (Izdatel'stvo 'Mezhdunarodnye Otnosheniia', Moscow, 1962), p. 211, quoted by Thomas W. Wolfe, *Soviet Power and Europe: 1945-1970* (Johns Hopkins University Press, Baltimore and London, 1970), p. 95.
15. Penkovsky, p. 207.
16. On possible linkages between Soviet domestic politics and Soviet foreign policy see Robert M. Slusser, *The Berlin Crisis of 1961: Soviet-American Relations and the Struggle for Power in the Kremlin, June-November 1961* (Johns Hopkins University Press, Baltimore and London, 1973), especially pp. 179-284.
17. *Department of State Bulletin*, no. 47 (15 October 1962), p. I.
18. Robert F. Kennedy, *Thirteen Days: The Cuban Missile Crisis, October 1962* (Norton, New York, 1969), p. 108.
19. *Pravda*, 14 December 1962.
20. *Krasnaia zvezda*, 4 February 1965.
21. Ibid, 25 April 1964.
22. *SShA*, no. I (January 1970), pp. 21-34.
23. G. Arbatov, 'O Sovetsko—Amerikanskikh otnosheniiakh', *Kommunist*, no. 3 (February 1973), pp. 105-6.
24. Compare pp. 13-14 of the original version of this paper, Adelphi Paper, no. 101; see also the chapters by Christopher Clapham and Mordechai Abir in *Conflicts in Africa*, Adelphi Paper, no. 93, especially pp. 17 and 26.
25. Robert Waring Herrick, *Soviet Naval Strategy: Fifty Years of Theory and Practice* (United States Naval Institute, Annapolis, Md., 1969), p. 149.
26. *Jane's Fighting Ships*, 1972-73 (Sampson Low, Marston, London, 1972), p. 80.
27. *Pravda*, 31 July 1960.
28. Ibid., 27 July 1969.
29. Admiral S. Gorshkov in *Morskoi sbornik* (February 1967).
30. Imre Pozsgay, in an interview published in *Magyar Hirlap*, 24 December 1972.
31. Allison, *Essence of Decision; Explaining the Cuban Missile Crisis* (Little, Brown, Boston, 1971), p. 182.
32. George F. Kennan, *Russia and the West Under Lenin and Stalin* (New American Library, New York and Toronto, 1960), p. 284.
33. Robert C. Tucker, *The Soviet Political Mind: Studies in Stalinism and Post-Stalin Change* (Pall Mall, London, 1963), p. 171.
34. *Oktiabr*, no. II (1965), pp. 147-8 and 171.
35. Roy Medvedev, *Let History Judge*, p. 362.
36. Khrushchev's 'Secret Speech'.
37. Djilas, *Conversations with Stalin*, p. 82.
38. *Pravda*, 9 February 1955.
39. As quoted by Uri Ra'anan, *The USSR Arms the Third World: Case Studies in Soviet Foreign Policy* (The MIT Press, Cambridge, Mass., 1969), p. 123.
40. *Pravda*, 30 February 1956.
41. Speech by A. I. Kirichenko to the XXIst Party Congress, ibid., 31 January 1959.
42. Michael Tatu, *Power in the Kremlin; From Krushchev to Kosygin* (Viking,

New York, 1967), pp. 364-428.

43. Irving L. Janis, 'Groupthink', *Psychology Today*, vol. 5, no. 6 (November 1971), pp. 44-6; see also the same author's *Victims of Groupthink: A Psychological Study of Foreign-Policy Decisions and Fiascos* (Houghton Mifflin, Boston, 1972).

44. *Pravda*, 30 March 1966.

45. Zbigniew Brzezinski, *Between Two Ages: America's Role in the Technetronic Era* (Viking, New York, 1970), p. 155.

46. V. Kudrov, 'Piatidesiatiletie SSSR i ekonomicheskoe sorevnovanie dvukh sistem', *Mirovaia ekonomika i mezhdunarodnye otnosheniia*, no. 10 (October 1972), p. 7.

47. For the 1972 economic results see *Pravda*, 30 January 1973.

48. Kudrov, 'Piatidesiatiletie SSSR: ekonomicheskoe sorevnovanie dvurh siste sistem', p. 9.

49. *Pravda*, 31 March 1971.

50. Ibid.

51. V. M. Kudrov, 'Glavnye kapitalisticheskie strany: sopostavitelnyi ekonomicheskii analiz', *SShA*, no. 6 (June 1972), pp. 36-40.

52. Yu. Zhukov in *Pravda*, 28 November 1972 and N. Shmelev, 'Novye gorizonty ekononicheskikh sviazei', *Mirovaia Ekonomika i Mezhdunarodnye Otnosheniia*, no. I (January 1973).

53. *The Military Balance 1973-74* (IISS, London, 1973), pp. 2, 5.

54. Colonel V. Bondarenko in *Krasnaia zvezda*, 20 August 1971.

55. M. Gladkov and B. Ivanov in *Kommunist Vooruzhennykh Sil*, no. 9 (May 1972), p. 12.

56. Brezhnev at the XXIVth Party Congress, *Pravda*, 31 March 1971.

8 THE RATIONALE FOR THE DEVELOPMENT OF SOVIET SEAPOWER

Michael MccGwire

My task is to explain the rationale for the development of Soviet seapower; to focus on the why of current developments rather than the what. This distinction is important, since it leads one to emphasize a different range of factors, each relevant to different levels of threat analysis.

The what of Soviet seapower provides the basis for contingency planning, where we focus on enemy capabilities and our own requirements, and the aim is to identify the most dangerous course of Soviet action, rather than the most likely. This can be labelled the military-tactical level of analysis.

By contrast, analysis at the politico-strategic level is primarily concerned to identify the most likely courses of Soviet action. This means we focus primarily on the why of Soviet policy and, by identifying the rationale behind past developments, we gain some understanding of the objectives and the constraints which will shape policy in the future. This requires us to look at Soviet interests, and while it is hard to be certain of what they see as being *in* their interests, it is much easier to identify what is *against* their interests. We also have to consider intentions which, given continuity of government, tend to be remarkably stable at the politico-strategic level. But probably the most important step is to assess Soviet capabilities in terms of the *requirements* they are designed to meet, and decide whether there is a surplus or shortfall of capabilities over these requirements.

A major difference between the two levels of analysis is the stance of the analyst. At the military-tactical contingency-planning level, he is looking at the situation primarily from the West's point of view and focusing on Western threat perceptions and vulnerabilities. At the politico-strategic level, the analyst is looking at it from the Russians' point of view and focusing on Soviet threat perceptions and vulnerabilities, before considering the range of opportunities that are open to them.

Obviously these different viewpoints yield very different pictures, and the level of analysis explains much of the apparent divergence of views concerning the Soviet threat. Both levels of analysis are essential, since they provide the two components of the threat equation: the type

The Rationale for the Development of Soviet Seapower

of enemy action which could take place, and the likelihood that such action will take place. The operational commander is required to focus on the first component, but higher level policymaking in peacetime requires the judicious balancing of both. Most of us are already well briefed on the first component; I am to give you my understanding of the second.

I am going to focus on the naval element of seapower, although towards the end I will touch briefly on other aspects of Soviet ocean policy. I will concentrate mainly on the last nineteen years, because contemporary naval policy, and indeed Soviet defense policy as a whole, stems from 1961; that is, the year before Cuba. But to understand this policy we must reach much further back in time, not least because most of the warships now in service stem from design decisions taken in the fifties.

For evidence, I draw on what the Soviets say and what they do. But I pay particular attention to their warship building programs, because these reflect high level decisions about the allocation of scarce resources. Detailed analysis of these programs allows one to identify the timing and the substance of past policy decisions and of subsequent shifts in policy, reflecting changes in Soviet perceptions of the threat, and the evolution of their naval requirements.[1]

Let me start by noting that for the last 200 years or so, Russia's navy has generally been the third or fourth largest in the world, although its effectiveness fluctuated widely. Russia used naval forces in the eighteenth century to help the army gain or increase her holdings on the Baltic and Black Sea coasts and, four times between 1768 and 1827, she deployed sizeable squadrons to the Mediterranean for a year or more. For three of these deployments ships were drawn from the Baltic Fleet and were used in operations against the southern side of the Black Sea exits during the wars with Turkey.

But increasingly thereafter, Russia found herself confronting predominantly maritime powers. In the Black Sea, Britain used her naval strength to prevent Russian gains at the expense of the failing Ottoman Empire; in the company of France, Britain intervened directly in what we call the Crimean War, extending her naval operations against Russia to the Baltic, White Sea, and Pacific, and the subsequent peace treaty forbade Russia a Black Sea Fleet. Twenty years later in the eighth Russo-Turkish War, British pressure ensured that Russia did not gain control of the Straits. In the Far East, Russo-Japanese rivalry culminated in the disastrous war of 1904-5, and the loss of two Russian fleets. In consequence, Russia's naval policy was increasingly dominated by the requirement to defend four widely separated areas against maritime powers who could concentrate their forces at will.

It is therefore wrong to suggest that Russia has only recently awakened to the significance of seapower. She used it in the past to her own advantage, but more often has seen its long arm used against her. Over the years she committed very substantial resources to naval construction, and the major warship building program, which was initiated after the Second World War, was the fourth attempt in 65 years to build up a strong Russian fleet: 1880, 1910, 1928, and 1945. But national strategy involves setting priorities and balancing competing claims for scarce resources. Russia was predominately a land power; the only threats to her territorial existence had come by land; the army was the basis of security at home, and of influence beyond her borders.

Substantial naval forces were indeed required to defend against assault from the sea, and to thwart attempts by maritime powers to dictate the outcome of events in areas adjoining Russia. But these forces were seen as an expensive necessity, rather than as a preferred instrument of overseas policy. One of the questions I will address at the end is the extent to which this attitude persists today.

These perceptions of Russia's naval requirements were reinforced during the interwar years. Between 1918 and 1921, Western navies provided vital support to the forces of counterrevolution. And then a naval arms race built up during the thirties. With traditional enmities now reinforced by a deep ideological cleavage, the Soviet Union was a beleagured state and had to take account of Japan in the Pacific, the Germans in the Baltic, and the possibility of the Italians joining the Turks in the Black Sea; plus, of course, the worldwide capabilities of the American, British, and French navies.

During the thirties the Soviet Union devoted substantial resources both to warship construction and to improving her naval capabilities: by linking the three western areas by inland waterway; by upgrading existing shipyards; and by building major new ones, safe from coastal assault, in the North, in the Pacific, and on the Volga. Throughout most of the thirties the Soviets only had the industrial capacity to build smaller units, and they concentrated mainly on submarines, torpedo boats, and naval aircraft. But by the end of the Third Five Year Plan in 1943 they planned to have a navy of 19 battleships and battlecruisers, 20 cruisers, 160 destroyers, over 1,500 naval aircraft, and no less than 340 submarines.

This sounds a substantial force, but in fact it would have been a fleet of short-legged ships sailed by inexperienced seamen under the

the command of novice admirals. It would have lacked carriers, radar, sonar, and much else. And, of course, this force had to be shared among four fleets. In June 1941 the Soviets had the most numerous submarine force in the world, but the great majority of these units had been designed to defend the home fleet areas against naval incursions.

The Second World War confirmed Russia's belief that ground forces were the basis of her national security. However, at the end of the war her most likely opponents were now the traditional maritime powers, who had not only been responsible for the capitalist intervention during the Revolution, but had recently demonstrated their capacity to project continental-scale armies over vast distances of sea, and to support their operations ashore. The likelihood of maritime invasion of the Baltic and Black Sea coasts was considered substantial. The Baltic gave access to the lines of communication with the Western front; the Black Sea would allow the invaders to bypass Russia's traditional defense in depth; and the rivers, instead of serving as defensive barriers, would provide the invaders with easy access to Russia's industrial heartlands. In enemy hands, the Black Sea becomes a grenade in Russia's gut.

In 1945, Russia had a powerful army but lacked a battleworthy fleet, and the navy therefore received relatively high priority in the rebuilding process, with force requirements largely carried over from before the war. Under the new, twenty-year naval construction program, no less than 1,200 submarines were to be built. We know that for certain. And I reckon that they also planned to build some 200 escorts, 200 destroyers, about 36 cruisers, 4 battlecruisers, and 4 aircraft carriers during this period, plus a mass of torpedo boats, gunboats, and subchasers, and some 5,000 aircraft in the naval air force. Large numbers; but of course nothing compared to the size of the combined Western navies at the end of the war, and even the submarines fall into perspective when divided among the four fleets. The prewar concept of defence in depth and coordinated attacks by air, submarine, and surface units were carried over. About 1,000 of the 1,200 submarines were intended for the defence of the home fleet areas, and the carriers were probably intended to extend fighter cover in the north and in the Pacific.

However, in 1954, as a consequence of the post-Stalin policy review, the Soviet leadership downgraded the threat of seaborne invasion and gave first priority to the dangers of a surprise nuclear attack by strategic bombers. The naval threat from the West was seen in more limited terms of nuclear strikes by carrier-borne aircraft, primarily against naval bases. This engendered a radical reappraisal of naval requirements and the decision to place primary reliance on long-range cruise missiles, which would be carried by small to medium surface ships, diesel submarines, and aircraft. The operational concept relied on the reach, the payload, and the accuracy of these weapons as a substitute for large numbers of weapon platforms. However, the missile systems had yet to be developed.

Khrushchev brought the 45-year-old Gorshkov to Moscow to implement these decisions. The building of cruisers was checked in mid-course; the mass-production of medium-type submarines, then building at 72 units a year, was sharply tapered to a halt; and while the destroyer, escort, and subchaser programs ran their full course, their successor classes were put back four years. This represented a sixty percent cut in annual production tonnage, enabling substantial resources to be released from warship construction to the domestic economy. Seven of the thirteen largest building ways were reassigned from naval use to the construction of fish factory and merchant ships. This shift of resources from naval to commercial construction was an important indication of Soviet priorities in the use of the sea.

The new concept of operations was predicated on engaging enemy carrier groups within range of shore-based air cover. It envisaged coordinated missile attacks by strike aircraft, diesel submarines, and large destroyers. These newly-designed units, the Badger C strike aircraft, the Juliett and Longbin missile submarines, and the Kynda missile ship, were planned to begin entering service in 1962.

However, by 1958 the key premise that shorebased fighter defence would be available over the encounter zone had been falsified by increases in the range of carrier-borne aircraft. This allowed U.S. carriers to strike at Russia with nuclear weapons from the Eastern Mediterranean and the southern reaches of the Norwegian Sea. To meet this threat from distant sea areas it was decided to place primary emphasis on nuclear submarines, which would be able to outflank the West's surface and air superiority. Plans were therefore put in hand to double nuclear submarine production (which was just beginning to yield the Hotel and November classes) to 10 boats a year, with deliveries due to begin in 1968. The recently authorized diesel submarine programs were cancelled and, as an expedient, their long-range missile systems were used to reconfigure nuclear submarines as SSBN: the Echo classes. Meanwhile, the development of a horizon-range submarine missile with its own target location capability was put in hand.

At this same period in 1957-58, a requirement to extend the range of ASW coverage beyond that provided by shore-based helicopters was identified, particularly in northern waters, where the Soviets assumed

The Rationale for the Development of Soviet Seapower 215

the U.S. Polaris submarines would patrol. This generated the requirement for the *Moskva* class of antisubmarine helicopter carriers.

So far, I have only talked of those forces directly involved in the defence of the home fleet areas, and I must now backtrack to pick up the task of "strategic", or long-range delivery. At the end of the war, the torpedo-firing diesel submarine was the only weapon system available to the Soviets which had the range and payload to bring atomic weapons to bear on North America. This, combined with the navy's tradition of daring attacks on enemy ports, led to the navy being given the task of long-range delivery. A nuclear warhead for a torpedo which, presumably, was to be exploded in such places as the approaches to New York or Hampton Roads, was probably developed by 1954, and a ballistic missile was fired from a submarine in 1955. This led to four classes of submarine which began to appear in 1958: two diesel, the Foxtrot and Golf, and two nuclear, the November and Hotel, one of each armed only with torpedos, and the other carrying missiles. However, problems (the nuclear classes were noisy and unreliable and the missile-armed classes had an unreliable weapon system), coupled with advances in American antisubmarine capabilities meant that at least three of these four classes were unable to meet planned operational requirements. The torpedo-armed Novembers were therefore re-tasked after Cuba), the role of the missile-armed submarines was curtailed, plans for the navy's future contribution to long-range nuclear delivery were cancelled and, as we have seen, the second half-generation of nuclear submarines, the Echo II class, was reconfigured for the anti-carrier role, as were the last five units of the first half-generation. The Echo1 Is were later converted back to straight torpedo-firing submarines.

This brings us up to the crucial year of 1961, but before moving forward let me summarize what I have said. During its first forty years, Soviet naval policy and the allocation of resources to naval policy and the allocation of resources to naval construction reflected their perceptions of the threat of assault on Russia from the sea. After World War II we see first the mass-construction programs designed to meet a misperceived threat, which was incorrectly inferred from the capitalists' war-inflated navies and from a Marxist prognosis of history. This is followed by savage cuts in shipyard allocations when the likelihood of seaborne invastion was realised to be low. And then we have the heavy investment in nuclear submarine construction facilities, responding to the new and correctly-perceived threat from carrier-borne strike aircraft, and to the need to oppose them in Western-dominated waters.

Meanwhile, Soviet efforts to develop a counter to the maritime capability of the West were continually thwarted by technological advances, which rendered program after program obsolescent before the units had even entered service. Of the 23 important classes of submarines and major surface ships whose construction was decided on in the late '40s, only five of the earlier surface types ran to schedule. By the middle '50s, all programmes had been radically altered. Nor did the decisions taken in 1954 and in 1957-8 fare any better, and we have a continuing picture of cancellations, adaptations, and expedients. These facts are important to current Western assessments since, in crude terms, about 75 percent of the Soviet Navy's distant-water surface ships and over 60 percent of their submarines stem from design decisions taken during these years. The remainder are of more recent origin.

As we move in to the current period, we must broaden our perspective and I want to focus briefly on a significant double shift (or wiggle) in Soviet defence policy during a twenty-month period in 1960-61. In January 1960, Khrushchev announced the result of what appears to have been a thoroughgoing defence review, which included the formation of the Strategic Rocket Force, its designation as the primary arm of the nation's defence, a substantial reorganisation of military research and development, and the cutting back of conventional ground forces. Given Khrushchev's faith in nuclear missiles and his belief that nuclear war would be suicidal, the new policy could only indicate a shift in emphasis towards the Western concept of nuclear deterrence, and away from the traditional reliance on balanced forces and a warfighting capability. But by October 1961 the shift had been reversed and at the 22nd Party Congress, Marshal Malinovsky's speech clearly indicated a return to the traditional military values. Meanwhile, a thoroughgoing reappraisal of what was involved in fighting with nuclear weapons and the development of a whole series of consequential policies appears to have been put in hand.

What caused this reversal? It was clearly a blow to Khrushchev's policies and vindicated those who argued that professional military opinion should prevail in matters of national defence. Bureaucratic politics is too facile an explanation; there must have been some significant change in what Soviets call the "objective factors" to have tilted a recently achieved balance of opinion within the leadership back to earlier policies, and by far the most plausible would be a change in threat perceptions. There is now a substantial body of evidence that the range of defence policy decisions announced by President Kennedy shortly after taking office in January 1961, engendered just such a reevaluation of the threat, and prompted the various measures which can be dated to this period. These included a very sharp acceleration of

The Rationale for the Development of Soviet Seapower

the Polaris program and a doubling of the planned production rate of solid-fuel ICBMs, which would be deployed in underground silos remote from centres of population. Perhaps equally important in terms of Soviet threat perceptions was the crusading rhetoric of the new administration, with its willingness to go any place, pay any price, and the detached logic of the tough-minded academic strategists who were thinking the unthinkable, and developing theories of limited nuclear war. In the circumstances it is not surprising that the Soviet leadership decided that they could not rely on nuclear deterrence, despite its obvious economic attractions, and applied themselves instead to the problems of fighting and winning a nuclear war, the likelihood of which appeared to have increased.

To understand the cluster of decisions that were taken in 1961, four related points concerning Soviet military doctrine must be borne in mind. First, Marxism sees international relations as conflictual, and the Soviet Union has always taken the possibility of major war very seriously. While its assessments as to the likelihood of war with the West have varied over the years, the Soviet leadership has never wavered in its belief that a strong military capability is the best way of making it less likely.

Second, Soviet military doctrine does not separate out the idea of "nuclear deterrence" from the general concept of defence. Defence of the Soviet Union depends on the capability to repel, or at least absorb any attack, and then go on to win the subsequent war. The Soviets obviously hope that their defence capability will be sufficient to dissuade an aggressor, which is of course deterrence in its traditional sense. But the crucial distinction between this and the Western concept of "nuclear deterrence" is implicit in the comment that "if the deterrent has to be used, it will have failed". The Soviets do not entertain such ideas. Should war come, their defence will only have failed if their armed forces are unable to recover and go on to final victory. This emphasis on defence through war-fighting is central to Soviet military doctrine. While Western theorists saw nuclear weapons as a means of threatening "unacceptable damage" to Russia, the Soviet Union saw them as integral to her fighting capability. Where the West thought in terms of credibility, argued about the arcane merits of counterforce and counter-value, or worried about stabilising and destabilising developments, the Soviets focused on achieving victory in war. It is true that Khrushchev, and Malenkov before him, expressed the opinion that there could be no winners in nuclear war, and as we have seen, advocated some form of deterrence policy, partly as a means of reducing military expenditures. But in the final analysis, neither was successful, because the security-conscious collective leadership was unwilling to base the defence of the homeland on an untested theory.

Which leads to the third point. This readiness to think through the implications of the nuclear arms race does not imply that the Soviet Union would willingly embark on nuclear war with the West. Marxist-Leninist theory lays down that the *initiation* of war as a deliberate act of policy can only be justified if (a) victory is virtually certain, and (b) the gains clearly outweigh the costs. War with the West meets neither of these criteria since by definition, such a war would be a world war and, again by definition, world war involves a fight to the finish between the two social systems. Defeat would be synonymous with extinction. Victory comes from survival. It is this catastrophic consequence of defeat which explains why, despite the admittedly low probability of such a war occuring, that preparations to fight and win one continue to be given such high priority within the Soviet Union.

Which brings us to the fourth point. Plans to cover the contingency of world war must provide for two equally important sets of objectives. The first focuses on *extirpating the capitalist system,* by such means as destroying its forces, its war-making potential, and its structure of government. The second set focuses on preserving the socialist system which, besides protecting the structure of government and ensuring the survival of some proportion of the working population and industrial base, must also aim to secure an alternative economic base which can contribute to the rebuilding of a socialist society. The implications of these dual sets of objectives are fairly self-evident, particularly in regard to the requirements for effective civil defence, the priority in locating ABM sites, the preferred size of missile inventories, and the importance of NATO Europe as an alternative economic base.

In the light of these four points, let us now consider the impact of the Kennedy decisions on Soviet naval developments. Acceleration of the Polaris program highlighted a trend which has been alluded to repeatedly in Soviet pronouncements, namely the shift in emphasis from land-to sea-based nuclear delivery systems, which the Soviets claimed constituted one-third of the U.S. inventory in 1966, rising to one-half in 1970. What underlay this shift in emphasis? When Polaris became operational, its most vaunted characteristic was its invulnerability which, in Western deterrence theory, provided an "assured response". But from the Soviet point of view, the more important implication of this invulnerability was that these missiles could be held back from the initial nuclear exchange, with the fair certainty that they would remain available for use at a subsequent stage of the war. So, too, could carrier-based nuclear strike aircraft.

The Rationale for the Development of Soviet Seapower 219

The capacity of sea-based systems to survive the initial exchange affected two aspects of Soviet military doctrine. First, strategic reserves. Largely ignored by nuclear deterrence theory, the requirement for strategic reserves is integral to the concept of war-fighting with nuclear weapons. Soviet strategy must assume that the availability of nuclear weapons may be critical at certain stages of a war, and that he who is in sole possession of a substantial capability is likely to determine both the final outcome of the war and the political structure of the postwar world. Since the West was acquiring sea-based systems which could be withheld from the initial exchange, the Soviet Union had at least to match this capability for deferred strikes. But the military planners had also to provide against the emergence of capitalist power bases outside the NATO area, such as Australia, South Africa, and Brazil.

The second aspect was the potential availability of NATO Europe as an alternative base from which to help rebuild the socialist system. This meant that Western Europe must be occupied rather than ravaged, and required a concept of political and military operations that limited battle damage to the minimum. The importance of Europe in this role was increased by the fact that America had no comparable option, since potential areas like Canada were targeted by Russia. However, this advantage would be lost if, after the Soviet occupation of Europe, Western sea-based strategic systems could deny Russia its use.

Of the problems which faced the Soviets in 1961, the simplest was to provide the sea-based weapons which would serve as the national strategic reserve. Although the navy had previously been relieved of its strategic role, the Soviets were already committed to increasing the rate of nuclear submarine construction from five submarines a year to ten, with deliveries starting in 1968. It was therefore possible to provide six ballistic missile submarines and four attack submarines annually for the ten-year production run 1968-77, although this change to the configuration-mix did cause major disruption to shipyard assembly facilities, the SSBNs being almost twice as large as the attack submarines which had already been intended.

Given their problems with the West's antisubmarine capability, it seems likely that the 1,600-mile SS-N-6 carried by the Yankee was an interim solution, with the 4,200-mile SS-N-8, which could be fired from home waters, as their final objective.

In contrast, the problem of providing a counter to Western sea-based systems was immensely complex. However, the triple potential of these systems, as part of the initial exchange, as the core of the West's strategic reserve, and as the means of preventing Soviet use of NATO Europe, meant they ranked high among the various threats to Russia.

And paradoxically, the most important objective, that of denying the West the option of withholding nuclear weapons for use at a later stage of the war, would be somewhat simpler to achieve than the less critical aim of limiting damage during the initial exchange. To achieve the first objective, it should only be necessary to pose a threat to sea-based systems that was sufficient to persuade the West to use those weapons while it could. This required that the U.S. submarines (and, for that matter, the carriers) be attacked at the very onset of war and meant that Soviet forces would have to be within weapon-range contact at the vital moment. Soviet surface ships and submarines must be predeployed in the seas where the threat lay.

Herein lies the genesis of the Soviet Navy's shift to forward deployment and, as I bring the story through to the present, let me emphasize that for the time being I will continue to focus exclusively on the navy's war-related mission. I will come back to the emergence of the peacetime role later on, but on the basis of a fair amount of evidence I remain convinced that strategic imperatives of the kind I have outlined provided both necessary and sufficient cause for the decision that, despite its manifest inadequacies, the Soviet Navy should be required to move forward in strategic defence.

The shift to forward deployment appears to have been decided upon in principle by the end of 1961, but the debate about means continued until 1963 or 1964 and, as Gorshkov has said, the new requirements demanded "the organic restructuring of the fleet and the reorientation of traditional naval policy and operational habits". The policy that finally emerged was shaped by several persistent tendencies. First, we have the traditional Russian spirit of technical and conceptual innovation and a readiness to adopt new but unproven technological advances. Second, a keen awareness that the best is the enemy of the good and, particularly where defensive responses are involved, a willingness to invest in ten per cent solutions, rather than wait until the complete answer is found. Third, a belief in the progressive application of new concepts and capabilities, as they become available; there are often discreet phases of initial, interim, and final application. In part, this is the "Don't just sit there, DO something" attitude, but it is also a conscious form of operational evaluation and development. Fourth, a readiness to take a very long view, and to persist with a problem until some type of solution is achieved.

Fifth, we have ground-force domination of military strategy and military policy which has, at times, required the navy to undertake tasks that violate traditional naval assumptions and has forced the navy to develop radical concepts. An example of this is the application of long-range surface-to-surface missiles to warships in the mid-1950s, overriding naval objections. Another is the deployment, ten years later, of ill-armed ships to the Mediterranean to act as forward observation posts to call down shore-based fire on U.S. carriers, although they themselves were easily sunk. Sixth, the heavy emphasis on a combined arms approach to military problems. This has had an invigorating effect on the development of Soviet naval doctrine, which has come to incorporate what are essentially ground-force concepts, such as theatres of military operations. It has also ensured that the resources of *all* relevant branches are deployed to meet any serious threat to the homeland, including those which come from the sea. And seventh, there is the concept of area defence which, though originating in the army, is fundamental to Soviet naval strategy, and is worth elaborating.

The concept of area defence is based on two main zones: an inner one, where local superiority of force allows command of the sea to be secured; and an outer zone, where command of the sea is actively contested. The greater part of Soviet naval policy and procurement since the 1920s can be explained in terms of the Soviets' attempts to extend their maritime defence perimeter and, within it, the zone of effective command.

As you know, the Soviet Navy is split among four widely separated fleets. If these individual fleets are to be ensured the superiority of force necessary to establish command in their respective areas, they must be able to deny the enemy the opportunity to concentrate his forces against any one fleet. This is most economically achieved by seizing the exits from the fleet areas, thus denying the enemy into those areas. In this particular respect, Russia is favoured by her geography. Three of her main fleet areas comprise semi-enclosed seas, and access to the Northern Fleet is canalised by ice during much of the year. Only Petropavlovsk lacks any geographical advantage of this kind.

Until 1961 the navy's primary concern was therefore to extend the inner zone of effective command to these natural defensive barriers, all of which now are held by NATO allies (Norway, Denmark, and Turkey) and would have to be seized by Soviet forces in the event of war. The outer zones did not reach far beyond these geographic constrictions and were primarily seen as areas where the reinforcement of the enemy forces defending these barriers could be interdicted. It was therefore natural that part of the Soviet response to the threat from Western sea-based nuclear weapons was to extend these outer defence zones, but this could only provide a partial solution. A comprehensive answer to the problem required some means of knowing continuously the location of the enemy's long-range nuclear delivery units wherever they might be, and the capability to strike them on command. This would be hard enough to achieve against carrier task forces; against ballistic missile submarines the problem was truly daunting. The Soviets nevertheless embarked on this difficult and expensive road and their incremental approach to the problem was typical. First, do what you can, with what is available. Meanwhile, put in hand a series of projects ranging from the short to the very long term, each aimed at progressively improving that capability and ultimately achieving an acceptable solution.

The Soviet response involved two overlapping concepts, area defence and long-range interdiction and, in terms of operational deployment, the ordering of priorities was fairly clear. Set at 1,500 miles (the range of the Polaris A-2 missile) and centred on Moscow, the arc of threat took in the Norwegian Sea and the Eastern Mediterranean, areas where Western strike forces were already operating. Extended to 2,500 miles (the range of the A-3 missile) the arc cut across the Atlantic from beyond Greenland to the African coast abreast the Canaries and then crossed the Arabian Sea between the Horn of Africa and Bombay.

The first requirement was to extend the limits of the outer defence zone to the 1,500-mile arc-of-threat and then progressively develop the capability to contest, and perhaps ultimately to deny, the use of these waters by Western long-range nuclear forces. Initially, this would involve an increasingly active naval presence, backed by shore-based missiles and aircraft. But new systems would be required to counter the submarines in these areas.

The second requirement was to acquire the capability for naval and air operations beyond this outer defence zone, in order to develop a counter to the longer-range Polaris A-3 system and its successors, and also to cover carrier deployments from American bases. In the short term these distant operations might have to depend on naval shore facilities in foreign lands. But in the longer term it was hoped to develop autonomous systems, such as reconnaissance satellites, anti-naval missiles emplaced ashore, and new classes of submarines, which would not have to rely on the good will of foreign rulers and would provide a truly worldwide response to the threat of strikes from the sea.

Such a policy is easy enough to describe but, besides the intrinsic difficulties of locating and destroying the targets, we must recall some of the circumstances. First, in 1961 the Soviet Navy was at an ebb as a result of the cutbacks in naval construction which stemmed from the 1954 decisions, and the further disruptions arising from the reversal of plans in 1957-58. All the existing surface ships and many of the submarines had been designed to operate within shore-based air cover, most of the ships, surface and submarine, in the current building programs were designed to fight carriers, and 60 percent of future nuclear submarine construction was reserved for long-range nuclear strike.

Second, the Soviet Navy was being required to move forward into seas where the West enjoyed overwhelming maritime preponderance. The concept of relying on the freedom of the seas and the "protection of peace" to safeguard the deployment of illarmed ships (particularly in the Mediterranean) was daring, given the tenor of debate in the West at that time, which included proposals for maritime countermeasures, such as seizing Soviet ships at sea, against Soviet pressure on Berlin.

And third, the army-dominated Soviet leadership was skeptical of surface ships, and even when they conceded a need for such ships it had to be met from within the navy's agreed-upon shipbuilding allocation.

The surface ships programmes give a good indication of the new priorities. During the 1960s we see a shift from anti-surface to anti-submarine systems of armament and an increased emphasis on the ships' survivability. As an interim measure, the ASW and SAM systems intended for the Kynda and Kresta programs were used to convert ill-armed Kotlin and Krupny class destroyers into effective antisubmarine ships. The Kynda class, the first of which Khrushchev described as a "floating coffin" at her commissioning ceremony, was cancelled at four ships, the yard facilities thereafter being used to build five extra Kashins. The *Moskva* program was cancelled at two ships. The cancelled ships' ASW and SAM systems were transferred to the Krestas, changing their primary role from anti-surface warfare to antisubmarine warfare. The *Moskva* class, designed to operate within a few hundred miles of friendly airfields able both to supply spare helicopters and provide air cover and support, would be inefficient for distant-water operations, and those ships therefore were succeeded by the *Kievs,* with over twice the aircraft capacity and a better defence capability.

Looking ahead to the end of the Kashin program, its successor, the Krivak, would be specialised for ASW, as would a new cruiser-size ship, the Kara. However, to start both Kara and Krivak and complete the Kresta II program, it would be necessary to drop the escort-sized ship from the inventory. This meant not providing a replacement for the Petya. The effect of these decisions was to introduce into the fleet a substantial number of ships intended primarily for distant deployments, ships which were quite different from those designed to operate within range of shore-based air cover and other forms of support. Meanwhile, no provision was made for any substantial increase in afloat support.

In relation to the new requirements being levied on the navy, the allocation of resources to shipbuilding was niggardly, the more so when we consider the scale of naval construction which had been authorised in the West at this time. We therefore can say with some certainty that in the first half of the sixties, the navy was still seen in Moscow as an expensive instrument of overseas policy.

The first phase of the shift to forward deployment, involving the progressive extension of the outer defence zone, lasted through 1967. In the Norwegian Sea it was not all that difficult to increase the range of Northern (and later Baltic) Fleet operations and it became standard practice for Northern Fleet ships and aircraft to deploy whenever significant Western forces operated in the area, with the NATO carriers being targeted by Soviet surface, air, and submarine missile systems.

In the Mediterranean, where the Sixth Fleet was deployed, and Russia had just been evicted from its Albanian base, the problem was immeasurably greater. The Soviet Navy did not attempt a sustained presence until 1964 and even then operational activity remained low and intermittent. The main emphasis was on trailing the U.S. strike carriers when they operated in the Eastern Mediterranean and, since missile-armed units were not always present, it can be assumed that the resulting target location data was for use by systems ashore such as ballistic missiles and strike aircraft based in southwestern Russia. The Soviets did not begin to be effective in the Mediterranean until they gained access to Egyptian ports and airfields following the 1967 war. Thereafter we see a progressive improvement in terms of numbers of ships and combat effectiveness until about 1972, when the trend levels off. By then, both in the Norwegian Sea and in the Eastern Mediterranean, the Soviet Navy could deploy an effective challenge to the strike carrier. The Soviets, however, had no comparable capability against the Polaris submarine in these areas, despite the steadily increasing emphasis on ASW.

The second phase of the shift to forward deployment began in 1967. This took in the 2,500 mile circle of threat and also addressed the problem of the U.S. Fleet's bases in North America and the U.S. Navy's transit routes across the Atlantic. After testing and rejecting the feasibility of providing mid-ocean support to anti-carrier submarines, we see the search for shore facilities with Cienfuegos in Cuba, Conakry in Guinea, and Berbera in Somalia, as the chosen hosts. A Cuban base would reduce submarine time-in-transit to America's eastern seaboard from twenty days to about four. West Africa, or better still the Cape Verde Islands, gave access to the Canary Basin, straddling the

Mediterranean approaches. Somalia provided a *point d'appui* in the northwest quadrant of the Indian Ocean. This latter is often misread as the Soviets rushing in to fill a vacuum left by the British, but the hydrographic precursors to the Soviet deployment were active in the area during 1967, at a time when British defence policy was still firmly committed to its role east of Suez. Meanwhile, the Arabian Sea provides better target coverage of Russia and China by a 2,500-mile missile, than does any other sea area. Long-standing Soviet suspicions about its use as a launch area for Polaris and Poseidon had been fueled by the 1963 agreement to build a U.S. Navy VLF communications station at North West Cape in Australia. Those suspicions were reinforced in 1966 by the agreement on the combined British and U.S. use of Diego Garcia near the centre of the Indian Ocean, with America paying the costs of developing the base.

By 1971, the worldwide Soviet pattern of deployment was clearly established, and within a year or two the buildup had levelled off. There is little doubt that during the later stages of this extended process some of the original reasons for the shift to forward deployment would have been eroded and overlaid with new ones, including the navy's emerging peacetime role. Nevertheless, we should not underestimate the persistence of the original rationale, which stemmed from the Soviet emphasis on contingency planning for world war. And while a fuller realization by the Soviets of the problems inherent in countering Polaris may have cast doubt on the value of these interim measures, the chastening discovery of just how long it took to develop any effective operational capability in distant seas meant that they had better start practising right away at what they could do, with the thought that thereby eventually they would develop suitable ships, equipment, and methods.

The decisions taken between 1961 and 1964 go a long way towards explaining both the present structure of the Soviet navy and a substantial part of its operational practices and patterns of deployment. But of course policies evolve and new requirements emerge, and towards the end of the sixties a cluster of developments combined to have a major effect on the navy's war-related priorities.

Probably the most significant were reports in 1967-68 that the U.S. Navy was intending to develop two new classes of submarine for service in 1973-74, one very fast and the other very silent, the latter being specifically designed to operate against Soviet SSBNs. This, of course, had major implications for the Soviet decision to embody a substantial part of the nation's long-range nuclear reserve in ballistic missile submarines. It highlighted the requirement to defend these new ships, just then beginning to enter service, against U.S. incursions. The important fact was that the Americans were actually talking about going after those submarines. That was what worried the Soviets. The fact that in due course the U.S. Navy built only one very silent submarine is not relevant to Soviet perceptions at the time.

Meanwhile, as more antisubmarine systems became available, mounted in surface ships, submarines, and aircraft, it must have become increasingly clear that however innovative their methods, the traditional ASW instruments embodied in these units had inherent limitations, and an effective solution to the Polaris and Poseidon problem would have to wait on the results of research and development still in progress.

Taken together, these two events engendered a shift away from developing a conventional ASW capability in distant waters (as part of the counter to Polaris) towards extending the inner defence zones in the Northern Fleet area and in the Pacific off Kamchatka, and providing them with watertight antisubmarine defences which would turn them into ocean "bastions" where SSBN could deploy in safety. Because ASW units can be brushed aside by superior forces, it would be necessary to establish command of both these sea areas.

To meet these changed requirements, the navy would need improved capabilities and, for a start, it was agreed that the follow-on classes to the Kara and Kresta programs (which would be due to begin delivery in 1980), would be some 25-30 percent bigger, allowing larger weapon loads and greatly increased combat endurance. A scaling-up process was also applied to the amphibious program, the Polnocny size being dropped from the inventory, the Alligator size carrying on (Ropuchka), and a much larger ship, the *Ivan Rogov* class, being added. The latter and the new *Berezina* class of underway replenishment ship are notable for being relatively heavily armed with self-defence systems, reflecting a new emphasis on being able to survive in hostile waters.

These follow-on classes would all be built within the navy's existing allocation of shipyard facilities. It was, however, decided to add a completely new type of ship to the surface program, a heavily armed nuclear-powered battle cruiser, which would be able to provide the command facilities which had been found so essential to forward deployment. This addition to the program required the return to naval use of construction facilities which had been turned over to civilian shipbuilding in the mid-fifties.

On the submarine side, it was probably already planned that at the end of the ten-year buildup of SSBN in 1977, resources would be moved across to correct the dearth of SSN for use in the ASW role. However, the final details of the follow-on programs were probably held over until the performance of the Alpha prototypes could be evaluated, and the full impact of the SALT negotiations was known.

This is what appears to have been agreed at the 24th Party Congress which approved the 9th Five Year Plan in the spring of 1971. However, the navy did not consider that these additions would be sufficient to meet the new demands being placed on it. Having lost the argument within the planning process, it decided to take its case against the army-dominated military leadership to a wider audience by means of the articles in *Morskoj sbornik* which we refer to as "the Gorshkov series". This debate had wide ramifications which I will come to later, but a major strand of the argument concerned the importance of general purpose forces and the need for a greater range of surface ship types, not excluding aircraft carriers.[2] It appears that by mid-1974 the navy had won at least part of its case, and an additional class of surface ship, comparable in size to the Kresta replacement, was added to the plan to allow for task specialisation between classes. More important, the leadership seems to have accepted that the new concept of operations would require effective seabased air support, and it appears that an aircraft carrier program was authorised, with the first ship due to enter service in the mid-eighties.

This brings my explanation of the Soviet navy's Western-oriented war-related role through to the present. Before turning to consider the implications of the added threat from China, let me touch briefly on specific missions in the event of war with the West. Bear in mind what was said about the reality of world war in Soviet contingency planning and accept that, irrespective of argument about the nature of nuclear war and its possible length, the Soviet planner must think not only of a post-exchange phase, but of subsequent phases through to its resolution. This emphasis on war-fighting, which must allow for the disruption of supply systems and base facilities, has major implications for the employment or withholding of forces in the initial stage of a war. It also heightens the awareness that war is in large part a matter of attrition and that victory goes to the side that gives up last. This awareness leads to the principle of never allowing an enemy weapon or force a free ride and to the continuing use of not-very-good and obsolescent weapons in order to complicate the enemy's problems.

The navy's most important mission is the contribution it makes to the Soviet long-range nuclear strike capability, and the SSBN force now has three overlapping roles: intercontinental strike, continental strike, and national strategic reserve. Endless permutations of targeting, deployment, and timing in these overlapping roles are possible, but they all raise the requirement that the submarines be kept secure against attack until such time as they have launched their missiles. As we have seen, the Soviets adopted the concept of ocean "bastions", which gave a new urgency to the requirement to establish command of the inner defence zones in the North and the Pacific. But it also gave a new importance to the outer defence zone and (to focus on the Northern Fleet area), whereas in the past, the Soviets have been primarily concerned to deny command of the Norwegian Sea to the West, they are now concerned to secure command for themselves, as a means of strengthening the outer defences of the SSBN bastions.

Soviet submarines would play a key role in these operations, but to be effective they needed surface ship support — a point emphasised by Gorshkov. This new concept therefore had its major impact on surface ship requirements, since Soviet naval constructors could no longer think in terms of some "D-Day Shootout", where ships only had to survive long enough to discharge their primary mission. Instead, the Soviets now had to prepare for the kind of sustained operations necessary to gain and maintain command of a large sea area, requiring long endurance, large weapon loads, and an underway replenishment capability. Further (as Gorshkov remarked in his book), command of a sea area is greatly facilitated by control of the adjoining coast, and this raised the new requirement for a long-range heavy assault lift, suitable for seizing key islands and/or stretches of the Norwegian coast. The Soviet navy also had to assume that in the post-exchange phase, it would be operating without shore-based air support, in the face of a U.S. carrier capability. This raised the requirement for a more ambitious type of sea-based air than that provided by the *Kiev* class, not so much to protect the major surface units (which could continue to rely mainly on SAM and other weapon sytems), as to deny the U.S. navy the use of the air in support of its ASW operations, and to allow the Soviets to use air ASW in their operations against U.S. hunter/killer submarines. Command of the sea subsumes command of the air above it and, army doubts notwithstanding, there was a clear requirement for air superiority carrier in the post-exchange phase.

So much for nuclear strike. The Soviets attach equal importance to the mission of countering Western sea-based nuclear strike systems. This is only common sense, given the concepts of war-fighting and of strategic reserves; moreover, the mission provides the bonus of damage limitation. However, we must distinguish between the priority the Soviets accord the mission, and their ability to discharge it, particularly as concerns the problem of countering Polaris, Poseidon and, in due course, Trident. Even today, we have difficulty in distinguishing between the evidence which reflects what the Soviets are *aspiring* to

The Rationale for the Development of Soviet Seapower

do, and that which reflects what their still limited capability *allows* the them to do. We know that from the start they recognised that the complexity of the Polaris problem would require the application of all available resources, including involvement by other branches of service besides the navy. On the basis of past practice, we can assume that they have pursued all three of the available lines of attack (exclusion, trailing, and area search/surveillance), and I have already described their initial and interim responses aimed at achieving a modicum of exclusion by extending their defence zones. It was probably hoped that ten years would be sufficient to develop a range of measures which, beginning in 1972-73, would allow some kind of final response along each of the three lines of attack, even if they needed further improvement. As usually happens when the Soviets try to move from an imaginative concept to its practical application, they were unable to meet their timetable and meanwhile circumstances changed, but hindsight allows us to postulate the outline of their final response, as originally envisaged.

To exclude Polaris/Poseidon from the more favourable launch areas, it was probably intended to start consolidating the ASW capability in the newly-extended outer defence zones. By 1972-73, the buildup of specialised ASW forces (surface, air, and submarine) would be significant, and it may also have been planned that a WIG-type vehicle with its capacity for high-speed low-level search, would add a new dimension to this essentially conventional capability. It was probably assumed that these measures, supplemented by those developed for the other two lines of attack, would prove a sufficient threat to encourage the United States to withdraw their SSBN from these forward areas. The second line of attack was trailing. Given their state of the art in the early sixties, the most readily available means of providing continuous target-location data was to use active sonar to trail a Polaris SSBN with another submarine. The essential requirement was a speed and depth advantage over the quarry, and it seems probable that the Alpha was designed with this task in mind, reflecting the natural (if incorrect) assumption that any successor to the Polaris submarine would have a significantly improved performance. The third line of attack was area search/surveillance. Russia's geographic situation, coupled with their technological disadvantage in acoustic detection, virtually forced the Soviets to place their major emphasis on discovering other ways of detecting a submerged submarine and developing original means of doing so. Western statements make it clear that the Soviets did indeed take this route, including the development of space-based systems. And finally, assuming that they could solve the problem of location, it seems likely that they intended to use ballistic missiles to sink the submarine, as I explain below.

It is difficult to assess the present state of Soviet progress in developing a counter to the Polaris/Trident systems. The adoption of the defended bastion concept for their own SSBN has placed an increased emphasis on the outer defence zones in the Norwegian Sea and Northwest Pacific, to the detriment of plans for the Eastern Mediterranean and the Arabian Sea. It would seem that the development of the Alpha proved more difficult than had been foreseen, seriously delaying the series production of this class, and meanwhile the problem of initial attachment has still to be solved. And while it is hard to be certain of their progress in non-acoustic methods of detection, there are as yet no clear indications of a major breakthrough in this field or in space-based surveillance systems. However, although it is difficult to know the present level of achievement, there is every reason to assume that the Soviets are persisting in their efforts to develop an effective counter to the SSBN, and are probably still pursuing all three of these mutually-supportive lines of attack.

Turning from Polaris to the strike carrier, the Soviets appear to have developed a reasonably effective range of responses to this threat, even though it took them the best part of twenty years to do so. The requirements for locating and attacking the carriers are handled somewhat differently in each of the three main types of scenario. We are all familiar with the meeting engagement or encounter, which would take place in the approaches to the Norwegian Sea or in the northwestern Pacific and involves in-depth defence with coordinated attacks. In the Mediterranean the continuous-company scenario presents the Sixth Fleet with a difficult problem, but I suspect the evolution of this successful concept was no more foreseen by the Soviets than by us. It raises a couple of points: first, the need to be able to strike instantaneously places a premium on deployed forces, particularly the missile submarines, and it seems likely that shorebased aircraft such as the Backfire will only have a follow-up role. I would, however, expect the ships of the Sixth Fleet to be targetted by IRBM and MRBM emplaced in southwest Russia. Second, the shift in priority from conventional ASW to securing the SSBN bastions in the Norwegian Sea and the Pacific, suggests that nowadays the primary role of Soviet ASW forces in the Mediterranean is to protect anti-surface missile units from preemptive U.S. attack.

The distant targeting scenario covers those carriers which do not immediately threaten Russia, but if not disposed of would contribute to the West's strategic reserve. Target location of these ships is provided by air and satellite reconnaissance, by surface and submarine pickets, and sometimes by trailing. Probably the Soviets hoped originally to meet the sink-on-command component of the anti-carrier and anti-Polaris missions with a common strike system. Two methods were probably envisaged, both relying on terminally-guided ballistic missiles: from ashore ICBMs and IRBMs; and from afloat shorter range weapons carried by submarines, strategically deployed. The present status of the concept is not clear. In 1972 the Soviets explicitly claimed they could attack surface forces from ashore. At this same period they were actively developing a submarine-launched tactical ballistic missile for use against ships, but the system appears to have been shelved in 1973. Quite apart from any technical difficulties with the latter, the Soviets may well have run into problems with SALT. If, as seems quite likely, it had been decided in the sixties to push ahead with the application of sea-based ballistic missiles against ships, the SALT limits may well have stifled the development just as it was reaching fruition and this would have created serious problems for the navy.

These, then, are the two main maritime missions: contributing to Soviet long-range nuclear strike and countering the West's sea-based strike capability. Of the other missions, I will only mention the interdiction of Western sea communications. There is some argument in the West as to the priority the Soviets accord this mission, and whether priority will be given to terminals or to ships in transit. There is also argument within the Soviet military about the importance of this mission. But this obscures the point that, irrespective of the significance the Soviets attach to Western sea communications, merchant ships are virtually certain to be attacked at the outbreak of war as a means of pinning down Western forces and, more important, of diverting them from assaulting the Northern Fleet's inner defence zone and attacking the ballistic missile submarines therein.

Let me also reemphasise how important the underlying concept of area defence is to so many of the navy's tasks, whether it be supporting military operations ashore, countering the projection of hostile military forces, or protecting coastal communications. Particularly in the inner defence zone, we are talking of establishing command of the sea, and it is relevant that in recent writings there is a new emphasis on the importance of this traditional concept.

Finally, a word about the naval implications of a war with China. Developments during 1969 increased the possibility of such a war. Taken together with the other political developments discussed below, this meant that it became a more likely contingency than war with the

West, and this was reflected in the adjustment of Soviet naval priorities which took place at the start of the seventies. It had to be assumed that in the event of a war with China, the Trans-Siberian railway would be cut and that the Far Eastern Front would be supplied by sea. This introduced the requirement to protect such shipments from the Chinese navy, which includes the third largest submarine force in the world.

But this threat to shipping reached back to the north-western parts of the Indian Ocean, where it could be posed by Chinese forces using friendly bases (eg. Pakistan or, in those days, South Yemen), by U.S. forces, or even by regional navies. The timely arrival of military supplies would be critical to the land battle in the Far East and, if circumstances prevented their shipment via the Red Sea, the Soviets would have to exploit the route used by the Allies in the two world wars, shipping down across Iran and out through the Persian Gulf. The Soviets have other naval requirements in that area since, in the event of world war, they most probably plan to move south to control the Gulf area and naval forces will be needed in the seaward approaches to fend off assaults by U.S. strike carriers and amphibious groups. But the heightened threat of war with China increased the strategic significance of the Arabian Sea, more than compensating for the shift in emphasis away from developing the means to counter Polaris in the area. The ground forces were now involved and the Soviet military investment in Somalia took off after Marshal Greckho's visit in February 1972, indicating that the provision of naval support facilities in the area was no longer a narrowly naval concern, but a matter of national defence requirements.

We can now go back to pick up the navy's peacetime role. Just as the wartime role can only be understood within the broader context of Soviet military doctrine, so must the peacetime mission be placed within the context of Soviet foreign policy. It is important to keep in mind the ordering of their primary foreign objectives. First, to avoid world war, but if it is inevitable, to win. Second, to ensure the Communist Party's retention of power in Russia. And third, to increase the Soviet Union's share of world influence at the expense of the West and of course China. More than for most states, these objectives involve major contradictions, as for example between the defence burden and the party's acceptability, between détente and ideological control, between the dangers of escalation and the need for confrontation, and between the ideological struggle with capitalism and the domestic requirement to upgrade technology and productivity.

For over twenty years the long-term strategy has been the acceptance of peaceful coexistence, a formula which rules out resort to interstate war with the West, but accepts other forms of international competition as legitimate and indeed inevitable. The term implies a mixture of competition, restraint, and cooperation with the capitalist bloc in general and the United States in particular. It is a multilevel relationship, part competition, part cooperation, and the interactions on the various planes often move in different and apparently contradictory directions. The West has difficulty with this concept, mainly because it believes normality in international relations to be the absence of conflict, and this despite its own record of the last 500 years. The Soviets have no such illusions. They see the status quo as a dynamic historical process of change. They have always been quite explicit that the ideological struggle (i.e., the fight for world influence) would continue, détente being aimed at avoiding the dangers of world war.

In considering the role of the military instrument in this struggle, it is useful to distinguish between the possession of military power and the use of military force, and between coercive force and military assistance. While the Soviets consider that military power is something you really can't have enough of, they have been very circumspect about the use of force outside their contiguous national security zone. They believe that history is going their way and, while happy to give it a nudge, it does not justify taking risks. In the past, the most useful approach was to frustrate Western attempts to interfere with this process, by strengthening the forces of world revolution through the supply of weapons, training, and equipment. On occasion this would also serve the more important objective of enhancing Soviet security, as in the cases of Indonesia, Algeria, and Egypt.

From 1961 onwards, a series of coincidental trends combined to favour a more active overseas policy. I list them in no particular order. First, the United States placed new emphasis on counterinsurgency operations and supportive intervention, which led finally to half a million men in Vietnam. Second, there was growing Sino-Soviet competition for leadership of the World Communist movement, accompanied by Chinese accusations that Russia was less than wholehearted in countering imperialist aggression. Third, we have the post colonial era, with the diffusion of power and the prolonged sorting-out process which follows a breakdown of structure. Fourth, we have the gradual maturation of Soviet policy towards the Third World, moving from ideological determinants to national interests concerning access to markets and certain raw materials. Fifth, as a by-product of decisions concerning the security of the Russian homeland, we have the emergence of a capability to project force overseas, the buildup of a long-range lift for the airborne forces, and the navy's shift to forward deployment. And sixth, there is the renewed emphasis within the Soviet military on contingency planning for world war, highlighting the requirements for a worldwide infrastructure.

These were all enabling factors, but it seems that Soviet ideas about a more assertive use of the military instrument began to be shaped by various developments between 1967 and 1972. Achieving parity in long-range nuclear weapons increased Soviet self-confidence, while a series of events caused them to downgrade the dangers that confrontation with the West would escalate to nuclear war. Among the latter, I would list the 1967 Arab-Israeli war, the Czech crisis in 1968, and the Jordanian crisis in 1970; but probably the more important was the SALT negotiation process, which led to a greater certainty of U.S. restraint. Meanwhile, the exaggerated response of the Western press to the Soviet Navy's impotent involvement in the 1967 crisis highlighted the political potential of this instrument. Then, the Egyptian war of attrition and the Israelis' deep penetration raids forced the Soviets to a decision of direct involvement in Egypt, with substantial air defence forces. And finally, the evidence of Vietnam, backed by the Nixon doctrine, suggested that the risk of direct confrontation with U.S. forces was on the wane.

Given this situation of increased opportunities and lowered risks, the overseas role of what they call a "Soviet military presence" appears to have been a major element in the sustained debate on defence and foreign policy which rumbled on from 1969 to 1973. The policy which seems to have emerged was that, anyway for the time being, direct Soviet involvement overseas would be limited to advisers, weapons, and logistic support, including the provision of adequate military supplies in the course of the battle. The combat role would be delegated to the Soviet-equipped forces of revolutionary states such as North Korea, Vietnam, and Cuba. This allowed the Soviet Union the best of both worlds; to affect the outcome of an overseas conflict with direct battlefield support while ensuring that political commitment and liability remained strictly limited.

What we see, then is a progressive shift in overseas policy towards an increasing readiness to use a "Soviet military presence" in support of foreign policy objectives. In assessing this development and the navy's role in particular, I find it useful to distinguish between four types of objectives which underlie this peacetime employment of military forces, because each type involves a different level of risk and degree of political commitment.

At the low end of the scale of political commitment, we have

"Protecting Soviet lives and property". This objective is referred to, but has received little priority to date. Landing ships are positioned to evacuate Soviet nationals in third party conflicts, but the only case of property involved Soviet fishing vessels seized by Ghana in 1969. At the high end we have "Establishing the strategic infrastructure to support war-related missions". This objective is not referred to directly, but can be inferred from the pattern of overseas military involvement during the last 20 years, and is implied in some of their more recent writings. Such an infrastructure can also serve peacetime policies, and the pattern suggests a readiness to incur high political and economic costs in pursuit of this objective. However, so far the Soviets have not used military force to maintain their position when the host country has withdrawn its agreement to their presence, although on at least two occasions, once in Egypt, once in Albania, they have sought to engineer a coup to bring a more sympathetic regime to power. Neither effort was successful.

In between these extremes we have the general objective of "Increasing Soviet prestige and influence". In naval terms this encompasses a wide span of activities ranging from showing the flag and port clearance to providing support for revolutionary forces or to regimes threatened by secessionist elements. They are prepared to commit substantial resources to this objective, such as their minesweeping activities in Bangladesh and the Gulf of Suez, but while the propensity for risk-taking has risen steadily, the underlying political commitment remains strictly limited.

Overlapping this general influence-building objective is the more restricted one of "Countering imperialist aggression". Despite much bombast in talking of this task, I believe that in terms of risking a major confrontation with the West, Soviet political commitment is low. The first clear cut example was the establishment of the Guinea Patrol in December 1970, since when we have the deployments of warships to the Bay of Bengal in 1971, to the South China Sea in 1972, and to Angola in 1975, as well as the three Middle East crises in 1967, '70, and '73. The latter series did show a shift from a narrow concern with the carriers towards a more general concern for the overall capability of the Sixth Fleet. But none of these examples provide evidence of Soviet readiness actually to engage Western naval forces in order to prevent the them from intervening against a Soviet client state.

However, what we do see is progressively greater involvement by the Soviet Navy in the provision of logistic support both before and during third party conflicts. In 1973, Soviet landing ships, escorted by combatants, carried Moroccan troops to Syria. Landing ships were also used during the subsequent war to ferry military supplies from Black Sea ports to Syria. More significantly, SAM-armed warships were stationed where they could protect aircraft making their final approaches to the main resupply airfields in Syria and Egypt, as if to cover against Israeli air attack. And most recently, we have the escorting by Soviet warships of military supplies being ferried from Aden to Ethiopia, and the use of landing ships to deliver such supplies.

The evidence suggests a policy of incrementalism, which explores and takes advantage of opportunities as they occur or are created, a policy of probing Western responses and establishing precedents. The role of a "Soviet military presence" in support of overseas objectives will therefore be shaped by the scale and style of the Western response to the various Soviet initiatives. In this context the distinction I have just drawn between the employment of Soviet warships to ensure the safe arrival of logistic support, and their employment to prevent Western intervention against a client state is important. So, too, is the distinction between the Soviet Union's willingness to risk hostilities with a third-party state, and their continuing reluctance to engage U.S. naval forces. Meanwhile we should bear in mind that the Soviet Navy's role in this assertive policy is secondary. The primary instruments are arms supply; military advice and training; the transport of men, munitions and equipment by merchant ship and long-range air; and direct participation by the combat troops of revolutionary states. The primary role of the navy is to provide protection and support and to serve as an earnest of Soviet commitment.

This brings us to the question of whether there is some grand Soviet design driving a coordinated oceans policy in support of overseas objectives. I think the short answer is no, but we must distinguish here between the operational aspects and the setting of objectives. The military style organisation of the merchant, fishing, and research fleets means that it is relatively simple to make use of their ships in peacetime for naval support tasks such as replenishment and forward picketing, and they all make some contribution to the generalised requirement for worldwide intelligence and information gathering. There are also the geostrategic advantages to be gained in terms of a worldwide infrastructure, actual or potential. The latter includes the provision of improved harbour facilities in locations which would assume great strategic significance for Russia in the event of world war, as for example the fishing port at Gwadar in Pakistan.

But when we turn to objectives, we see that the long-term interests of the three main fleets often diverge. The buildup of the fishing fleet stemmed from a decision in the late forties that fisheries were a more

cost-effective source of protein than collective farming. The buildup of
the merchant fleet reflected the post-Stalin shift in the middle fifties
towards trade, aid, and arms supply, and the consequential requirement
to earn hard currency and avoid dependence on foreign bottoms. The
navy's shift to forward deployment reflected the new threat to the
Soviet homeland from distant sea areas. Inevitably there is some
conflict among these interests and, at the Law of the Sea negotiations,
the narrow domestic concerns of the Soviet fishing industry, which
likes to work as close as possible to foreign shores, thus irritating local
fishermen, ran counter to the foreign policy objectives of increasing
Soviet influence. Similarly, security concerns and the concept of
strategic infrastructure have led the Soviet Union into political
entanglements which would seem to be against her broader interests.
Only the merchant fleet, which brings in military supplies, takes out
local commodities such as bauxite or sugar, and is generally a pacific
and well-disciplined instrument, consistently serves these more general
foreign policy goals, and I see it as the principal maritime instrument of
Soviet overseas policy.

Of course these judgments are based on past evidence, and we
cannot be sure how things will develop in the future. It is clear that a
policy towards the employment of forces in peacetime has been evolved
progressively and, although the navy's political role stemmed from the
presence in distance seas of warships which had been deployed forward
in "strategic" defence, changes in threat perception, risk and
opportunities meant that this role had become increasingly important.
This brings us back to the question of whether the Soviet navy is still
perceived as an expensive necessity, whose forces are procured
exclusively for war-related tasks, or whether it is coming to be seen as a
preferred instrument of policy for pursuing overseas objectives in
peacetime. This is hard to answer, not least because the Soviets do not
seem to have made up their minds on the matter. There is, however,
some evidence that Soviet attitudes to the navy's role in war and peace
may perhaps be changing, and it is to that I now turn.

Evidence that there was disagreement within the military leadership
over the navy's role and the resources being allocated to naval
construction surfaced in an unprecedented series of eleven articles
published under Gorshkov's name in *Morskoj sbornik* (the navy's
professional journal) in 1972. Entitled "Navies in War and Peace", the
dominant tone of the series was defensive advocacy, which went
beyond the contention that the Soviet Union needed a powerful navy,
to criticising the formulation of naval policy and the composition of
the fleet. Using selective historical analysis, Gorshkov's central theme

was the increasing importance of naval forces as an instrument of state policy in peacetime, and as a means of influencing the course and outcome of wars. A powerful fleet was a necessary adjunct of great power status, but this required a conscious policy regarding the role of seapower in each nation's plans. Gorshkov asserted that the Soviet Union lacked such a policy. In consequence, it had an unbalanced fleet that was deficient in surface ships, both as to numbers and the range of different types, and the navy had been shaped too closely to a single, restrictive and largely defensive mission. At the core of the navy's argument lay three complaints against the army-dominated military leadership: the latter was unable to grasp the significance of naval operations in a war with maritime powers; it was unable to understand the importance of general purpose surface forces; and its concept of the armed forces' "internationalist mission" in peacetime was too timid and restrictive.

Halfway through the series' publication, *Morskoj sbornik* began to encounter unprecedented delays in being released to the press by the army-controlled military censors (delays which extended into 1974), and during the same period there were major turnovers of the journal's editorial board, which were again unprecedented. These concrete reactions, reinforced by other circumstantial evidence, confirmed the strong textual indicators that a major debate was underway, with powerful coalitions on either side. However, a compromise biased in the navy's favour appears to have been reached by mid-1974, when Marshal Grechko acknowledged that the external function of the armed forces had been expanded, and Gorshkov acknowledged that operations against land (rather than enemy fleets), now comprised the main naval mission in war, an explicit statement that the military leadership appears to have been seeking since at least 1967. Meanwhile, a significant increase in the future allocation of resources to surface warships had been approved and (presumably) the preparation of the book *The Seapower of the State* had been authorised.

Although the book originally was not scheduled for publication until the second quarter of 1976, it appeared without warning in February, just two weeks before the 25th Party Congress. The underlying message was much the same as the Gorshkov series, but the book's scope and structure differed considerably. It was almost three times as long, with significant additions and deletions to the original material, it was much more carefully written, and the style was less polemical. The historical analysis, which made up 80 percent of the articles and provided the basis for Gorshkov's original argument, reappeared as the second chapter of the book, although with substantial amendments. Of the remaining two-thirds of the book, 85 percent was essentially new material, and fell into two categories. The first chapter was devoted to an extensive discussion of the importance of the ocean and of the non-military aspects of seapower, subjects which had been treated very cursorily in the articles and, unlike the latter, the chapter read as if the different sections had been written by specialists. For example, the book had almost 11,000 words on maritime transportation (compared to only 75 in the articles), and a former Minister of the Merchant Fleet was a contributing author to the book. The other two chapters focused on naval matters and comprised a not very interesting review of naval developments since World War II (Chapter 3) and a discussion of contemporary problems in naval warfare (Chapter 4). The latter included three significant items.

A new section entitled "Fleet against Fleet and Fleet against Shore" is nominally devoted to stressing the priority of naval operations against targets on land, but devotes most of its space to illustrating the importance of the traditional naval role. This is achieved first by extending the definition of fleet-against-shore to include landing operations and attacks on sea lines of communication. Next, by establishing two categories of fleet-against-fleet operations: the "pure" form intended to gain and maintain command of the sea; and those operations which are "tied to the simultaneous accomplishment of other missions". It is then shown that this second category of fleet-against-fleet, which comprises the vast bulk of naval operations, is in fact supporting operations against the shore. This allows the navy's main objective to be redefined as "securing the fulfillment of all missions related to operations against enemy land targets, and to the protection of one's own territory against attacks from his navy". This extensive definition permits full discussion of the traditional role played by navies in World War II, including the importance of carriers. And under the guise of exceptions to the general rule, this section of the book smuggles in numerous examples of traditional naval operations which have had strategic significance, or have even been *more* important than the battle on land.

The same general thrust can be seen in the section on the "Problems of Balancing Navies", which provides a critical analysis of great power fleet structures since 1905 in terms of their capacity to handle the unforseen demands of war, and it is clear that Gorshkov is arguing for maximum flexibility. As in his article, he stresses the limiting effect of Germany's concentration on submarines, which was exacerbated by its failure to provide anti-ASW forces for their support, points which are very relevant to the Soviet circumstances. However, in discussing the

the priority given to the development of submarines and aircraft in the Soviet navy, there is a definite muting of tone in his comment on the need for "a matching development of the other arms of the navy" (especially surface forces), which presumably reflects the navy's successful battle on this issue, whereas in the articles Gorshkov was still arguing the point. This success may also explain why Gorshkov reverts to his 1967 tautological definition of "balance" as denoting the capability to carry out assigned missions in different circumstances. In the articles he saw "balance" as stemming from the *choice* of mission, which he argued should be defined in as general terms as possible, in order to exploit the navy's inherent versatility and to allow for unforseeable developments. However, the choice of mission may now be less important, given Gorshkov's ability to redefine its meaning in terms which suit the navy's purposes, as he did with "fleet against shore".

And lastly, the section entitled "Command of the Sea", a concept which Gorshkov asserts is the most vital in naval warfare. The discussion brings out all the classical advantages of gaining command, comes close to explicitly advocating the "pure" form of fleet-against-fleet operations, and in the process provides powerful support to the arguments in the other two sections for the continued importance of general purpose surface forces, particularly in the anti-ASW/pro-SSBN role. Gorshkov argues that the strategic significance of sea-based long-range nuclear systems makes it essential to ensure a "favourable operating regime" for ones' own forces, and asserts that undoubtedly, the West will seek to wrest such command for themselves at the very outbreak of war.

The book, then, is not just a simple exposé of the role of seapower in the contemporary world, but part of a continuing argument about the navy's role and the resources being allocated to it. The nub of the argument is summed up rather nicely in the "Fleet against Fleet" section, where Gorshkov criticises Napoleon for blaming his admirals for repeatedly failing, whereas the fault really lay in his own "inability to make a timely analysis of the French navy's capabilities, and to use it in the struggle with the enemy." Napoleon's failure to invade England in 1805 was not due primarily to Britain's unchallenged maritime superiority but to his "one-sided strategy, which stemmed from his preoccupation with operations in the land theatres and his lack of understanding of the navy, his disregard for its capabilities in war, and as a result, his inability to use it in a struggle with a naval power, such as England was at the time". The analogy with present circumstances is striking. In Gorshkov's view, the failure of the Soviet military

The Rationale for the Development of Soviet Seapower 241

leadership to understand or even to analyse properly the navy's role, coupled with its prejudices concerning particular weapons and platforms, has meant that on the one hand the fleet has been configured for a relatively narrow span of specific missions, and on the other hand it lacks the full range of forces with which to discharge these missions effectively. In peacetime, this inability to comprehend the navy's potential leads to its underutilisation as an instrument of overseas policy. In a war with maritime powers, it could lead to national disaster.

This critical tone, including the pointed reference to Napoleon's failures, is preserved in the second edition of the book and is carried even further in a ten-page addition. This new section, entitled "The Strategic Employment of the Fleet" argues the importance of a country having a unified maritime strategy, and it mainly consists of a historical critique of the traditional tendency towards separate continental and maritime strategies. Gorshkov notes that the Soviet Union does have a unified strategy but it becomes clear that he is dissatisfied with its overall structure and method of application, and considers that the maritime aspects of the strategy are neither properly integrated nor given sufficient attention. Gorshkov reminds the reader that there is now no sphere of armed conflict where any one branch of service can exercise absolute sovereignty and that all military operations now involve the employment of several branches of service to achieve a common goal. Using circumlocatory language and rather obscure argumentation (p. 317), he goes on to make two related proposals which can be read as criticism of the existing situation.

In one, I understand him to say that, since naval operations are becoming increasingly important and since they rely on support from other branches of service, it is therefore desirable, when considering strategic missions in oceanic theatres, to review the ways of employing *all* the armed forces and not just the navy. From his full argument I infer that Gorshkov considers that the other four branches of service give insufficient priority to naval missions when shaping their strategic concepts and employment policies, and perhaps are reluctant to subordinate themselves to naval requirements when supporting operations in the oceanic theatres.

In the other, I understand him to say that, given the continuing growth in the role of the Soviet navy (which stems from the increasing importance of sea-based strategic nuclear systems), it is necessary to formulate a multi-faceted military strategy which will provide for the most expedient employment of all branches of service, while allowing that the relative importance of the continental and oceanic theatres may vary during the course of a war. This last point is particularly significant and, while Gorshkov is unlikely to be challenging the overriding priority accorded to the European land battle in the initial stages of war with the West, I infer that he is arguing that in other circumstances the oceanic theatres may be more important. Two come readily to mind: the initial phases of such a war in the Pacific theatre; and the subsequent phases of such a war in the Atlantic theatre. However, Gorshkov is flouting one of the armed forces' most basic dogmas by questioning the perennial primacy of the continental theatres of operation.

The debate continues, but if we consider where it started from, the navy has made remarkable gains. Albeit addressed to a wider audience, the navy's case was first deployed in its "own" journal during 1972-73, as some 54,000 words spread over 11 issues and 13 months. Three years later, the argument was extended, improved, and restated in a book of 151,000 words, which had an unusually large printing of 60,000 copies, and was brought out ahead of schedule to meet a political deadline. Within four years a second 60,000 copy edition had been published, which is one-eighth longer and includes a new section which extends naval claims even further. The military publishers categorised the first edition of the book as being for "the military reader"; the second edition is specifically for "admirals, generals and officers of the Soviet Army and Navy". The argument evolved from defensive advocacy of the navy's role, to a more rounded discussion of the importance of the ocean and of seapower in its broader sense, to challenging the primacy of the continental theatres in war. And as a final mark of approval, three of the contributing authors were promoted between the first and second editions, two to Vice Admiral and one to Rear Admiral.

But the most persuasive evidence that Soviet attitudes to the navy's role may be changing comes from the reviews of the first edition of *The Seapower of the State*. These are exemplified by Marshal of the Soviet Union Bagramyan's comment in *Izvestiya* that "for the first time in Soviet literature, the author formulates the concept of seapower as a scientific category". This judgement was echoed by other reviews, all of which stressed the book's contribution to military science and noted that the role of maritime power had, for the first time, been given a scientific formulation. This does not mean that all the ideas in the book have been fully accepted, but it does imply that the concept is now established in the mainstream of Soviet analytic discourse and (to quote Admiral of the Fleet Lobov), "the book will be an important source for developing a correct viewpoint of the seapower of the state". This is significant, because up to now Soviet theorists have had an ideological aversion to the concept, which they equated with Mahan, capitalism, and colonialism. Just as Keynes' "General Theory" legitimised the idea of deficit financing and induced a shift in national economic policies, so may this "scientific formulation" engender a shift in Soviet perceptions of the navy's role in war and peace.

The shipbuilding evidence and the brazenness of Gorshkov's most recent argument suggest that some such shift is taking place with regard to the navy's wartime role. The evidence regarding the peacetime role is much less clear, as are Gorshkov's own opinions in the matter. We should bear in mind that until the publication of his articles in 1972, there were few indications that Gorshkov was a long-standing advocate of far-flung, balanced fleets; one could well argue the reverse. Twenty-five years ago he was brought to Moscow by Khrushchev to implement decisions which were primarily designed to release resources from naval use to the civilian economy. If they had been carried through, they would have resulted in a task-specific, defensively oriented navy, more firmly tied to home waters than at any time in its history. The 1957-58 decisions (which were prompted by Western technological advances rather than any change in Soviet objectives), would have partially broken these ties, but only to end up with an unbalanced fleet, depending wholly on submarines and aircraft for distant operations. While it can be argued that these particular procurement decisions derived directly from the political leadership, no such defence can be offered where combat capabilities and operational readiness were concerned. Yet the shift to forward deployment seems to have come as an unwelcome surprise to the Soviet navy, which was operationally ill-prepared for the move. As late as February 1963, seven years after he had taken over as Commander in Chief of the navy, Gorshkov had to lecture the fleet on the need to get to sea and stay there, so as to develop an ocean-going all-weather capability. Writing in 1968, Gorshkov noted there had been a need to "meet the qualitatively new requirements" which had involved the "organic restructuring of the navy and the reorienting of traditional naval policy". This is hardly the picture of a navy straining at some political leash which was thwarting its peacetime aspirations. It also gives the lie to self-serving claims that contemporary Soviet naval policy stems from the mid-fifties, when Gorshkov took over.

Nevertheless, in his articles Gorshkov was clearly arguing for an assertive foreign policy and for the importance of navies as an instrument of state policy in peacetime. This might seem to fit with the policy announced at the 24th Party Congress in 1971, which was amplified in the book *Military Force and International Relations* edited by V. V. Kulish, except there is distinct difference in treatment. While not underplaying the naval contribution, Kulish discusses the role of a "Soviet Military Presence" in general terms, referring to the increased importance attached to strategic mobility, and the possible future requirements for "mobile and well trained and well equipped forces". Gorshkov places all his emphasis on the navy's unique qualifications and is at pains to point out the inherent limitations of other forms of military force in this role. We should remember, however, that one of the main purposes of his articles was to release more resources to naval construction and all arguments were grist to that mill. We do not know the exact make-up of the powerful coalition of interests which emboldened Gorshkov to make this untypical stand against agreed policy. There is, however, evidence that there was a major cleavage of opinion within the Soviet leadership at this period over foreign and defence policy questions and their impact on the domestic economy, and Gorshkov could only hope to draw support for the navy's case from the "harder". side of the debate. It may therefore be that he angled his argument regarding the navy's peacetime role in that direction.

If anything, the book can be seen as supporting this suggestion. The material from the relevant article is reproduced in heavily amended form, and the tone is less assertive. On the other hand, there is a new section devoted to Western naval involvement in "Local Wars of Imperialism". However, these two sections make up less than seven percent of the whole and the navy's peacetime role is much less prominent than in the articles, the bulk of the book being devoted to war-related subjects or the non-military aspects of seapower. The latter takes up one fifth of the book, the emphasis on marine transportation being particularly noticeable. In terms of the books's title and the place of the sea in Soviet foreign policy, it is surely significant that the authors' collective included V. G. Bakaev, a former Minister of the Merchant Fleet.

Turning to the shipbuilding evidence, we see that there are clearly defined war-fighting requirements for all classes which are currently building or forecast. The longer range amphibious ships are configured for opposed assault in hostile waters, which argues against them having been built primarily for a peacetime role. We also have evidence which indicates that the new large carrier was justified in terms of defending the SSBN bastions and not for peacetime intervention. Writing in February 1967, Gorshkov gave the standard line of disparaging the carrier's vulnerability and reaffirming the correctness of the Soviet decision to rely on missiles. At this date, the Soviet navy had three years experience in the Mediterranean and in less than a year would be moving to the second phase of its shift to forward deployment and the greater political exploitation of naval forces in distant sea areas. But Gorshkov did not argue for a proper aircraft carrier at this time; indeed, his remarks can be interpreted as stifling suggestions in that direction. However, writing in 1972, he makes no reference to the carrier's vulnerability and was silent about its contemporary tasks and capabilities; he did however deploy a rarely quoted Leninist principle which argued (by implication) that since the enemy had carriers, so must the Soviet Union. And this was part of the larger argument for general purpose surface forces which were needed for the defence of the SSBN bastions.

Lastly, we need to consider the Soviet Union's geostrategic circumstances. It stretches from Western Europe to Japan, borders twelve states, and another seven are directly accessible across short stretches of sea. The country spans 170° of longitude (a full 180° if we include the Warsaw Pact), and thus looks south at half the globe. About 85 percent of the world's population lives within 3,000 miles of Soviet territory, although China blocks immediate access to Southeast Asia. Western Europe, North Africa, the Middle East, and the Indian subcontinent are all within 2,000 miles of the Soviet Union, while the territories of its national security zone are contiguous. In terms of strategic access, Russia is Mackinder's heartland, and the availability of strategic air lift backed by merchant shipping means that the navy's role in projecting Soviet military power is relatively less important.

To sum up. Additional resources have been allocated to naval construction and there are clear indications that the Soviet leadership has accepted that the importance of the navy's role has increased significantly, both absolutely and relative to the other branches of service, and this process may continue in future. Meanwhile, a policy for the employment of Soviet naval forces in pursuit of peacetime objectives has evolved progressively, but there is as yet no evidence that this is seen as a primary (as opposed to supporting) means of projecting Soviet power in distant parts of the globe. However, the concept of seapower has now been accepted as relevant to the Soviet Union's circumstances, and while the theoretical implications are probably still being worked out, one of the upshots in the future may be a new willingness to use Soviet naval forces to counter Western military intervention.

Having outlined the reasons underlying the development of Soviet seapower, I conclude by considering briefly some of the implications for the West. But first we must review the main naval capabilities which will face us in the years ahead.

On the submarine side, U.S. statements indicate that nuclear construction has dropped from ten to seven units a year, and that missile tubes are being removed from Yankees. This suggests that SSBN production is now running at three a year, and in measure as Deltas join the fleet, Yankees are being converted to SSN so as to remain within the SALT limit of 62 hulls. This implies that by the end of 1987 (the end of the ten-year programme) the SSBN force will still stand at some 60 units carrying about 950 missiles, i.e., still within SALT 1. Allowing a 25-year hull life, the Soviets may plan to stabilise their force by the end of 1992 at 75 submarines carrying 1,200 missiles.

Turning to nuclear-powered attack submarines, the Yankee conversion program will mean that seven attack units will now join the force each year, compared to about four a year during the previous decade. Assuming that the overall production of nuclear hulls remains at seven a year, this will boost the attack submarine force to about 135 nuclear-powered units by the end of 1987, reducing thereafter to stabilise at about 100 units by the end of 1992. The future of the diesel submarine force is much less clear. If current building rates continue, the force could dwindle to about 75 in the mid-nineties. It would, however, be prudent to assume a substantially larger number since the Soviets have the experience of higher force levels, they have spare building capacity and they could easily boost production in the years ahead. Within the Soviet concept of operations, submarines are an all-purpose defence unit and it is hard to have enough of them. Nor should we forget that the Soviet Union was tooled up to build 72 Whiskies a year in the mid-fifties, and had originally planned to build 100 submarines a year in the early sixties.

The new surface ship programs represent both an increase in the number of ocean-going warships delivered each year and in the size of the various ship types. In the past, the Soviets have been mainly successful in holding down the growth in size of successive classes, and for several decades the parameters of the main ship types have remained roughly constant, most notably the "destroyer-sized" type at about 4,000 tons and the "escort-sized" type at about 1,200 tons, and it was analytically useful to make use of those categories. However, some two or three years ago, the Soviet navy redesignated the destroyer-sized Krivak as an "escort ship" and at the same time altered the type-designation of various other classes to reflect a distinction between anti-submarine and anti-surface capabilities. Bearing in mind Gorshkov's original argument that all-purpose ships had never proved successful,

The Rationale for the Development of Soviet Seapower

plus U.S. press reports that of the two smaller new classes of cruiser, one will carry anti-surface systems and the other will be primarily ASW, it seems likely that these redesignations presaged the future structure of the fleet.

On this assumption, when looking to the nineties it is useful to think in terms of four main sizes of ship, with the type designator indicating the general role: a battlecruiser size; a cruiser size of about 12,000 tons; a destroyer size of about 8,000 tons; and an ocean-escort or frigate-size of about 4,000 tons. I assume that the battlecruiser and cruiser sizes will have a general purpose capability and that only one class of each will be built at the same time, whereas there will be at least two classes of destroyer-size ship under construction, each optimised for different aspects of maritime warfare. The destroyer-sized ships will be able to operate as fleet escorts, whereas the frigate-sized will lack the long range anti-air and -surface systems required for such a role. I am not suggesting that this categorisation will apply immediately, but this could be the general fleet structure by 1990, at which date the present inventory of antisubmarine and anti-surface ships will be obsolete or obsolescent, except for the Kara and Kresta II classes, both of which would be treated as destroyer-sized types.

What sort of numbers are we talking about? Counting only those ships which were built or converted after 1957, but using the *former* categorisation of types (where the cruiser size is around the 8,000-ton mark), at the beginning of 1980 the Soviets had about 27 cruiser-ships (Kynda, Kresta, Kara), about 60 destroyer-size ships (including Krivak), and about 100 escort-size units. They also had two modified *Sverdlov* command cruisers and four air capable ships (2 *Moskva* and 2 *Kiev*). By 1995, allowing a 25-year life cycle and using the *new* categorisation, we could expect about 15 cruiser-size ships, 65 destroyer-size (including Kara and Kresta II), and 55 frigate-size ships (Krivak and successor). There would also be 5 battlecruiser/command ships and perhaps 7 or 8 air capable ships, comprising 2 *Moskva*, 4 *Kiev* and 1 or 2 new type large carriers. To put it another way, every three years the Soviet navy will acquire a powerful new battle group comprising a heavily armed battlecruiser, 3 cruisers, and about 10 large destroyers. The first three or four of these battle groups will rely on a *Kiev* to provide a modicum of seabased air support, but thereafter we might expect to see one fully capable air-supriority carrier for every two battle groups.

On the land-based air side, we can expect Backfire to replace Badger as the primary strike aircraft, but it is not clear whether the naval force will remain at its present strength of about 350 aircraft. Although the navy is getting half the Backfires which enter service, the annual production rate is low and at present two old aircraft are being retired for every new delivery. On the other hand, the improved aircraft now entering service with frontal aviation make it likely that the tactical air force will take over ground targets which were formerly the responsibility of the long-range air force. This may well release additional strike aircraft for naval missions.

So much for the numbers involved, but there are implications concerning capabilities which can be drawn from the preceding analysis. First, submarine technology. The Alpha represents an important breakthrough for the Soviets, since it can go faster and dive deeper than the latest U.S. submarines, although it is still noisier. However, the wider significance of the Alpha is that it represents the first real end-product of the 1957-58 decision which singled out the submarine as the key component of the Soviet navy, with all that implies in terms of priority for research and development resources. Bearing in mind the Soviet capacity for innovation and their penchant for adopting unconventional means to outflank a superior capability, we should expect the Alpha to be only the first of a series of advances, which could challenge our technological lead in the submarine field, and may also affect our future antisubmarine capabilities.

Second, nuclear propulsion. Gorshkov stressed that surface ship characteristics should provide for good seakeeping and long endurance, and long range at high speeds. If nuclear submarine construction has dropped from ten to seven units a year, past shipbuilding practice would lead us to expect that the other three nuclear propulsion systems are still available to the navy. If we allow that perhaps four of these are being used for the battlecruiser program, this would leave another five systems available over three years. While we would expect the new large carrier to be nuclear powered (given the operational concept), this program was approved out-of-plan, whereas the reallocation of propulsion systems is more likely to have been part of the original plan approved in 1971. We might therefore find that the cruiser-size follow-on to Kara is nuclear powered.

Third, the tactical employment of ballistic missiles and the use of shore-based systems. We should pay serious attention to what the Soviets have written about the employment of ballistic missiles against ships and submarines. There tends to be substance in their technological claims, even though they often advance the claim when the capability is in sight rather than in service. It is quite likely that the Yankee was originally conceived as a tactical missile battery for use against carriers. It is quite likely that the SS-NX-13 terminally guided SLBM was shelved because of SALT and not because of insuperable technical problems. It is clear that important elements of the military leadership have always been attracted to the concept of "calling down fire" from land-based systems on naval targets, using satellite surveillance systems, or ships and submarines as forward observers. Even if the Soviets have yet to develop a fully successful system, there is every reason to suppose that they will persist in their efforts because of the operational and political advantages such a "global system" would bring.

We can now move on to the implications of this analysis in terms of general war with the Soviet Union. First, we see that their definition of world war generates massive doctrinal pressures to avoid war with the West; on the other hand, should circumstances arise where a NATO war seems absolutely inevitable, there will be equally massive doctrinal pressures to preempt, whether or not the United States has an assured second-strike capability. Meanwhile, no efforts are spared from developing the means of degrading that capability. This has focused Soviet military thought on "the initial stages of a war" and the importance of getting in the first blow, should war be unavoidable. This leads them to stress the importance of achieving surprise in as many ways as possible . . . technological, temporal and spatial, and through novel operational concepts and unexpected systems combinations. This is not something you dream up on the day, but something you plan for long in advance.

A second and more tangible implication is the "Battle for the Norwegian Sea". For the Soviets, this sea area had moved from being nice-to-have to need-to-have, with all that implies in terms of military resources being allocated to seizing key islands and stretches of Norwegian coast in order to establish command at the outbreak of war. It can be assumed that the Soviets will seek to establish their defence perimeter on the G-I-UK gap and, while it will be difficult to resist the initial thrust, it would be much harder for the West to try and fight its way back once the Soviets were firmly esconced.

Thirdly, the Soviet requirement to protect their SSBN bastions and establish command of the outer defence zones demands a very large number of forces. It is therefore in the West's interests to sustain a sufficient level of explicit threat in those directions in order to tie down those forces. At the same time the West has to challenge any Soviet attempt to establish in peacetime implicit dominance of such sea areas as are flanked by its member nations.

And fourth, the West should look seriously at the implications of the Soviet Union's determined attempts to develop some means of countering Polaris and Poseidon. One of the reasons why the U.S. navy stayed ahead in the past was that the routine process of technological innovation often outflanked Soviet efforts to respond to the maritime threat, sometimes inadvertently. I use "outflanked" literally, since it was frequently the change in a geographically specific scenario which brought Soviet efforts to naught. But for twenty years now, the U.S. SSBN force has placed primary reliance on the concealment offered by ocean space and plans to carry on doing so for the next ten years at least. Meanwhile, the Soviets have spent the last eighteen years seeking the means of breaching that concealment, and doing the basic research which may lead them to some breakthrough in non-acoustic and/or space-based methods of detection. We may be right in our judgement that the Soviets will not be able to beat the problem, but it has two snags. One is that basic research is a Soviet forte, and while they will undoubtedly have difficulty in the technological application of any theoretical breakthrough, we have not been investing in the scale of research on our side to be certain of where they are at. The other is that if our assessments of Soviet progress are wrong, we are making it easier for them to arrange a successful interception, by maintaining essentially the same course for thirty years or more. One of the great attractions of deploying our SLBM in penny packets in coastal waters is that it would largely nullify a massive Soviet investment in R&D (involving four of the five branches of service), and force them to rethink the requirement to counter Western SSBN.

We now turn to the peacetime activities of Soviet naval forces in distant sea areas. The most significant development is that Soviet wartime requirements have justified the procurement of powerful new general purpose forces which will greatly increase the peacetime potential of the fleet. For the first time the Soviets are now developing a genuine worldwide naval capability. And while the concept of defended SSBN bastions will tend to work against continuous distant deployments, concern for the Chinese threat acts in the opposite direction, drawing forces into the South China Sea and the Indian Ocean. In terms of the Western response to these developments, what are the implications of the preceding analysis?

First, we would limit the forward deployment of Soviet naval forces in peacetime if we maintained an active naval presence in the outer defence zones of their SSBN bastions. At the same time we would be bolstering our allies and supporting our wartime objectives.

Secondly, we should exploit the fact that the peacetime role of Soviet naval forces is still in its formative stages. There is a continuing debate in Moscow on the nature of seapower and its potential role in state policy, on the value of a Soviet military presence in the pursuit of overseas objectives, and on the broader objectives of Soviet foreign policy. The nature of the West's response to Soviet initiatives will be a factor in the outcome of the debate and our aim should be to reinforce those who claim that for the Soviet Union, naval forces are not the most cost-effective instrument of overseas policy, while disapproving those who argue that such forces are essential to the normal pursuit of overseas objectives. Unquestionably, this will be hard to achieve, but there are three things we must certainly avoid. We must not allow the employment of Western forces to be inhibited by a Soviet naval presence; indeed, we should go out of our way to demonstrate the opposite. We must not exaggerate the scale and nature of the Soviet navy's peacetime capability; rather, we should actively publicise their operational inadequacies and material failures, we should highlight their limited commitment to client's interests and their narrow national security concerns. And, except in a narrow range of carefully considered circumstances, we must refrain from denying the Soviet Union maritime access to distant states; the casual use of Western naval power to prevent legitimate access by Soviet merchant ships can only reinforce the argument that a strong naval presence is required to protect the Soviet Union's state interests in peacetime.

And third, we must face up to the problem of incrementalism, or the Soviet practice of developing policy step by step. Sometimes the process is forced on them by limited resources, as in the Mediterranean deployments. In other cases, the process is deliberate, as in Cuba, where we see at one time a pier for submarines, another time a recreation field for Soviet sailors, and still another a squadron of Soviet interceptors near Havana. This can only be dealt with by deciding ahead of time where we will draw the line. To an extent, we already do this, but it seems that the contingency planning process starts too high up the crisis scale to cover the problem. We need to fill this gap between the Soviet navy's routine activities and the scenarios underlying our contingency plans. Besides allowing us to work out the appropriate responses ahead of time, this would highlight the longer-term consequences of allowing Soviet naval forces to establish apparently innocuous precedents. The Soviets are well aware that the West's interest in the use of the sea is of a different order to their own. They are very conscious of our worldwide maritime preponderance. They also understand toughness. The question is, when and where we draw the line. However, for such a policy to be successful, the line must reflect a substantive Western interest (as opposed to passing political petulance), and the Soviet Union must be made aware ahead of time, where the line has been drawn.

Finally, we must look at the implications of the preceding analysis in terms of arms control as a means of increasing Western security. One of the lessons we can draw from the past 25 years is that when we devise new ways to discomfort the Soviets in war, or to deter them from attacking us in peacetime, attention must be given to the response it will evoke. For example, it is questionable whether the additional security provided us by the Polaris-Poseidon system compensates for the practical disadvantages arising from the Soviet navy's shift to forward deployment. Similarly, the Soviet response to the threat to their own SSBN force has been to shift resources into building powerful general purpose surface forces which will result in a genuine worldwide naval capability which may well discomfort us in the years ahead. Looking to the future, we need to ask ourselves what would be the Soviet response if we introduced the strategic version of the Tomahawk cruise missile to the fleet, and would that be to our long-term advantage.

But the arms control implications of the analysis go beyond these peacetime inconveniences to the more fundamental questions of threat perceptions and the likelihood of war. For some time there had been a growing disjunction between the very high nuclear inventories on both sides and the level of middle-of-the-road threat assessments. As the arms buildup continued, this disjunction became increasingly hard to bridge and the last few years have seen a steady upward shift in threat perceptions, even though the objective circumstances governing intentions have not changed. On the Soviet side, a major engine of the arms buildup is their war-fighting doctrine. On the U.S. side, a second-strike doctrine requires a matching response and meanwhile, as threat perceptions have risen, so has there been a movement towards an increased war-fighting capability. The cycle continues and, as threat perceptions are drawn inexorably upwards, it becomes more difficult to apply controls to the arms procurement process.

One means of breaking this cycle is to engender a shift from war-fighting doctrines to policies of mutual deterrence, and the West has some leverage in this direction which stems from the importance of sea-based nuclear strike systems as strategic reserves in a world war. In the post-exchange phase the Trident SSBN, with its autonomous capability and 240 nuclear warheads, becomes the war-fighting machine *par excellence*. If this same missile capability were deployed in spartan diesel submarines which were operationally tethered to U.S. home waters, it would provide unambiguous evidence that the U.S. was discounting war-fighting as a strategic option. More important, it would effect the kind of fundamental change in the situation which would force the Soviet leadership to review their policies and programs for countering Polaris and Trident, and to make new decisions. The need to start again from the beginning, coupled with the even greater difficulties of developing a counter to the spartan SLBM system, would reinforce the case of those in the Kremlin who argue that it is time for the Soviet Union to adopt a posture *vis-à-vis* the West of mutual deterrence based on MAD, and to play down the requirement to fight a general war. It is at this stage, when new alignments are formed and Soviet policy is in a state of flux, that further proposals for naval arms control (involving both sides' SSN and the security of the bastions) could shape the final outcome. While important in their own right, such measures could provide the catalyst needed to break the arms race cycle and open up new opportunities for arms base control in other fields, including land-based systems.

We have, however, been discussing what could be rather than what is likely, and despite the current talk about SUMS, U.S. domestic factors would prevent any such political initiative in the foreseeable future. This is unfortunate because developments in East-West relations over the last few years evoke disturbing echoes of the 1960-61 period, in terms of their impact on Soviet weapons procurement decisions. From the Soviet standpoint, things were not going particularly well before 1979, but last year was an especially bad one, which saw a growing rapprochement between China and America, increased defence spending throughout the West, "provocations" over troops in Cuba, stalling of SALT in Congress, the promise of new U.S. strategic systems, and a commitment to upgrade NATO's theatre missile force with weapons which will target Soviet territory and reduce strategic warning time to a few minutes. And then, to cap it all, came Afghanistan, a major setback to the Soviet Union's broader foreign policy objectives, which also served to rekindle the crusading rhetoric of the Kennedy era.

We can therefore assume that as the Soviets finalise the details of the 11th Five Year Plan for presentation to the Party Congress next spring, worst-case assumptions will hold the field and, despite the growing competition for investment funds to develop key sectors of the domestic economy, defence procurement may well increase. Given the recent additions to the surface warship program, naval procurement is less likely to be affected than the strategic rocket and air defence forces, despite the fact that there is probably some slack in naval building capacity, and of course, additional facilities can be diverted from civilian ship construction. However, while the delivery rates remain unchanged during the next decade, the tough-minded decision-making climate may be favourable to incorporating improved characteristics (such as nuclear propulsion in surface ships), and the ratchet effect, which is present both in arms racing and in the Soviet planning process, may ensure that such systems will continue to be provided in the future.

Given these circumstances, the West has no option but to gird itself for a sustained, if low key naval buildup. We are faced by a substantial increase in the allocation of resources to Soviet surface ship construction, in part through the five-year planning process, in part through an out-of-plan addition, which not only increases the annual delivery rate and tonnage, but introduces powerful new types of ships into service. Besides this practical recognition of increased naval requirements, there is a new theoretical acceptance of the concept of seapower and its relevance to the Soviet Union in war and peace. And finally, we are faced with a period of revived East-West antagonism, which is likely to be characterised by increasing military intransigence. Respond we must, but it needs to be a measured response, and we should not allow ourselves to be mesmerised by the new surface programmes. The Soviets continually stress that the submarine force is the primary arm of the fleet, an assessment we should heed, and we should also concern ourselves with the threat from land- and space-based global systems. The response should be measured because we do not wish to encourage naval confrontation in all corners of the globe. We should avoid the rhetoric of an arms race and as we build up our forces, we should talk in terms of arming to parley.

Notes

1. The analyses on which this article is based can be found in "Naval Power and Soviet Global Policy", *International Security,* Spring 1979, and the various chapters of *Soviet Naval Developments* (1973), *Soviet Naval Policy* (1975) and *Soviet Naval Influence* (1977), all published by Praegers and edited by the author (with others). The references in these works give some indication of the author's debt to the other analysts working in this field, not all of whom are mentioned.

2. For a summary of the evidence that Gorshkov was arguing for carriers, see my "Naval Power and Soviet Oceans Policy" in *Soviet Oceans Development,* John Hardt (Ed.), U.S. GPO, October 1976, pp. 118-119. Prepared by CRS for the Senate Committee on Commerce and the National Ocean Policy Study.

CONTRIBUTORS

Hannes Adomeit is a research fellow at the Stiftung Wissenschaft und Politik, Ebenhausen, Munich. He has written on general aspects of Soviet foreign policy.

Robert Arnett is currently working as a specialist on Soviet Strategic forces for the Office of the Assistant Chief of Staff for Intelligence, Headquarters, Department of the US Army. He received a PhD in Political Science from Ohio State University in 1979. His dissertation examined Soviet views on nuclear war survival 1962-77.

John Baylis is a lecturer in strategic studies at the University College of Wales, Aberystwyth. He has written generally on British Defence policy and is the author of the forthcoming book *Anglo-American Defence Relations 1939-1980* (London, Macmillan, 1981).

Ken Booth is a senior lecturer in strategic studies at the University College of Wales, Aberystwyth. He has written generally on strategic studies and Soviet foreign policy with special reference to naval policy. His latest book is *Strategy and Ethnocentrism* (London, Croom Helm, 1979).

Raymond Garthoff is a research associate at the Brookings Institution, Washington. He is a leading authority on Soviet defence policy and has written widely on the subject for over 20 years.

Benjamin Lambeth is a staff member of the Rand Corporation, Santa Monica California. He has written generally on Soviet foreign and defence policy for various publications.

Michael MccGwire is a research associate at the Brookings Institution, Washington. He is a leading authority on Soviet defence policy with special reference to naval policy.

Dennis Ross is a member of the Defence Department (US) Office of Program Analysis and Evaluation. He has written generally on Soviet foreign policy issues.

Gerald Segal is a lecturer in strategic studies at the University College of Wales, Aberystwyth. He has written generally on Chinese defence policy and is the author of the forthcoming book *The Great Power Triangle* (London, Macmillan).

INDEX

Abakumov 200
Aden 236
Adomeit, H. 30, 31, 32
Afghanistan 17, 30, 31, 32, 89, 253
Afonsky, I.A. 164, 178
Aircraft 79, 82, 115; B-52 155, 157; Backfire 20, 230, 247; Badger 214, 247; Mig 139, 140; Yak-25 140
Akhromeyev, S.F. 164
Albania 192, 224, 235
Alekseyev, N.N. 163
Alexander, A. 28
Algeria 233
Andropov, Y. 61, 167, 204
Angola 17, 31, 235
Anti-Ballistic Missile (ABM) 87, 105, 142, 154-7, 161, 165, 166, 168-9, 171-3, 175, 180, 218; Agreement on 21, 26, 27, 92, 94, 128, 176; Treaty 107, 120, 159; *See also* Missiles, SALT
Anti-Submarine Warfare (ASW) 37, 166, 214, 219, 23-4, 226, 228-9, 230, 239-40, 247
Anuytin, V.N. 165
Arabian Gulf 31-2, 232
Arbatov, G. 135, 136, 137
Armenia 61
Arms Control 14, 19, 20-26, 41, 94, 181, 252; Agreements 93, 115, 179-80; Proposals 84, 86-8, 141; USSR role in 10, 14, 15, 27-9, 93-6, 154-81; *See also* SALT
Arnett, R. 11, 12, 55-74
Australia 219
Austria 84, 185

Bagramyan, Marshal 242
Bakaev, V.G. 244
Bangladesh 235
Beletsky, I.I. 163-4
Berezhkov, V.M. 63
Beria, L. 198, 200
Berlin 82, 84, 187-93, 200, 203
Berman, R. 38
Biological weapons 314

Bolshevik Revolution 76-80, 112
Booth, K. 15, 16, 45-101
Bovin, A. 62
Brazil 219
Brezhnev, L. 61, 65, 119-20, 130, 131, 136, 167-8, 178, 186, 200, 204-5
Brown, H. 166
Bulganin 188, 201-2
Bulgaria 187, 188

Canada 219
Cape Verde Islands 224
Carter, J. 24
Chemical Weapons 34, 35
China (People's Republic of China) 58, 156, 171, 185, 195, 225, 231, 232-3, 245, 250; Domestic problems 89, 90; Nuclear policy 24, 86-8, 89, 95; US and 88, 89, 94; USSR and 14, 15, 19, 20, 24, 30, 76, 85, 86-8, 89, 158
Civil Defence: Expenditure on 24; USSR and 12, 14, 17, 22-4, 41, 55, 111-12, 121; West and 22-4, 55-6; *See also* US Strategic Thought, USSR Strategic Thought
Clausewitz 10, 56, 58, 91, 109
Cold War 13, 80-6, 200; *See also* US-USSR Relationship
Cominform 82
Comintern 78
Communist of the Armed Forces 57, 65
Compellence 191-2
Crankshaw, E. 75
Crimean War 211
Cuba 224, 234, 251, 253
Cuban Missile Crisis 14, 87, 95, 116, 119, 190-3, 195, 203, 211
Czechoslovakia 30, 31, 82, 87, 157, 200, 234

Détente 17, 18, 26, 87, 92, 94, 105, 115, 116, 121, 136, 188, 232-3; *See also* US-USSR Relationship

Deterrence 10, 14-26, 107-8, 117, 125, 127, 135, 138, 145, 147, 177, 180, 188, 190-1, 192-3, 216-17, 219; Active 14, 22, 89; Asymmetrical 83, 106; Credibility of 55, 85, 105-8; Defence and 10, 13-14, 16-17, 20-6, 75, 79, 80, 81, 83, 84, 85-6, 90, 96, 106; By denial 17, 22, 41, 130, 132, 133, 134, 135, 136, 137, 138, 146; Effectiveness of 55-6, 75-80, 84, 85, 105-8, 109-11; Mutual 566, 58, 107, 134, 160, 252; Passive 14, 22, 114; By punishment 22, 26, 41, 130-1, 132-3, 134, 135, 146, 147; Strategic 14-26, 83-6, 87-90, 91; US 13-14, 17, 20-6, 55, 83, 109, 130-1, 146, 217-18; USSR 10, 13-17, 20-6, 27-8, 32-4, 40-1, 75, 79-81, 83-6, 90-1, 106, 108-11, 114, 121, 122, 125, 127, 128, 129, 130-8, 145-7, 160, 180, 194, 217
Diego Garcia 225
Djilas, M. 189, 200
Dmitriyev, A. 65
Dobrynin, A. 178, 192
Dulles, J.F. 188
Dyusheyev, Zh. 62

Eden, Sir A. 188
Egypt 31, 195, 224, 233, 236
Erickson, John 32-3, 36, 40
Escalation: Crisis Management; 24, 114; Nuclear War 20, 24, 36-7
Ethiopa 31, 236
Ethnocentrism 3, 16, 21
Europe 12, 19, 33, 34, 35, 36, 83, 119; Military balance 13, 94; US and 13, 84; USSR and 12, 14, 82-4, 87
Europe, Central 76, 77, 80, 86
Europe, Eastern 14, 30, 31, 37, 82, 83, 84, 87
Europe, Western 14, 37, 80, 82-4, 87, 94, 245
European Defence Community 84

Far East 78, 86, 89, 186, 189, 211, 232; *See also* China, Vietnam
Fedenko, A.A. 165
Fedorov, Ye. 62
France 19, 34, 76, 95, 189, 211-12

Frunze, M.V. 77

Gallagher, M. 139
Garthoff, R. 27, 29, 154-82
Gerasimov, A.V. 163
Germany 13, 78, 79, 80, 82, 83, 84, 112, 116, 185, 186, 187, 190-1, 195, 212
Ghana 235
Golovin, I.N. 187
Gorbunov, A.M. 165
Gorshkov, Admiral 37-40, 130, 196, 214, 220, 227-8, 237-44, 246, 248
Graham, D. 55
Grechko, Marshal 61, 112, 120, 128, 159, 167, 176, 178-9, 195, 204, 232, 238
Greenland 222
Grishin 203
Gromyko, A. 61, 167, 192, 204
Gryzlov, A.A. 163-4
Guinea 224, 235

Heikal, M. 202
Helsinki 136
Herrick, R.W. 196
Hiroshima 187
Hitler, A. 78, 79, 186
Horelick, A. 197
Hungary 30, 187, 188, 197

Ideology 10-13, 17, 21, 23, 26, 30, 32, 56-7, 58-60, 64, 76, 77, 80, 81, 83, 96, 124, 125, 126, 131, 134, 136, 137, 138, 218
India 89
Indonesia 233
Institute for the Study of the USA and Canada 63
Institute of Military History 65
Institute of World Economy and International Affairs (IMEMO) 63
Intentions: Capabilities and 18, 23, 25, 29-32, 105-6, 107-23, 124, 185; Estimation of 9, 105-6; Worst case 23; *See also* US Military Capability, USSR Military Capability
Inter-Continental Ballistic Missile (ICBM) 14, 18, 19, 22, 24, 84, 87, 94, 96, 113, 115, 120; *See also* ABM Missiles, SLBM
Iran 185

Index

Israel 236
Italy 192, 212

Japan 76, 78, 79, 80, 89, 185, 205-6 212, 245; *See also* China, Far East
Jellico, Admiral 37
Johnson, A. 126
Jones, T.K. 55
Jordanian Crisis 234
Jutland, Battle of 37

Kaganovich 202
Kahn, H. 91
Kaplan, F. 23, 24
Karenin, A. 134
Keegan, G. 23, 55
Kennan, G.F. 199
Kennedy, J.F. 14, 86, 91, 192, 216, 218, 253
Keynes, J.M. 243
Khalipov, V.F. 63, 64
Khrushchev, N.S. 14; 75, 84-5, 86, 116, 118, 119, 186, 188, 199-204, 214, 216-17, 243
Kirilenko, A. 61
Kissinger, H. 178-9
Kohler, F. 55
Kondratkov, T.R. 65
Konev, Marshal 191
Koralersky, M.A. 164
Korea 82, 185, 188, 199, 200, 234
Kosygin, A. 61, 119, 154, 167, 175, 178
Kozlov, M.M. 164, 168, 178
Krylov, N.I. 59
Kudrov 205
Kulakov 203
Kulikov, V.G. 159
Kulish, V. 38, 135, 244
Kunaev 203
Kurchatov, I.V. 187
Kuznetsov, N.G. 199

Lambeth, B. 15, 16, 20, 105-23
Lenin, V.I. 63, 198, 202-3;
 Inevitability of war theory 14, 76-7, 84-6
Leningrad 196
Lenin Military Political Academy 63-4
Lobov, Admiral 242

MccGwire, M. 38-40, 210-54

Mackinder, H. 245
Mackintosh, J.M. 92
McNamara, R. 86, 91, 154-6
Mahan 243
Main Operational Directorate 109
Main Political Directorate 65, 109
Malenkov 198, 201-2, 217
Malinovsky, Marshal 35, 216
Manchuria 79, 185
Marshall, G. 188
Marshall Plan 82
Marxism-Leninism 56-7, 58, 59, 64, 66, 76-7, 199; *See also* Ideology, Lenin
Marxism-Leninism on War and the Army 35, 57, 60, 66
Medvedev, R. 186
Middle East 30, 31, 34, 195, 224, 234, 235
Mikoyan, A. 204
Military Force and International Relations 38, 244
Military Historical Journal 57
Military Strategy 33, 56
Milovidov, A. 63, 64
Missiles 18, 21, 25, 37, 92, 125-6;
 ABM 138, 143, 154-8, 168-9, 172-3; Air to Surface 96; ALCM 171; Anti-tank 34; Cruise 105, 147, 214, 252; Frog 139; ICBM 140, 155-8, 168-70, 172-4, 176, 189, 190, 194, 217, 231; IRBM 171, 173, 230-1; MRBM 29, 115 171-2, 230; M-X 105, 147; Poseidon 174, 225-6, 228-9, 249, 252; SAM 173, 223, 228, 236; SLBM 129, 130, 147, 155-8, 168-9, 194, 248, 250, 253; SS-6 28, 140; SS-7 140, 160; SS-8 140, 169, 174; SS-9 126, 138, 142, 143, 169, 170, 174; SS-11 20, 142, 168, 171, 174; SS-13 169; SS-16 115; SS-17 173-4; SS-18 126, 138, 174; SS-19 171, 173-4; SS-20 20, 115; SS-N-6 219; SS-N-8 219; SS-NX-13 248; Throw-weight 18, 94; Trident 174, 228, 230, 252-3
Mollet, G. 188
Molotov, V. 187, 198, 201-2
Morskoj sbornik 196, 227, 237-8
Multi-Independently Targeted Re-Entry Vehicle (MIRV) 94, 95, 96, 120, 171-2, 174, 194;

See also ICBM, Missiles, SLBM
Mutual Assured Destruction (MAD) 13-14, 16, 21, 22, 23, 24, 41, 61-5, 93, 95, 124, 133, 134, 176, 253; *See also* US Military Thought, USSR Military Thought

Nagasaki 187
Napoleon 240-1
Nasser, G.A. 202
Navies in War and Peace 37, 237
Nazi-Soviet Pact (1939-41) 79
Nitze, P. 124, 144-7, 145
Nixon, R.M. 89, 92, 167, 234
Non-Proliferation Treaty (1968) 86; *See also* Arms Control
North Atlantic Treaty Organization (NATO) 13, 33, 37, 82, 84, 87, 218-19, 224, 249, 253; Theatre weapons of 19, 37
Norway 39, 222, 224, 228, 230, 249

Organakov, N.V. 162-4, 167-8, 178

Pakistan 89, 232, 236
Partial Test Ban Treaty (1963) 14
Penkovsky, O. 191
Pipes, R. 10, 11, 56, 58, 124
Pleshakov, P.S. 166
Poland 76, 77, 187
Polaris 22, 24, 192, 215, 217-18, 222, 224, 228-9, 230, 232, 249, 252, 253; *See also* Missiles, SLBM
Potsdam Conference 187
Pravda 62, 189, 190
Pugwash Conferences 163

Red Sea 195, 232
Ross, Dennis 20, 25, 26, 28, 124-53
Rotmistrov, Marshal 193
Rumania 187, 192
Rybkin, Ye. 57, 58, 65

Sanakoyev, Sh. 62
Schmidt, H. 163
Seapower *see under* US, USSR
The Seapower of the State 238, 242
Semonov, V.S. 135
Shcherbitskii 203
Shchukin, A.N. 166
Shelepin 204
Shelest, P. 204
Shelyag, Admiral 63, 64

Shepilov 202
Signalling 36-7, 114
Simonyan, R.G. 65
Sinetsky, P.V. 164
Sino-Soviet Rift 14, 86-8, 89-90, 158, 233
Smirnev, L.V. 120, 166-7
Sokolovsky, V.D. 33, 56
Somalia 31, 195, 224-5, 232
South Africa 219
South Asia 89
Southeast Asia 89
Spielman, Karl 28
Stalin, J.V. 11, 13, 75, 78, 81, 83, 85, 126, 185-8, 198-200, 213
Stalingrad 80
Standing Consultative Commission 165, 180
Starodubov, V.P. 164-5
Steinbruner, J. 147
Stockholm Peace Appeal 84
Strategic Arms Limitation Talks (SALT) 16, 18-21, 26-7, 92, 105-6, 110, 115, 116, 121, 126, 135, 136, 141, 154-81, 207, 227, 231, 234, 246, 248, 253; SALT I 15, 27-8, 92-6, 115, 157, 158, 159, 160, 166, 170-1, 173, 194, 246; SALT II 15, 17, 95-6, 105, 157, 164; Soviet Objectives in 159-62; US and 154-81; *See also under* US, USSR
Strategic Forecasting 80, 83
Strategic Rocket Forces (USSR) 35, 59, 140, 143, 216; *See also* USSR Military Capability
Strategic Stability 144-8; *See also under* US, USSR
Submarines 78, 82, 212-16, 220, 222, 225-8, 240, 246, 248, 251, 252; SLBM 22, 37-8, 92, 118; 'Y' Class 169; *See also under* Missiles, US, USSR
Suez Crisis 188
Surikov, B.T. 165
Surprise Attack Conference (1958) 163
Suslov, M. 85
Syria 31, 235-6

Taiwan Straits Crisis (1958) 189
Talensky, N.A. 156
Tanks 33-4, 79, 115, 139
Terminology 19; Definition problems

Index

19, 20; *See also under* US, USSR
Theatre Nuclear Forces: China and 20;
  Europe and 18-19, 37; *See also
  under* US, USSR
Trans-Siberian Railway 78
Trofimenko, G.A. 134, 141, 145
Trotsky 77, 200
Truman, H.S. 187
Truman Doctrine 82
Trusov, K.A. 163-4
Tucker, R.C. 199
Turkey 192, 211-12, 221
Two-Camp Theory 85
Tyushkevich, S. 65

Union of the Soviet Socialist Republics
  (USSR): Academy of Sciences
  63, 166, 204; Arms Control Section
  164; Civil War 76, 77, 79; Council
  of Ministers 201, Czarist Empire
  76, 90; Defence Council 136;
  Domestic politics of 30, 75-80,
  81, 82, 89, 119; Europe and
  14, 19, 33-6, 82-4, 87, 119, 158;
  Europe (Central) and 76-7, 80-6,
  189, 190, 192, 194-5, 200; Europe
  (East) and 13-14, 30-1, 37, 82-4,
  87, 185, 186, 200; Europe (West)
  and 14, 19, 37, 82-4, 87, 186,
  205-6, 219; Insecurity, feelings of
  132, 133, 136, 146; Threat
  perception 13-15, 19, 21, 25-6,
  75-80, 81-6, 87-8, 89-90, 107,
  121, 126, 131, 132, 136, 137,
  141, 142, 157-8, 213, 217, 219,
  221, 237, 150
United Kingdom (UK) 76, 186, 189,
  211-12, 225, 240; Nuclear
  capability 19, 24, 95
United Nations 88
United States (US): China and 88-9,
  94, 253; Congress 96, 253; Defence
  Department 24, 105, 106-7, 109;
  Defence Intelligence Agency
  23; Rand Corporation 126;
  Strategic Air Command 118
US Military Capability: ABM 157,
  169; Air based systems 18, 81,
  83, 118; Aircraft carriers 173,
  214, 222-4, 228, 236; Conventional
  147, 192; Counterforce 146;
  Credibility of 55; Deployment of
  18, 81, 83, 225; Deterrence
  capacity 14-20, 55, 62-4, 83,
  109, 146; First Strike 113, 129;
  Forward Based System 19, 20,
  95, 96, 173, 178; Land based
  system 18; Naval power 18, 94,
  113, 118, 195, 212, 236; Nuclear
  monopoly 187-8; Overinsurance
  86-7, 91-2; Second strike 17,
  96, 112, 113, 146-8, 249, 252;
  Soviet 'superiority' 144-8;
  Strategic forces 14-20, 55-6, 62-5,
  67, 81, 83, 88-96, 105-6, 154-81,
  190; Technological superiority of
  133; Warfighting 16, 44, 55, 252
US Military Strategy: Alliance policy
  13, 83; Analysis of 13-15, 20, 21,
  22, 23, 26, 40-1, 105-7, 108-14;
  Bases 83, 171, 173, 192, 222, 224;
  Changes in 15-16, 36, 40-1, 46;
  Civil Defence 21-4, 111-12;
  Convergence with USSR 16, 20-6,
  41; Debate in 9-11, 13, 15, 22-9,
  31, 55-61, 63, 105, 127; Essential
  equivalence 25, 41, 106, 109,
  160; Presidential Directive 59,
  13-14, 16, 36, 41; Roll-back 83,
  188; Sufficiency 26, 109;
  Superiority 18, 25-6, 41, 90, 91,
  92, 116, 136, 142, 156, 192;
  Worst case paradigm 82, 91; *See
  also* Deterrence, Missiles
USSR Armed Forces: Buildup of
  29-38, 80, 87, 90, 105-6, 115-16,
  121, 156; General Staff 122;
  High Command 111; Main
  Political Directorate of 65, 109;
  Modernization of 33-4, 87, 90,
  105-6, 116
USSR Communist Party of the Soviet
  Union (CPSU) Central Committee
  62, 109, 111, 166, 167, 201-3
  204; 20th Party Congress 199;
  21st Party Congress 189; 22nd
  Party Congress 191; 23rd Party
  Congress 203-4; 24th Party
  Congress 130; 25th Party Congress
  238; Politburo 28, 61-2, 107,
  135, 137, 167, 177, 203-4
USSR Defence Council 28, 167
USSR Military Capability, Airforce
  30, 33, 79, 106, 113, 115, 118,
  165, 172, 174, 174, 193; Air-
  defence 14, 17, 22; Airlift 30,
  31, 82, 84, 87, 113, 120; Assured
  Destruction 23, 87, 95, 96, 121,

132-3; Conventional 13-14, 17, 22, 32-8, 78-81, 83, 84, 115, 118, 119, 187, 190, 229; Defensive 32, 40, 55, 75-80, 83-6, 90-1, 194; Deployment of 18, 25, 29, 30-1, 35, 36, 37, 38, 40, 79, 83-4, 88, 107-8, 115, 121, 137-8, 141; First Strike 18-19, 23-5, 89, 91, 92, 112-14, 128, 142; Intentions of 18, 23-5, 30-2, 33-40, 82, 91, 105-6, 144, 143, 145, 210; Nuclear 10-12, 13-14, 16-17, 34-8, 55-74, 80-1, 84-6, 87, 90-1, 94, 105-23, 124, 143, 164, 165, 194, 227, 231; Offensive 32-4, 55, 125, 127, 194; Overinsurance of 90-1, 92, 126; Projection of 29-32, 38-40, 79, 82; Proliferation of 25, 29-32, 33-8, 75-80, 82, 86-8, 90-2, 95, 105-7, 110, 116, 121, 124, 136-7, 156, 168, 170, 185, 193-4, 252; Restraints on 18, 31, 32, 87-9, 114, 115; Second Strike 17, 21, 96, 129, 130; Theatre 18-20, 36-7, 115-16; Utility of 29-32, 33-40, 79-80, 108-117, 135; War Fighting 14, 16, 19, 22-3, 29, 34, 36, 39-41, 55, 105, 109-11, 112-14, 119, 124, 132, 194, 216-17, 219, 227-8, 252; Western response to 34, 35, 36-8, 40, 55, 82-6, 105-6

USSR Military-Industrial Commission 120, 166-7

USSR Navy 10, 14, 30, 32-3, 37, 38-40, 84, 118, 170, 210-54; Area defence 221-2; Blue-water role of 14, 80, 194-8, 226; Build-up of 39, 84, 212, 219, 221-3, 226, 237, 247-54; Fleet areas 221, 224, 236; Forward deployment 39-40, 220, 224, 234, 237, 243, 252; History of 211-17; Peacetime role of 33, 38-40, 195-6, 232-45, 250-1; Wartime role of 37-8, 39-40, 220, 227, 243, 250; Withholding strategy 37, 38, 218-19

USSR Strategic Policy-Making: Arms Control 10, 14-15, 27-9, 93, 94-6, 154-81; Civilian analysts 28-9, 62-3, 107, 134, 135, 136; Crisis diplomacy 10, 13, 107, 117; Defence Industrialists 28-9, 120; Economic determinants of 18, 110, 117, 121, 160-1; Expansionism 76, 80-6; Interest groups 10-11, 15, 27-9, 55-74, 83-4, 107-9, 119-20, 133, 140, 198, 203, 216; Inter-service rivalry 27; Military and 10-11, 15, 21-2, 27-9, 28-40, 63-6, 75-101, 107-9, 110-12, 118-19, 127, 133, 135, 136, 137, 194, 232-7; Ministry of Foreign Affairs 166, 177-8; Procurement and 18, 30, 84, 91, 105-7, 110, 115, 117-18, 139-40, 141-4; Rationality in 25, 84-5, 91-2, 113; Risk Taking in 185-205; Technological determinants of 25-7, 80-1, 92, 94, 96, 109, 110, 115; Worst-Case planning in 80, 82, 83, 91, 253

USSR Strategic Thought: Analytical approaches 9, 55, 91, 105; Civil Defence 12, 14, 17, 22-4, 41, 55, 111-12, 128-9; Conceptual problems 9, 55-74; Convergence with US 16, 20-6, 41; Counter-force 128, 132, 135, 138, 145; Damage limitation 128-9, 130, 133, 134, 138, 146, 176, 220; Debates 63-4, 83, 111-12; Definition 108; Development of 11-15, 32-40, 55-101, 105-23, 127, 132; Doctrinal determinants of 15-27, 107, 110-11, 114, 115, 117-23, 124-53; Essential Equivalence 25-6, 41, 106, 110, 115, 180, 197; First Strike 128-9, 131, 142, 143, 146, 159, 175, 194; Historical determinants of 12-15, 18, 21, 37, 75-101, 125, 126, 132; Inevitability of war 14, 76-8, 80, 84-5; Institutional determinants of 10-11, 15, 18, 21-2, 27-9, 55-74, 91, 107-9, 117, 119-20, 121-2, 125, 126, 134, 138, 139; Offensive in 127, 138; Masterplan 13, 25, 31, 108; Permanently operating factors 11, 13, 25; Pre-emptive 112-14, 127, 130, 132, 176-7; Psychological determinants of 21, 76, 113, 125-6; Socio-cultural determinants of 21, 121, 126; Soviet literature on 33, 35-6, 55-6, 58, 59, 61-6, 106,

Index

107, 108, 109, 112, 114, 116-18, 121, 122, 159; Superiority and 18, 25-6, 41, 9-92, 110, 112, 114, 115, 116, 124, 126, 134, 148, 175, 188-93, 207; Surprise 213, 249; Technological determinants of 25, 81, 92, 105, 107, 109, 110, 121; Victory 175, 217-18; Warfighting in 127, 132, 194, 216-17, 219, 227-8, 252; Withholding strategy 218, 227; *See also* Deterrence, Missiles
USSR Supreme Soviet 159, 167, 189, 192, 201
Ustinov, Dimitri 120, 163, 165, 167-8
US-USSR Relationship: Analysts of 9, 11, 13, 16, 18, 21, 22-7, 30, 31-41, 55, 60, 61, 80-6, 105-23; Defence and Deterrence 10-13, 14, 16-17, 20-6, 83-6, 90-1, 96, 106, 108, 110-11, 127, 131; *Détente* 14, 17-18, 26, 87, 72, 94, 105, 115, 116, 232-5; Dialogue in 27, 84, 87, 92-4, 117, 177, 179, 180-1; Differences in thinking 138, 143, 145, 147, 176, 194; Essential equivalence 25, 41, 106, 109, 115, 134; Mutual perceptions 13, 21, 60, 75, 77, 80, 82, 83, 84, 86, 89; Parity 12, 15, 18, 20, 21, 25, 26, 30, 32, 86-7, 88, 92, 94-6, 115, 124, 142, 156, 158, 159, 195; Relative capability 55, 62-5, 85-6, 92-4, 105, 106, 134, 142, 154-81; Stability in 17-19, 41, 87, 91, 92; Technology 19, 21, 25-6, 27, 80-1, 92-4, 96, 105, 109

Vance, C. 167-8
Van Cleave, W. 124
Vietnam 89, 233-4

Voprosy Filosofii 206

War: Defensive Operations in 33-4, 75-80; Inevitability of 14, 33, 76, 77, 78, 80, 84, 85, 131; Offensive Operations in 33-4; Surprise in 11, 13, 14, 17, 32, 106, 112; USSR literature on 32, 33-6, 55; USSR view of 10-12, 32-8, 55-74, 76-8, 80-3, 105, 106, 107-23, 131; Victory in 11-12, 26, 106, 11-12, 117; *See also* USSR Strategic Thought
Warner, J. 168
Warsaw Pact 84, 87, 245; *See also under* USSR
Weapons Acquisition 39, 84, 91, 105, 107, 110, 115, 117, 120, 139, 140-3, 144; *See also under* US, USSR
Weber, M. 202
Wigner, E. 55
Withholding Strategy 37-8, 218-19; *See also* USSR Military Capability, USSR Navy
Wolfe, T.W. 96
World Economy and International Relations 205
World War I 32, 34, 61, 65
World War II 13, 32, 35, 61, 62, 65-6, 82, 212-13, 215, 239
World War III 61, 65

Yakolev, A. 140
Yemen 195, 232
Yugoslavia 186, 188, 192, 199-200

Zakharov, M.V. 162, 193
Zhdanov 198
Zhilin, P.A. 65, 131
Zhukov 187, 202

RAYMOND H. FOGLER LIBRARY